A Spy for the Union

A Spy for the Union

The Life and Execution
of Timothy Webster

COREY RECKO

McFarland & Company, Inc., Publishers
Jefferson, North Carolina, and London

Library of Congress Cataloguing-in-Publication Data

Recko, Corey, 1974–
    A spy for the Union : the life and execution of Timothy
Webster / Corey Recko.
        p.   cm.
    Includes bibliographical references and index.

    ISBN 978-0-7864-7490-5
    softcover : acid free paper ∞

    1. Webster, Timothy, 1822–1862.   2. Spies—United
States—Biography.   3. United States—History—Civil War,
1861–1865—Secret service.   I. Title.
    E608.W43R43 2013
    973.7'85092—dc23
    [B]   2013030877

British Library cataloguing data are available

On the cover: Timothy Webster, 1860 (Records of Pinkerton's
National Detective Agency, Library of Congress); *bottom*
Richmond Civil War ruins, including the Confederate Capitol
building 1865 (National Archives); background, vintage paper,
spyglass (iStockphoto/Thinkstock)

Manufactured in the United States of America

McFarland & Company, Inc., Publishers
  Box 611, Jefferson, North Carolina 28640
  www.mcfarlandpub.com

To Gwendolyn and Hanna,
Follow your dreams

"His name is unknown to fame; but few were truer or more devoted to the Union cause than was Timothy Webster."— Allan Pinkerton, *History and Evidence of the Passage of Abraham Lincoln...*, 11.

Table of Contents

Preface   1

Introduction   5

  1. From Newhaven to Princeton   7

  2. Officer Webster   12

  3. A Pinkerton Detective   22

  4. Resurrectionists   29

  5. The Rock Island Bridge   39

  6. Plot to Assassinate the President-elect   49

  7. Work in Maryland Continued   59

  8. A Spy in Memphis   68

  9. Operations in Baltimore   85

10. Tim Webster in Richmond   92

11. Timothy Webster Returns to Richmond   101

12. Pinkerton's Blunder   111

13. April 1862   127

14. Post-Mortem   131

*Appendix I: Timothy Webster's Testimony in Front
of the New York City Board of Aldermen, 1855*   139

*Appendix II: Timothy Webster's Reports from
Maryland, 1861*   144

*Appendix III: Timothy Webster's Reports from
Kentucky and Tennessee, 1861*   147

Appendix IV: Timothy Webster's Reports from Baltimore, 1861   151

Appendix V: Allan Pinkerton's Reports (from Tim Webster's reports) to George B. McClellan, 1861–62   153

Chapter Notes   185

Sources   199

Index   207

Preface

Timothy Webster, who is best known for his work as a spy for the Union during the American Civil War, began his career as a New York City policeman during the department's formative years, and followed that by joining Allan Pinkerton's newly created private detective agency. The purpose of this biography is to tell of the life of Timothy Webster, while focusing on his career, the important and interesting events and cases he was involved in, and his place in the time in which he lived and in American history. It is also to separate fact from the fiction that has made its way into his story.

I first learned about Timothy Webster when I was researching Pinkerton's National Detective Agency in the early 2000s for my book *Murder on the White Sands: The Disappearance of Albert and Henry Fountain* and subsequent articles I wrote about Pinkerton operative John C. Fraser for the Wild West History Association *Journal* and *Wild West* Magazine. Unfortunately, what I soon discovered was that much of what had been written about Webster was untrue. This started with Allan Pinkerton's book *The Spy of the Rebellion*, in which Webster is a main focus. The problem is many of the incidents in the book were exaggerated or completely made up, but that hasn't stopped them from spreading since the book's 1883 publication. To avoid repeating the same mistakes, I had to rely on primary sources whenever possible and question anything that was too far removed from actual events. While too many original sources were used in reconstructing Webster's life to mention here (see the Sources section in the back of the book for a complete list and the endnotes for more specificity), his story from Abraham Lincoln's election through his Civil War service was put together starting with his handwritten field reports and, where those do not exist, with Allan Pinkerton's reports to General George B. McClellan. Other sources were used to confirm the content of these reports whenever possible.

Such an undertaking required the assistance of many people. It is with gratitude and appreciation that I recognize the contributions of the following people: Jennifer Nash, Senior Search Room Supervisor, East Sussex Record Office, UK; Jeanette Cafaro, Museum Assistant, Historical Society of Princeton; Marcus A. Berry, Special Collections and Preservation Division, Chicago Public Library; Roberto Rincon, Jeffrey K. Wade, and Joanne Cartalino, interns at the Illinois Regional Archives Depository, Ronald Williams Library, Northeastern Illinois University; Lois Travis, Clerk of the Circuit Court of Cook County; Diane Lanigan, Graceland Cemetery, Chicago; Bonnie B. Coles, Senior Searcher Examiner, Library of Congress Duplication Services; Carol Kroeger and Janet Meyer, Rock Island County Historical Society; Karen Anderson, Executive Director, Scott County Historic Preservation Society, Inc.; Ronald F. Fournier, Bob Romic, and Michelle Hukvari, USACE Technical Library, Rock Island District; Bob Cavanagh, Abraham Lincoln Presidential Library; Linda Bailey, Curator of Prints and Photographs, Cincinnati Museum Center; Colleen McKnight, Special Collections Librarian, the Historical Society of Washington, D.C.; Darlene Leonard, St. Lawrence University Archives, Owen D. Young Library; Vincent J. Sansone, Diocesan Theologian/Archivist of the Catholic Diocese of Richmond; Katherine Wilkins, Assistant Librarian, Jeffrey Ruggles, Curator of Prints and Photographs, and Jamison Davis, Visual Resources Manager/Exhibit Specialist, Virginia Historical Society; Beth Petty, Research Assistant, Valentine Richmond History Center; Ed Margerum; Lucille Campbell; Mark Collins; Graham Amy; Cheryl Rabe; Leo Lawton; Janelle Bartlett Mummey; Paul Burkholder, Cleveland Civil War Roundtable; David Gaddy; Al Kissane; everyone in the Cleveland Public Library interlibrary loan department for tracking down so many books and microfilms, including Sue Kleme, Eddie Johnson, Tonya Jenkins, Michelle Makkos, Pamela Benjamin, Melanie Guzman McCarter, and Kelly Ross. Thank you to Michelle Davis for the great work creating maps. Thank you Jane Singer, who has spent much time searching for the identity of Hattie Lewis/Lawton and who was always willing to discuss her, Tim Webster, and other topics related to the book; Mel Maurer, Historian for the Cleveland Civil War Roundtable, and Frank Morn for reading an early draft of the manuscript and providing detailed feedback; Patricia Goff for discussing many aspects of Webster's life and Onarga with me, for her great research into Webster's genealogy and for reading a draft of the manuscript; John Brenner for his feedback; Louis Gerteis for detailed feedback and valuable suggestions; and my wife Meg for reading a draft of the manuscript and providing valuable feedback, and for everything else she does for me. I'd also like to thank my family who mean so much to me: my father Alan and mother Linnea, my sister Hayley an her husband Nick, our pets, cats Sally and Molly (who sat on my lap during the writing of much of this), and our rabbit Lobo (1999–2012). Finally I'd like to thank the most recent additions to our family, Gwendolyn Ellie Recko and Hanna Katrina Recko, for the happiness they bring us.

Introduction

As a New York City policeman in 1853, Timothy Webster was assigned to work the Crystal Palace Exhibition, which became known as America's first world's fair. While at the Crystal Palace, Officer Webster was introduced to Allan Pinkerton, a Scottish immigrant who had recently founded his own private detective agency in Chicago. Neither man could have known the importance of the meeting at the time.

In the 1850s Pinkerton's National Detective Agency laid the foundation for what would become the most famous private detective agency ever. Refusing such ordinary cases as divorce, Pinkerton's detective agency focused on criminal matters and was often employed by government agencies. In putting together what proved to be a talented team of detectives, Pinkerton often turned to policemen. Timothy Webster, who was recommended to Pinkerton by another member of the New York City police force, was one of these men. Though he did not join Pinkerton's detective agency immediately following the initial meeting with Allan Pinkerton, the England native decided to accept the job offer after continued harassment by New York politicians investigating "foreigners" in the New York Police Department. Webster moved his family to Illinois and went on to become one of the agency's best detectives.

Though quiet and reserved personally, when on a case Webster used an outgoing personality to gain friends and to get people to share information he needed. The skilled detective worked on such interesting cases as tracking the famed forger Jules Imbert, uncovering a plot to destroy the Rock Island Bridge, and investigating grave robberies in Chicago. He also did the more mundane work of keeping watch for thieving conductors as a railroad detective. Then everything changed.

Abraham Lincoln was elected the president of the United States and southern states seriously considered secession. There were even threats to assassinate the president-elect before he took office. Luckily for the United States, Timothy Webster, Allan Pinkerton, and other Pinkerton operatives uncovered and foiled the assassination plots. Webster's service to his country did not stop there. The southern states soon seceded and the United States fell into civil war. Men from both sides joined the military and prepared for battle. Tim Webster did not hesitate when the time came to defend his country, but he would not be meeting the enemy on a bloody battlefield. Timothy Webster put his special skill set to use not as a soldier, but as a spy.

Allan Pinkerton was put in charge of espionage for General George B. McClellan, and Tim Webster, who gathered much important information leading up to McClellan's Peninsula Campaign, became Pinkerton's top spy. Webster's work behind enemy lines included multiple trips to the Confederate capital of Richmond. He even acted as a courier for members of the Confederate army and once took official correspondence from a Confederate general to a colonel. On top of that, he received passes to cross enemy lines from the Confederate secretary of war. The secessionists saw him as one of them.

Webster's family immigrated to the United States when Tim was young. Webster was raised primarily in New Jersey and married a local woman. The couple had four children. Family was important to Webster. He always lived close to some of his siblings and his father went with him when he moved to Illinois.

Professionally, Timothy Webster — whom New York City police officer Tom Sampson called "the bravest, coolest man, I think, that ever lived,"[1] — worked as a New York City policeman, a private detective, and served his adopted country in its most desperate hour, first as part of a small group of detectives who may have saved Abraham Lincoln's life in 1861 and then as a spy for the Union. It is for Timothy Webster's brave and honorable service to the United States of America that he is remembered.

1

From Newhaven
to Princeton

Newhaven, Sussex County, sits on the southern coast of England, slightly more than fifty miles from London. In the first half of the nineteenth century the small town of Newhaven was slowly increasing in size. Its 1801 population of 584 increased to 927 by 1821. The town's most important feature was its port in Newhaven harbor. Not only did the harbor have a great deal of import and export traffic but, because of the location, was also a useful stop for ships that needed to escape dangerous weather. While most of Newhaven's economy centered around port activity, the town also had two large breweries for which it was known and four inns. The rural coastal town was described by one visitor at the time as "extremely neat and clean."[1] Living in Newhaven in the early part of the nineteenth century was Timothy Webster, who (at least in later years) worked as a tinsmith. Timothy and his wife Frances already had three children, Mary, Maria, and Samuel, when their son Timothy was born on March 12, 1822.[2]

The family grew even larger with the birth of Esther, Godfrey, and twins James and Jonathan before the end of the decade. Unfortunately, Godfrey lived for less than two months and James lived for only twenty days.[3] Outside of this family information, nothing else is known about the Websters during this period or how Timothy spent his first eight years of life in this rural community.

In 1830 the Webster family immigrated to the United States of America, where the opportunity to improve one's lot was much greater than where they had left. It was this hope for a better life that likely brought the Websters to their new country. The United States was made up of twenty-four states and numerous territories at the time they arrived. The president was Andrew Jackson, who would have a big effect on the development of young Timothy's political views. The Webster family was

St. Michael, 2004. Timothy Webster was baptized in this church (photograph by Mark Collins, www.roughwood.net).

undoubtedly spared some of the prejudice aimed at other immigrant groups because of their country of origin. Because of cultural similarities, English immigrants, who generally did not group together in ethnic settlements, blended into American culture and society much easier than other immigrants. They also arrived at a time when there was not much public opposition to immigration. This welcoming attitude would change over the next few decades. The Websters settled in Princeton, New Jersey. Shortly after arriving they celebrated the birth of Fanny. She was followed by three more children: Helen in 1833, Daniel in 1835, and Elizabeth in 1838. The family also lost a child when three-year-old Jonathan drowned in 1831.[4]

Princeton, where Timothy would arrive as an eight-year-old boy and leave as a man, was a growing city thanks to the construction of the Delaware and Raritan Canal and the Camden and Amboy Railroad. Settlement in the area began in the late seventeenth century, but Princeton Township, which was just over 16 square miles, wasn't formed until Mercer County was created in 1838. The city was home to people of English, Dutch, Scottish, and African descent. The African American population

Interior of St. Michael, circa 1900 (courtesy of Graham R. Amy).

included many former slaves, the result of the gradual emancipation laws the state had when the Webster family arrived.[5]

Timothy was raised at a time when schools were run by the local community. When children during this period were not doing schoolwork or chores, they often played games such as jackstraws (now known as pick-up sticks). It was common for families to find much of their entertainment at home during this period.[6]

The next documented event in Timothy Webster's life is his marriage. Nineteen-year-old Timothy married twenty-three-year-old Charlotte Sprowls of Monmouth County, New Jersey. The couple was married by Justice of the Peace Thomas Blake in Cabbagetown, New Jersey, on the twenty-third day of October 1841.[7]

The husband and wife appear to have made their first home in Princeton, as this is where their first child was baptized. The couple's son, Timothy, was born in 1842 or '43. Their second child, Sarah, was born — possibly in the family's next residence in New York City — about 1845.[8] Family appears to have been important to Timothy Webster, as shown not only by the children he had with Charlotte, but by the fact that close family members followed him with every move. The Webster family suffered a loss on February 19, 1848, when Timothy Webster's mother Frances died in Princeton.[9]

Webster showed an interest in politics and became a Jacksonian Democrat. Jacksonian Democrats followed the political philosophy of Andrew Jackson, the president of the United States from 1829 to 1837. Jackson supported greater rights for the common man — including voting rights for all white men, not just landowners — and individual rights. For Andrew Jackson, individual rights did not extend to blacks or Native Americans.[10] There is no record of Timothy Webster's beliefs on specific issues, which is unfortunate because it would be interesting to know how his views fit in not only with those of the divided nation, but also how they fit with those of his future employer, Allan Pinkerton, who was an ardent abolitionist and defender of black rights.

It is written that as a young man Webster was trained as a machinist. How long he was employed at this trade — while becoming an adult at a time when the country was suffering a depression that began because of the panic of 1837 and wouldn't end until 1845 — is not known, but it wasn't to be a lifelong vocation. Sometime between 1843 and 1850 Timothy and Charlotte moved to a new home and Tim started new job as an officer on the New York City police force.

During the second half of the 1840s the United States gained more land as a result of the acquisition of Oregon territory and the Mexican-American War. With this new land, now extending all the way to the Pacific Ocean, came new problems. Chiefly among them was whether the territories would ultimately allow slavery. This debate would grow over the next decade. Meanwhile, a potato famine in Ireland drove many from that country to the U.S. The migration of this large, mostly poor and uneducated ethnic group brought out resentment from many Americans. They were not

Timothy Webster, Sr., father of Timothy Webster (courtesy of Lucille Campbell).

Nassau Street, Princeton, pre–1870. The building on the left is an early tavern in Princeton, maybe the first. Records show the tavern's existence as far back as 1787. How much earlier it was built is unknown. The building on the right is the post office, which was removed before 1870 (collection of the Historical Society of Princeton).

only accused of stealing jobs, but some thought the Catholics (which almost all the Irish were) could not be trusted as Americans because they were under the power of the pope.[11] Webster would soon find himself a victim of the xenophobia this mass immigration caused.

2

Officer Webster

Exactly when Timothy Webster moved to New York City and became a police officer is unknown. We know from the federal census he was a policeman living in New York by 1850. That same year Timothy and Charlotte added a third child to the family with the birth of Eleanor. Sadly for the Webster family, she died sometime during her first decade. Living with Webster, his wife, and their children at that time were some of Webster's younger siblings and his brother James's family. Another family member of note is Timothy's brother Daniel, who turned 15 in 1850. He didn't live in New York then but would later move there and follow Timothy's footsteps by becoming a New York City police officer. The 1850 census shows that Webster lived in the Eighth Ward, which was on the southwest section of Manhattan Island bordered by water on the west, Broadway on the east, Houston Street on the north, and Canal Street on the south. Because police officers were required to live in the ward they worked in, we know Officer Webster worked in the Eighth Ward in 1850. At some point during the next couple of years Timothy Webster moved his family north to the Twenty-second Ward, which was bordered by 40th Street on the south, 86th Street on the north, Sixth Street on the east, and water on the west.[1]

It is not known if Webster had any police experience before becoming an officer in the nation's largest city. New York City's 1850 population was 515,547. To accommodate the city's increasing population and businesses, one-thousand six-hundred and eighteen buildings were erected in 1849 alone. It was already a dense metropolis when Webster arrived.[2]

Joining the New York police force before 1850 meant that Webster was an officer during the early days of the New York Police Department. Prior to 1845 the police force was much too small to have a meaningful effect preventing crime in such a largely populated area. To deal with the crime in this growing city, the Municipal Police Act was signed into law in 1845. The bill set up a police department in New York City that was similar to the successful police department that London had for the previous sixteen years. The new force began with eight-hundred men. The officers wore a star shaped badge. They were not initially armed, but this changed in 1853 when policemen were armed with clubs. Uniforms were also introduced that year.[3]

Why Timothy Webster chose to move to New York and go to work in law enforcement is a mystery. Whether it was a desire to combat crime, the danger and excitement, or some other reason, the fact is that Tim Webster spent the rest of his life doing police and detective work.

Not much has been recorded of Webster's experiences as a policeman. Former Pinkerton operative Pryce Lewis wrote in his memoir that Webster spent part of his time with the police force as a dog catcher. In 1853 Webster worked as a policeman at New York City's Crystal Plaza Exhibition, which was known as America's first world's fair.[4]

The event was significant in the history of the New York Police Department because the officers working the exhibition were the first to wear uniforms. Because the reception to the uniforms was so favorable, the entire police force soon wore them.[5]

The Crystal Palace exhibition began on July 14, 1853, and ran through November 1, 1854. The Palace itself was an impressive structure that included 15,000 panes of glass. Inside were 4,390 exhibits, which included industrial products, consumer goods, art, guns, clocks, boats, minerals,

Uniform of the Crystal Palace Police, *Gleason's Pictorial Drawing Room Companion*, September 17, 1853, pg. 185 (author's collection)

and various inventions.[6] In a letter to his sister, Mark Twain described the Crystal Palace Exhibition: "From the gallery (second floor) you have a glorious sight—the flags of the different countries represented, the lofty dome, glittering jewelry, gaudy tapestry, &c., with the busy crowd passing to and fro—tis a perfect fairy palace—beautiful beyond description."[7]

One of the many who attended this celebration of progress and industry was Allan Pinkerton, who recruited a few of the officers stationed there for his new private detective agency. Pinkerton later wrote that while at the Crystal Palace, Captain James Leonard introduced him to Timothy Webster.[8] Pinkerton was impressed by Webster and likely offered him a job with his detective agency at this time. If he did, Webster declined. He would stay on with the New York police force for a few more years. In time, Webster's meeting with Allan Pinkerton would change the course of many lives.

The next documented event in Timothy Webster's career is his testimony in front of New York City's Board of Aldermen. The board was conducting a wide-ranging and bizarre investigation into the city's police department. The broad scope of the investigation was corruption in the

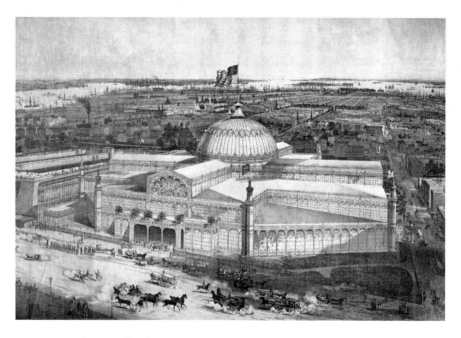

New York Crystal Palace, 1853 (Reproduction number: LC-DIG-pga-00099, Library of Congress Prints and Photographs Division).

Interior of the Crystal Palace, 1853 (Reproduction number: LC-DIG-ppmsca-08321, Library of Congress Prints and Photographs Division).

department, but it became centered on alleged perjury in a report by the chief of police as to the number of "foreigners" in the department, and the nativity of the chief himself—not that being foreign born and serving in the department was actually illegal.

Living in such a diverse city meant that Webster was witness to the anti-immigrant sentiment of this nativist movement, although, by this time he should have had nothing to fear from the nativists. He had been in the United States since he was a young boy and was, by all appearances, and American. Still, he would fall victim to their paranoia. Even though the strongest anti-immigrant feeling was against Irish immigrants and Catholics (as most Irish were), who some believed were more loyal to the pope than the United States, the movement targeted all people born on foreign soil.

One nativist protest in New York City led to what became known as the Astor Place Riot. In 1849 nativists intent on driving an English actor off stage protested outside the opera house where he was performing. This led to a riot in which over twenty people were killed and over one hundred injured. The nativist movement led to the rise of what would become the American Party in the early 1850s. Sometimes called the Know-nothing Party because in its early days members said they "knew nothing" when asked about the organization, the group stood against foreign born persons voting or holding public office and wanted to extend the period a person had to live in the United States from five to twenty-one years before they could become a citizen. Many involved in this movement also hoped to deny immigrants jobs, which they argued cost Americans (by their definition of Americans) jobs. The Know-Nothing Party was near its zenith in 1855.[9] This was the environment when the New York City Aldermen began their investigation.

The inquiry, spearheaded by Alderman John H. Briggs, focused on a report made by Chief of Police George W. Matsell on March 19, 1855. A month earlier the aldermen asked for a breakdown of the nationality of officers in the department. They wanted to know just how many were foreign born and of those, how many had been in the country for less than five years. They were especially concerned with the number of Irish policeman. The completed report showed that of the one-thousand, one-hundred and thirty-five officers, four-hundred and seventeen were foreign born (which roughly corresponded to the percentage of foreign born New Yorkers). Alderman Briggs charged Chief Matsell with perjury, alleging there were "at least 600 foreigners" in the department. Although this difference may not seem like a big deal, it was to Briggs, who claimed to be concerned about what impact a large number of foreign born officers could have on the city's protection. John Briggs fought the police department and some of his fellow aldermen throughout this year long investigation.[10] His fear of foreign policeman was shown earlier in what the New York *Times* called "a lengthy speech." The *Times* reported Briggs's opinion that

> the police formed a foreign standing army. An important foreign nabob — His Honor the Chief—fetches them out to drill as the Russian armies are drilled under their Czar. The police was not American — but Americans were often arrested by them without cause, and taken before an Irish judge and summarily consigned to the Tombs. He [Briggs] was once collared, himself, in the Park, by one of these foreign functionaries without show of cause, and came near being thrust into the Tombs.[11]

One wonders what Briggs was "collared" for, and how much the bitterness over this affected his attitude. Much later in the investigation Briggs stated, "This ... is the anniversary of the day on which the British evacuated this City, and I think it is very proper that it should be the day when an English Chief of Police vacates the office which he holds."[12]

One of the few men from the force called to testify was Lieutenant Timothy Webster. Each of the men who were called refused to cooperate with the investigation, and Webster was no different. The New York *Herald* reported Webster's May 2nd testimony. "Mr. Timothy Webster, lieutenant of police, made his appearance at the conclusion of the foregoing testimony, and was sworn by Ald. Briggs, but he proved as refectory as Mr. [William] McKellar."

Briggs, preparing to administer the oath, asked Webster, "You do solemnly swear that you will answer all questions?"

Responded Webster, "I solemnly swear that the evidence I shall give will be the truth, the whole truth, and nothing but the truth, so help me God."

"Put your hand on the book. Now, you do solemnly swear that the evidence you will give shall be the truth?"

Webster repeated the oath, and immediately followed it by stating, "Now, I decline answering any questions put by this committee."

Ignoring Webster's statement, Briggs began the inquiry by asking, "What is your name?" Webster sat silent.

The clerk spoke up, "Give us your name, can't you?" Webster gave no answer. "Timothy Webster — is that your name?" the clerk asked.

"That is the name on the subpoena I received," Webster responded.

Alderman Briggs asked, "Have you ever answered any questions put to you in the station house in regard to your nativity, et cetera?"

"I refuse to answer."

"What country are you a native of?" Briggs asked.

"I positively decline to answer any question this committee puts to me," Webster stated. "I wish that to be distinctly understood."

"Have you been posted up by Mr. McKellar, outside?" Webster gave no answer. Briggs then left the room and Webster took a piece of tobacco.[13]

Later in the month Webster again appeared before the board. He still refused to answer questions about his country of birth.[14]

Lieutenant Webster appeared before the board again on the last day of June 1855 as one of three the *Times* called "contumacious witnesses." These three witnesses—Webster, William McKellar, and Michael McCann—along with Chief Matsell, took up the vast majority of the board's time during the investigation. Webster's only recorded testimony at this appearance was a few wisecracks at Alderman Briggs's expense, including telling him, while referring to an affidavit stating that Matsell

New York City Hall, circa 1855. Photograph by Silas A. Holmes. This is where the board of aldermen met (Reproduction number: LC-USZ62–22024, Library of Congress Prints and Photographs Division).

was born in England, "Why, Alderman, I could go down into Jersey and get an affidavit that you were born in Ireland."[15]

Before their next appearance in front of the aldermen, Webster, McKellar and McCann appeared before Judge Charles P. Daly to argue that they should not be forced to answer certain questions from the board of aldermen. After hearing the arguments, Judge Daly ruled that "the examination of the witnesses must be confined to the subject which is under investigation, and cannot be asked any question not relating to it.... Nor is he bound to answer any question that would tend to criminate him ... or that would tend to degrade him, unless the question asked is essential to the direct proof of the matter under investigation."

Turning specifically to the testimony of Timothy Webster, Daly addressed two questions asked of him: "Have you ever answered, in the Station-house, any question as to your nativity?" and "What country are you a native of?" Judge Daly ruled that "these questions are irrelevant," and Webster was not compelled to answer them. Daly's decision continued, "But this witness refused to answer any other question the committee might ask him, a refusal entirely unwarrantable, and which renders him liable to be proceeded against as for a contempt."[16]

In early September, Webster and the other "contumacious witnesses," Matsell's clerk William McKellar and Lieutenant Michael McCann, appeared before the board yet again. McKellar and McCann were slightly more cooperative this time, but Webster, whom the New York *Times* described as being "very stubborn," didn't give an inch.[17]

Confrontation began immediately when Webster refused to read the oath, then said, "I should like to have counsel in this matter."

Briggs responded, "Oh, we cannot allow a witness to leave the stand. You need not say anything criminating yourself or anything of that kind. We want plain facts."

"Yes, Sir, I know that," said Webster.

"Any honest man ought to be ready to tell the truth without the aid of counsel, and that is all that is required."

"All I want is that you shall proceed legally, and not usurp powers that do not belong to you."[18] After receiving permission to refer to Alderman William Tucker as his counsel, Webster agreed to take the oath, but made it clear that he would follow the decision by Judge Charles P. Daly as to what he would testify to.[19]

Briggs asked the opening question. "What is your full name?"

"I will never deny that. My full name is Timothy Webster, sir."

"How long have you been attached to the police department?" Webster consulted Tucker, asking if the question was allowed under Judge Daly's decision. To this query Briggs responded, "I ask the question," despite having just agreed to let Webster consult with Alderman Tucker.

"I have a right to refer to your colleague, I believe," said Webster.

"Well, we will give you all the line you are entitled to, and a little more," Briggs said.

"I do not ask for more," Webster responded.

After reviewing the decision, Alderman Tucker said, "It is not enumerated in the questions, but it is my opinion that the judge goes on and gives us the power to examine witnesses on the matters referred to the committee."

Webster disagreed, saying, "Yes, sir, that is your opinion, but I do not read it as such."

Briggs told the witness, "We decide that you are bound to answer all questions relating to the subject now pending before the committee."

"I have no objection that you shall claim what you think is proper," said Webster.

"Then you refuse to answer my question?" Briggs asked.

"I do not see it here," Webster stated, referring to the judge's decision, of which he had a copy.

Briggs moved on. "What class of office do you hold in the police department?" After more discussion, Webster refused to answer the question. Next he was asked, "Were you ever attached to the chief's office?"

Webster held Daly's decision up as he declared, "It is not in the decision which I am governed by."

"Are you a citizen of the United States and of the State of New York?" Briggs asked.

That question brought a laugh from Webster as he responded, "Judge Daly refers to that point strictly, and I abide strictly by his decision."

Briggs was obviously annoyed by this point. "Perhaps you know more than the judge does himself, but that has to be settled some other time." Briggs went to his next query. "When were you naturalized, by whom, and in what court?" After a long silence, Briggs asked, "Do you decline answering that question?"

"I abide by the decision of Judge Daly."

"Then I understand you refuse to answer the question."

"I cannot help what construction you put upon what I say. I speak the plain English language."

"Well, Mr. Webster, that will do for today, sir. We shall require to call you some other day, I suppose." The committee adjourned for the day.[20]

Two days later, Webster, along with McKellar and McCann, appeared in the Court of Common Pleas before Judge Lewis B. Woodruff for charges stemming from their refusal to answer Alderman Briggs's questions. In the charges against Webster, it was stated that his "conduct was disorderly, that he used sneering language to the committee," and that he "was defiant towards them." Woodruff ruled in favor of the witnesses. Webster was not called to testify again.[21]

The investigation led to Chief of Police George Matsell being brought up on charges regarding his nationality. The Board of Police Commissioners ruled that the charges were not sustained. Matsell had been born in England, but his family came to the United States when he was a young boy. Much to Alderman John Briggs's chagrin, it was ruled that George Matsell was a citizen due to his father's naturalization. The decision came a full year after the investigation began.[22] Nothing else came of Briggs's efforts. Over the next half of the decade the nativist movement faded away as the country dealt with other issues.

A list of appointments and dismissals for the New York Police for 1855, published on December 28, show that Webster was on the force at that time.[23] After that, Lieutenant Webster disappears from the records. What effect the Board of Aldermen's investigation had on Webster's decision to leave the New York Police Department is unknown, but leave it he did. Timothy Webster next appears on the historical record as an employee of Pinkerton's National Detective Agency in 1856.

3

A Pinkerton Detective

Although 1850 is the official date Allan Pinkerton gave for his detective agency's founding, the actual date may have been as late as 1855. While it appears the agency existed in some form when Allan Pinkerton was being hired to take on cases in the early 1850s, the first official record of the agency is a document relating to the creation of the Pinkerton & Co. on February 1, 1855. The contract was for six railroads to give Allan Pinkerton $10,000 to hire detectives to protect railroad property and to watch for dishonest employees. When Timothy Webster joined the agency in 1856 it was known as the North-Western Police Agency. An agency document from that time states that the mission of the agency was "for the purpose of transacting a General Detective Police Business in Illinois, Wisconsin, Michigan and Indiana; and will attend to the investigation and depredation [*sic*], frauds and criminal offenses; the detection of offenders, procuring arrests and convictions, apprehension or return of fugitives from justice, or bail; recovering lost or stolen property, obtaining information, etc." Because police could not make arrests outside their own county and many rural areas had little or no police presence, the private detective was a necessary addition and often worked with local law enforcement or on behalf of local governments.[1]

Allan Pinkerton, the agency's founder, was born in Scotland in 1819. He grew up in a Glasgow slum known as the Gorbals. As a young man he learned the cooper's (barrel maker) trade. At some time around the age of twenty Pinkerton became a devoted follower of Chartism, a political movement based on a bill titled "People's Charter" which contained six demands: universal suffrage, abolition of property qualifications or members of Parliament, annual parliamentary elections, equal electoral representation, pay for members of Parliament (since under the no pay system common citizens could not afford to become members), and voting by ballot (as opposed to a public show of hands). It was at a Chartist related fund-raiser that Allan Pinkerton first saw Joan Carfrae, who, after Pinkerton's persistent courtship, agreed to become his wife. They were married in 1842 and less than a month later the newlyweds set sail for North America in search of a better life.

For a short time they lived in Montreal, but soon left Canada for the United States. They set their sights on the city of Chicago but something changed and they ended up in Warsaw, Illinois. After a brief stay there they moved to Chicago, and then to Dundee, Illinois, where Pinkerton set up a barrel making shop. It was in Dundee that Allan and Joan had William, their first of six children. It was also in Dundee that Pinkerton became involved in the abolitionist movement. He and his wife would often hide escaped slaves and Allan Pinkerton became extremely devoted to the cause. In the next decade, in his next home in Chicago, he would host such guests as Frederick Douglass and John Brown.

In Dundee, Pinkerton's career as a detective began with a chance discovery. Pinkerton took a raft to a small island on the Fox River because it had trees ideal for making barrel staves. While on the island he found evidence that someone had been using the island. Curious as to what they were up to, he returned often. His persistence paid off when, while hiding in the tall grass one night, a group of men came ashore. Though he was unable to determine what they were doing, he reported the suspicious behavior to Kane County Sheriff Luther Dearborn. The sheriff, with Pinkerton, moved in one night and caught what turned out to be counterfeiters.

The news of Pinkerton's role in uncovering the counterfeiters spread and led to a request from a local shopkeeper to find the person who was passing him counterfeit bills. Pinkerton quickly cracked the case and his reputation as a detective grew locally. This led to freelance work as an investigator and eventually a job as a police officer in Kane County, Illinois. He failed in a bid for sheriff of Dundee on the Abolitionist ticket, but continued on as a deputy and doing freelance detective work. He went on to work as a deputy sheriff in Cook County and soon was named the first ever detective on the Chicago police force. He resigned a year later and was appointed as a special agent for the Chicago Post Office to investigate mail thefts. It wasn't long before he went into business for himself. Allan Pinkerton established his detective agency in Chicago.[2]

Chicago at the time was a small but rapidly growing city. Its population rose from 4,470 in 1840 to 29,963 in 1850 to 112,172 in 1860.[3]

After being hired by Pinkerton, Timothy Webster chose not to move his family to the city of Chicago, but instead to tiny Onarga, Illinois. His

Allan and Joan Pinkerton (date and photographer unknown; Records of Pinkerton's National Detective Agency, Box 4, Folder 6, Library of Congress).

father and his sister Helen's family came with them.[4] The rural town of Onarga formed because it was chosen for a stop for the Illinois Central Railroad, which was put down in 1853. The town was laid out the following year and a post office was opened in 1855, which meant the town was still in its infancy when Webster arrived. Onarga was over eighty miles south of Chicago, so Webster had to travel to the city by train.[5]

Much of what Webster did as a Pinkerton operative will never be known. Many of the records of Pinkerton's National Detective Agency were destroyed in the Great Chicago Fire of 1871. Allan Pinkerton did write books about cases from the early years of the agency, but Pinkerton cared more about telling a good story than he did about historical accuracy. Much of what he wrote is either exaggerated or made up completely, as will be seen.

One case the agency is known to have worked on early in Webster's employment was the tracking and arrest of a forger known as Jules Imbert. According to Pinkerton, Webster had a role in the case, but there are no primary sources to prove or disprove this claim.

Imbert, who was born in the French West Indies, had been known by many aliases, including John Hart, Henry Donnell, Alexander Gay, Mouline Dutton, and Cephas Beaumas. Imbert's career as a forger and swindler brought him to America around 1850. His forgeries took him to places such as Key West, Charleston (where he sent a fake letter to his wife stating that he had died), Wilmington in North Carolina, Baltimore, New York, St. Louis, and Chicago. He made a good deal of money along the way. It was when he attempted to swindle R. K. Swift, Brothers & Johnson in 1856 that Pinkerton's National Detective Agency was brought in.[6]

That the Pinkerton National Detective Agency and operative George H. Bangs worked on the case is fact, but the only record of Timothy Webster's involvement and the specifics of tracking and capturing Imbert is Allan Pinkerton's 1875 book *Claude Melnotte as a Detective, and Other Stories.* As previously stated, Pinkerton is known for fictionalizing his accounts, but, because this was such a highly publicized case, there is at minimum some basis of fact in Pinkerton's story. Where the facts end and the fiction begins will never be known.

According to Pinkerton, he took George H. Bangs and Timothy Webster

George H. Bangs (photograph by F. Gutekunst in Philadelphia, date unknown; Records of Pinkerton's National Detective Agency, Box 27, Folder 5, Library of Congress).

with him when he went to the office of R. K. Swift, Brothers & Johnson to meet with them to discuss Imbert.[7] Bangs, who was about nine years Webster's junior, had a career in journalism, but changed paths and, like Webster, became a New York City policeman. In 1853 he was assigned to work at the Crystal Palace, where he was introduced to Allan Pinkerton. He soon began what would be a long and successful career with Pinkerton's National Detective Agency.[8]

When Pinkerton, Webster, and Bangs arrived at the office of R. K. Swift, Brothers & Johnson, Richard K. Swift was standing in the doorway. According to Allan Pinkerton, Swift's first words were "Run! Pinkerton! Run!" Pinkerton asked what he meant, and Swift pointed and exclaimed, "That's the man! I want you to spot him." Webster and Bangs followed the man while Pinkerton went with Swift to his office.[9]

Swift explained to Pinkerton why he was suspicious of the man who called himself Alexander Gay. Gay had come to the bank and, after receiving forty dollars for a draft by the Peninsula Bank of Detroit, told them he wished to sell a bill of exchange for £2,800 that he possessed. He said he wanted to sell it at a low rate because he needed quick cash for a real estate deal. The bank did not purchase the bill because they did not deal much in exchanges.

Two weeks later Gay returned to the bank with $14,000 and wished to purchase an English bill of exchange. He said he had received the money when he sold his previous bill of exchange to the E. W. Clark & Bro. bank in St. Louis. Swift was suspicious because Gay had so recently wanted to sell a bill of exchange but now wanted to buy one. Swift telegraphed the bank in St. Louis and confirmed that they had purchased the bill of exchange from Gay. Swift did agree to sell Gay the English Bill of Exchange but, because he was suspicious, sent for Pinkerton.[10]

Webster and Bangs followed Gay that night and Webster stayed on Gay's trail as Gay took a train to Detroit. Gay, obviously aware that he was being followed, leapt off the moving train a short distance from the Detroit depot. Detective Webster jumped from the opposite side of the train and kept on his man. He followed Gay to Hamilton, Michigan. There Webster telegraphed Pinkerton, who asked the operative to return to Chicago.[11]

Things quieted down until R. K. Swift, Brothers & Johnson received a telegram from Montreal asking about a draft they sold because, as Pinkerton put it, "there were suspicious circumstances connected with the purchaser." Pinkerton sent Bangs to Montreal. Bangs presented the case

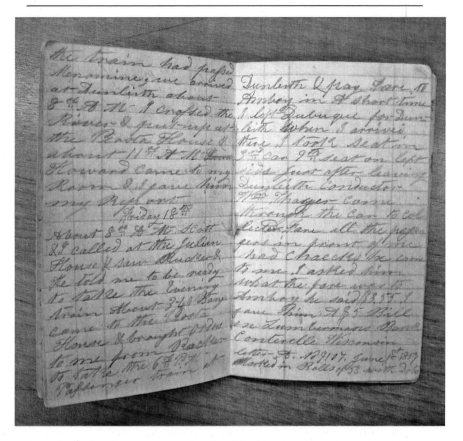

Timothy Webster's 1857 casebook. The closed book measures 3¾ × 5¾ inches (Records of Pinkerton's National Detective Agency, Box 25, Folder 4, Library of Congress; photograph by author).

to the Montreal authorities and Gay, now going by the name of Jules Imbert, was detained. Imbert voluntarily returned to the United States with Bangs. On the way back Imbert confessed to some of his crimes in an effort to make a deal for himself.[12]

Jules Imbert was taken to St. Louis for trial, convicted of forgery, and sentenced to seven years in the state prison. He was released after five years for what a newspaper called "exceedingly good behavior." It would not be the last time that Imbert was jailed for forgery.[13]

Most private detective work for the North-Western Police Agency was not this exciting. A more mundane example of detective work that was common for Pinkerton agents was the conductor testing for the Illinois Central Railroad. The job was simple. The operatives would pose as passengers to catch theft by conductors. The Pinkerton operatives not only recorded what they and other passengers paid for fares, but sometimes paid with marked bills. This use of labor spies was hated by the labor movement and was just one of several activities that would turn organized labor against Pinkerton's detective agency in the coming years.[14]

One of the few items of Webster's that has survived is a notebook he kept detailing a ten-day railroad assignment in 1857.[15] This assignment also serves as just one example of how detective work could keep someone away from their family for extended periods of time. In Webster's case, longer absences from home were soon to come.

4

Resurrectionists

In the nineteenth century one of the biggest problems in the advancing field of medicine was the archaic laws which made it difficult, and sometimes impossible, for medical schools to obtain the cadavers they needed for research and education. So medical professors turned to resurrectionists for their body supply. Resurrections were grave robbers. They would steal recently buried bodies and sell them to medical schools. This phenomenon was not exclusive to the United States of America, but was a problem anywhere that the laws had not caught up to research needs.

The most infamous men known as resurrectionists, William Burke and William Hare, were, in fact, not grave robbers at all. Burke and Hare, who operated in Scotland in the late 1820s, turned to murder for fresh bodies and the profit they could bring. The outrage of their actions led to the passage of the Anatomy Act of 1832 in the United Kingdom, which gave anatomists access to unclaimed bodies.[1] In the U.S. laws took much longer to catch up to the needs of medical schools.

It was in late October of 1857 when it was discovered that four graves had been opened and the bodies removed from the Potter's Field section of the Chicago Cemetery, which contained paupers' graves. The Chicago City Council didn't go to the local police, but to Allan Pinkerton, to solve the case.[2]

The deceased had been buried on or about October 25. A day or two later the grave digger noticed that the graves appeared to have been disturbed. He reopened them and found empty coffins. He informed the city undertaker of his findings, who, in turn, informed the city aldermen.[3]

Aldermen Russell Green and Artemus Carter hired the North-Western Police Agency to investigate. The aldermen may have turned to Pinkerton's agency rather than the city police because of the suspected involvement of Martin Quinlan, the city sexton, in the body thefts. The sexton was the government official in charge of the cemetery. Among the powers granted to the Sexton was the power to arrest anyone causing a disturbance or otherwise violating regulations in the cemetery.[4] This may have resulted in a friendly relationship between him and the city police. It is not known what aroused suspicion in Quinlan, but the fact that the undertaker went to the city aldermen instead of Quinlan suggests the suspicion of Quinlan began with the undertaker.

All that survives describing the operatives' movements are Pinkerton's reports to Green, brief coverage in Chicago newspapers, and the recollection of one incident from the case by Allan Pinkerton in an 1878 book. To further complicate the reporting of this story is Pinkerton's use of letters to identify his operatives in reports to Green. We know from these reports that ten operatives worked on the case. Newspaper reports tell us that three were James Finncan, George H. Bangs, and James R. Howard. Timothy Webster's name gets added to the list by Allan Pinkerton in the 1878 book *Criminal Reminiscences and Detective Sketches*. Pinkerton wrote that Webster was in charge of the force stationed at the cemetery. Another detective Pinkerton added to the list in this account was an operative named O'Grady (no first name was given), who may or may not have existed, as his addition to the story was only to tell of a practical joke. From the brief actions reported in the newspapers that match Pinkerton's reports, it can be concluded that George Bangs is operative C in Pinkerton's report and James Finncan is A. Webster, if he was indeed in charge, was B or D.[5] The fact that D was one of two operatives to plan the surveillance of the cemetery increases the likelihood that D was in charge of the surveillance and was Tim Webster.

On the day the North-Western Police Agency was hired, October 27, Allan Pinkerton assigned operative James Finncan to the task of watching Martin Quinlan. Finncan also watched Quinlan on the following day, with a second operative joining him during the second half of the day. The men reported no suspicious behavior from Quinlan.[6]

Pinkerton reported to the aldermen, "On the morning of the 29th of October, I detailed two of my men, here designated as "C" [Bangs] and "D"[Webster?], for the purpose of visiting the cemetery, to make an examination of the grounds, select such positions as would best secure the object desired to be attained, and make all necessary arrangements for the watching of the grounds, which watch it was deemed best to commence on that night."

That night six operatives (designated as A through F in the reports) watched the cemetery. They reported that "all had been quiet."[7] Years later Pinkerton wrote about the methods the operatives used in this case.

Pinkerton recalled that the men in the cemetery were under the charge of Timothy Webster. The detectives were stationed throughout the cemetery to watch every entrance and pay extra attention to fresh graves. Pinkerton wrote that, as no words could be spoken between the operatives for fear of being heard, he decided that they would run chalk lines (a type of string), attached to stakes each spaced about three feet apart, to each operatives' station. Then, to make sure each detective was at his station and awake, each of them was required to gently pull the line three times to signal to the next operative that he was there. This was repeated from post to post, then, after about a minute, was repeated in reverse order. The signal was repeated every fifteen minutes. A signal was also worked out to inform the other operatives if one of them spotted anyone entering the cemetery.[8]

After the first quiet night, a seventh operative was added to the cemetery watch. For a week the detectives spent the chilly late October and early November nights in the Chicago City Cemetery on the windy shores of Lake Michigan.[9]

Pinkerton remembered that spending night after night in a cemetery had a negative effect on a few of the men. He wrote that some of the operatives "began to notice ... indications of weakness on the part of the more susceptible among them. These braver fellows immediately commenced, with solemn tones and long faces, to relate hobgoblin tales of ghosts and materialized spirits which came from their silent resting-places for unearthly strolls among them."[10]

One of the weakening men, according to Pinkerton, was an Irish immigrant named O'Grady. Pinkerton said that O'Grady had talked much about his bravery. Because of O'Grady's bragging, Pinkerton admitted to taking delight in O'Grady's suffering and claimed that he decided to play a joke on O'Grady. He remembered, "I determined to play ghost for one night, show O'Grady a genuine goblin, and put his often-told tales of personal bravery to a practical test."

According to his story, Pinkerton arrived at the cemetery before his operatives one night and hid "within a heavy clump of *arbor vita* ornamenting a family lot" about twenty feet from O'Grady's nightly position.[11]

Shortly after Pinkerton arrived, the detectives, "one by one, and all in stealth ... began coming in from every direction ... while Timothy Webster noiselessly sped from point to point, stretching the line which held the men silently to their work." When O'Grady took his place he was "groaning and muttering," according to Pinkerton's account.

Once the sun had completely set Pinkerton moved from his hiding place so that he could feel the signals being sent by the string. He quietly sat and watched O'Grady. Then he saw O'Grady do something which a man hiding in the dark should not do. He lit a pipe. He also took out a black bottle of alcohol and began drinking, then set it on the base of the monument of the grave over which he was sitting. Pinkerton wrote, "I was indignant, and yet interested. I felt like dragging the brave O'Grady from his comfortable quarters to give him a good drubbing for his utter carelessness of the interests of the operation, and I am certain that in my then state of mind I would have done so if my desire to nearly scare the life out of him had not been uppermost."[12] While Pinkerton was rightfully upset, there is some irony because his plan to "scare the life out of" O'Grady certainly could not have been done quietly, and, if the grave robbers were near the cemetery at that time, would have put the mission in danger.

After watching O'Grady for a short time, Pinkerton accidentally broke the silence when he knocked a stone from where he was hiding to the graveled path below, frightening the target of the joke. O'Grady's reaction caused Pinkerton to change his plan. Rather than simply rushing at O'Grady while covered in a sheet, Pinkerton decided to "bring on the climax in a gradual accumulation of horrors." Pinkerton "gave a well-defined moan, and watched for the results."[13]

O'Grady began "trembling violently." Pinkerton claimed that O'Grady was shaking so badly that he could hear O'Grady's bottle knocking against his teeth as he took a drink. Pinkerton let out another moan. This, he wrote, "caused Mr. O'Grady to industriously begin crossing himself, and at the same time mutter some prayers as rapidly as his half-drunken lips could dole them out." Then came what this all led up to. Pinkerton remembered, "I suddenly rose in my ghostly attire and in a moment was upon him, waving my arms and gesticulating very savagely for any sort of ghost that was ever manufactured, but never uttering a word." O'Grady yelled as he jumped into the air, and fell back, doing "a complete back somersault over the base of an uncompleted monument."[14]

O'Grady took off running with the "ghost" following after him. The other operatives heard this and were quickly on their way. As O'Grady sprinted toward the western boundary of the cemetery, Pinkerton followed. O'Grady jumped the fence to exit the cemetery. Pinkerton claimed that as he leapt over the fence the operatives behind him opened fire. The detectives followed them over the fence, but because he and O'Grady were too far ahead, the operatives soon gave up the chase.

O'Grady ran northwest. He led his pursuer out of the city, passed an area "containing but a few scattering residences," and later into "the open prairie." Pinkerton remembered that O'Grady was "still yelling and cursing and praying" as he ran. He soon "came to the north branch of the Chicago River, then hardly more than a creek, into which, with a wild cry of despair, the Irishman plunged, swimming and scrambling to the other side" as Pinkerton reached the shore. Pinkerton gave another yell and watched as O'Grady "was tearing and bounding through the hazel brush" to escape his pursuer.[15]

Allan Pinkerton wrote that he never again heard from O'Grady. It needs to be noted here that operatives E and G disappear from Pinkerton's reports to Alderman Green before the conclusion of the case.[16] Could one of them have been O'Grady? Pinkerton left no record of the reaction by the other detectives in the cemetery when he told them he was the "ghost."

Six operatives spent October 29, and then seven operatives spent October 30 through November 5, at the cemetery. Nothing happened during this time. On the 6th Pinkerton was only able to send out four operatives, A [Finncan], B, D [Webster?], and F. Because there were only four detectives available this night they did not follow their normal routine. Instead, they took up positions near the northwest corner of the Catholic Cemetery, near the exit on North Avenue. They did this because when the four bodies disappeared there were tracks of a wagon on the ground through this exit.

The detectives took their positions at about ten o'clock on what was reported to be an unusually dark night. It is possible that the grave robbers were already in the cemetery when the detectives arrived because no one was seen entering, but between 11:30 and midnight a buggy was seen traveling away from the cemetery on North Avenue toward Clark Street. Finncan and operative D [Webster?] stealthily followed the buggy. The detectives kept their distance and stayed hidden, sometimes even crawling on their hands and knees. As the buggy turned south on Clark Street, the horse pulling it increased speed to a "brisk trot." The detectives ran after it.

Finncan caught up to the buggy and grabbed hold of the rear axle, slowing it down, then let go and went to the side of the road, not wanting to be seen. Finncan's action appears to have disarranged the horses' harness, and the buggy stopped at Chicago Avenue. A man exited the buggy to fix the harness. The detectives, who knew they were after the correct men because they could smell the corpses, rushed up and arrested the man who was outside the buggy. They immediately recognized him as City Sexton Martin Quinlan. It was said that Quinlan not only recognized the arresting officer, but called him by name. Was this officer Finncan, or D — possibly Tim Webster?

The other operative drew his pistol on the two men who remained in the buggy. Suddenly the horse backed up and the detective got his leg caught in the buggy's wheel. As he attempted to remove his leg from the wheel, the men in the buggy jumped out of the opposite side and took off running.

The detectives, knowing the identity of Quinlan, left him and chased the others. A few shots were fired, but neither man was caught. When the operatives returned to get Quinlan he was gone. He was soon found heading to his house. Along with Quinlan, the operatives had all the evidence they needed. Inside the buggy were two corpses: one male and one female. Both were in canvas bags, carefully packed, and tied down. Quinlan and the buggy were held at the Pinkerton office until morning.[17]

Quinlan appeared in court on the 7th and his case was held over for trial.[18] Meanwhile, Pinkerton detectives worked to identify the two men who had escaped. George Bangs and another detective sat in the captured buggy and let the horse take them where he may.

The animal took the detectives to Wright and Currier's livery stable on Michigan Street. Here the detectives received a description of the man who rented the horse and buggy. Soon Bangs, who had been deputized for this case, arrested Eli York, a student from Rush Medical College. York appeared in court that day. Justice Isaac L. Milliken released him on $800 bail. Dr. Daniel Brainard, the president of Rush Medical College, posted the bail.[19]

On November 21 the grand jury found nine indictments against Martin Quinlan, four of which included Eli York. This did not sit well with the attorney hired to defend Quinlan. The Chicago *Daily Times* reported his reaction to the nine indictments:

This was more than the counsel bargained for. He was only retained to defend the city sexton, and had reason therefore to suppose the city office-holders who have agreed to foot the bill, would decline to pay for defending York. The counsel did not feel very good-natured about it, and having been notified that the case was about to be called for trial, he proceeded to the courtroom and expressed his opinion of the matter. His opinion did not happen to be very complimentary to the detectives, whom he berated roundly for having given such evidence before the grand jury as caused that body to include

A pre-1871 Chicago street scene. Lake Street, east from State Street, date and photographer unknown (Chicago Public Library, Special Collections and Preservation Division, CCW 5.104).

York in the indictment. York, he said, had been examined before a magistrate, who had acquitted him on account of the insufficiency of the evidence to justify holding to bail. Yet, in the face of this, the grand jury had indicted him in no less than nine different bills. It was a personal matter with these detectives, and he continued to speak of them for some minutes.

When he had done, the representative of the detectives [Edward A. Rucker] asked permission to say a word. He said several words, among which were words to the effect that the true number of indictments against York

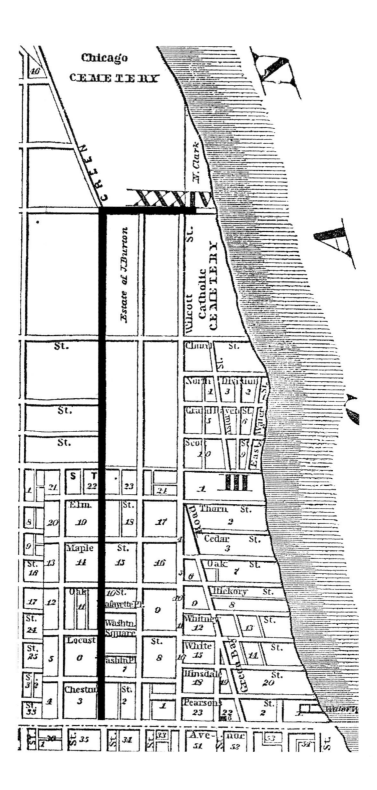

being but four, the counsel in saying there were nine, had uttered five falsehoods.

At this moment the indictments flew from the legal gentleman's hand in every direction, and his fist made a singularly rapid forward movement toward the other party's nose. The other party dodged the blow and was about to return it in kind, when the medical student "went in" on the other party's anatomy. "Mr. Sheriff!" shrieked the court, as the coat-tail of a portly individual disappeared through the door. "Police!" shouted the state's attorney. "Two upon one — take 'em off!" bawled the spectators. At this critical juncture, a policeman jumped up from somewhere in the crowd, and seized the belligerent attorney by the collar. "You're my prisoner!" he screamed, tugging and pulling with all his might to get the man off. That ended the fight.[20]

Chicago Courthouse and City Hall, 1850s (Chicago Public Library, Special Collections and Preservation Division, CCW 1.118).

Opposite: Map of cemetery and surrounding area. The black line follows the grave robbers' path from the cemetery to where their buggy was stopped (courtesy of the David Rumsey Map Collection, www.davidrumsey.com).

The victim of the attack, Edward A. Rucker, was a founding partner in Pinkerton's National Detective Agency.[21]

The case came to a close when, on January 11th, York and Quinlan appeared in court. The state announced that it would not pursue charges against Eli York. Martin Quinlan pled guilty to two of the indictments and was fined $500.[22]

Grave robberies in Chicago continued for decades because of antiquated laws that made it impossible for medical schools to obtain the cadavers needed for research and study.[23] The resurrectionists were necessary for the advancement of medical knowledge.

5

The Rock Island Bridge

Timothy and Charlotte had another child, Eva Lewes, in 1857 or '58. The only appearance of her name in any record is the 1860 census.[1] How much longer she survived is unknown, but she likely died young. Unfortunately for Timothy Webster, his job appears to have kept him away for a significant amount of the life of his little girl. During the next few years he did not spend much time at home because of a case that required him to take up residence in Iowa. While slavery was further dividing the country because of the Supreme Court's 1857 Dred Scott decision and the blood spilling in Kansas territory as a result of the Kansas Nebraska Act of 1854, Tim Webster's job pushed him into another of the regional battles in the country. This battle to protect self-interest over progress had to do with railroad expansion and bridging the Mississippi River. Webster was sent to Davenport, Iowa, after an attempt was made to burn down the Rock Island Bridge.[2]

The Rock Island Bridge, which connected Rock Island, Illinois, with Davenport, Iowa, while passing over Rock Island, was the first railroad bridge to cross the Mississippi River.[3] While bridging the Mississippi had obvious benefits—such as moving people and large quantities of goods quickly by rail to facilitate western growth, rather than having to unload in Rock Island, haul goods and people across the river by ferry, and reload in Davenport—not everyone supported the bridge. Those whose income and economy depended on the steamboats that carried passengers and cargo up and down the Mississippi fought the bridge at every step. They feared this expansion of the railroad over the Mississippi would give train travel and shipping an advantage and severely injure, if not completely destroy, the steamboat industry. The legal excuse they used to oppose the bridge was that it obstructed the river.[4] An editorial in the Rock Island *Argus*, commenting on a lawsuit that claimed the bridge obstructed boat traffic, showed not only how strongly some opposed the bridge, but expressed this view with baseless accusations and paranoid delusions of a conspiracy by railroad companies that desired nothing more than to destroy their competition by shutting down river traffic.

> It was an outrageous violation of law to place the bridge in the river, and it has already been the cause of the death of many men; the loss of an immense amount of property, and a great injury to the business, not only of Rock Island and Davenport, but of the whole valley of the Mississippi, Nor has it brought a corresponding benefit to anybody. Not an extra passenger or pound of freight has been brought to the railroad in consequence of the bridge, — but it has been an enormous bill of expense to the railroad companies, and made them liable for heavy damages which must ultimately be paid.
>
> But, we suppose the railroad interest will manage to keep the case in court as long as possible. We presume they cannot hope to realize any present pecuniary benefit from the bridge, but they do hope, by keeping the obstruction in the river, to materially cripple the navigation interest, and establish a precedent whereby the great river of America will be rendered comparatively useless. It is favored by those who seek, by special privileges and charted monopolies, advantages over the mass of community; and it is opposed by those who would sustain the freedom of the seas, the lakes and the rivers — by those who advocate free ships, freedom in trade, and equal privileges to all.[5]

There were also those who favored bridging the Mississippi yet opposed this bridge. They saw the enormous potential of the railroad in a country that was quickly growing its population and expanding its borders. They believed that whichever railroad took the lead linking east to west, the Chicago and Rock Island Railroad which was to connect to the Mississippi and Missouri Railroad at Rock Island in the north, or a proposed southern route, would greatly benefit its regional economy. As plans for a southern route were delayed, those who wanted the south to take the lead in connecting to the west, including then secretary of state Jefferson Davis, joined steamboat interests in opposing the Rock Island Bridge.

Another north-south battle was that between the northern city of Chicago and the southern city of St. Louis. Chicago stood to become a huge beneficiary of this new link to the west. The ability to move people and goods quickly to and from Chicago set up the city to take over as a dominant transportation center. On the other side, the city of St. Louis, Missouri, stood to lose substantial income if the riverboat industry shrank. Because of its location, St. Louis had become the center of steamboat commerce during the 1840s and remained so in the 1850s. Steamboat and St. Louis interests opposed the bridge from its inception, which led to the lawsuits claiming the bridge interfered with navigation of the river. Despite the opposition and lawsuits, construction of the bridge, which began in 1854, was completed in 1856.[6]

On May 6, just fifteen days after completion of the bridge, the steamboat *Effie Afton* crashed into one of the bridge's piers. *Effie Afton's* crew and approximately two-hundred passengers escaped unharmed, but the ship caught on fire because, it was claimed, a stove tipped over. All its cargo, except for a few cattle that made it to the shore, was destroyed. Also destroyed was part of the Rock Island Bridge. The bridge caught fire, which caused a section to collapse. The destruction of this portion of the bridge brought cheers, the ringing of bells, and the blowing of whistles from other boats on the river and spectators on both shores. The screams of the dying cattle, horses, and oxen that were on board the ship did not seem to dampen the mood.[7]

Following the collision with the bridge, Jacob Hurd, captain and co-owner of the *Effie Afton*, sued the Rock Island Bridge Company, claiming that the bridge was a hazardous obstruction to the navigation of the river. The case went to trial in Chicago in 1857. Norman B. Judd and Abraham Lincoln, both of whom would be connected to different operations later in Detective Webster's life, and Joseph Knox represented the Rock Island Bridge Company. The trial ended with a hung jury, nine to three in favor of the bridge company. The fight continued both in the courts and in the United States House of Representatives while the bridge was repaired.[8]

In the meantime some sought a quicker method to get rid of the bridge. According to some sources, an unsuccessful attempt was made to burn down the bridge in the summer of 1858. A second attempt to burn the bridge occurred on June 5, 1859. It was written in 1862 that it was the attempt in the summer of 1858 that brought Timothy Webster to Davenport. Whether there was an 1858 attempt to burn down the bridge or just threats that caused the detective to be brought in, he was undoubtedly there by the June 1859 attempt, because it was a bridge watchman — most likely a Pinkerton patrolman (there is no record of any other group guarding the bridge) — that found the combustible material on the bridge that night.[9]

The North-Western Police Agency had been hired to protect the bridge and to find those plotting to destroy it. There are no records telling how many operatives engaged in this work, but any operatives that undertook this task reported directly to Timothy Webster. We know this because Webster was placed at the center of the investigation when, under the alias J. R. Reed, he was named as superintendent of the bridge. Under Webster, along with any detectives that might have assisted on the case, were a group of uniformed guards.[10] Pinkerton's detective agency had recently created a uniformed guard force that would become a major part of the agency's business in the coming years.[11]

Timothy Webster moved, at least part time, to Davenport, an Iowa city with an 1860 population of 11,267.[12] Iowa had become the twenty-ninth state in 1846 (there were thirty-three states by 1859). Actually his residence was a lone house on a pier at the midpoint of a section of the bridge, but he spent much of his time on the Davenport side of the river and made a big impact on the community. A mention of Webster in a local newspaper showed that it was known that Webster had a wife and children back in Illinois.[13] During this time Timothy's family suffered a loss. On March 27, 1860, his father, Timothy Webster, Sr., passed away.[14] It is possible that Tim spent many hours on the train making frequent visits to his family in Onarga, but we also know that he spent much time, including many off-hours, in the city of Davenport, and that he became a part of the community. He was remembered in *History of Davenport and Scott County Iowa*, published in 1910, as follows: "[Timothy Webster] was well known in this city during his residence here and in 1860 was elected

The Rock Island Bridge, circa 1860. The house in the center is the superintendent's (reprinted from *Rock Island Arsenal: In Peace and in War*, by B. F. Tillinghast).

alderman from the fifth ward, but for reasons best known to himself at the time he declined to qualify for the office. He was a Jacksonian democrat, a great admirer of Stephen A. Douglas [Democratic nominee for president in 1860] and took an active part in the presidential campaign of 1860."[15]

What clues Webster found during the investigation, or if he did the work himself or took a supervisory role while other operatives investigated, is unknown. What is known is that the investigation eventually focused on two men, Josiah W. Bissell and Walter E. Chadwick. Bissell had been hired by the St. Louis Chamber of Commerce to collect evidence — which consisted mostly of taking affidavits—for cases pending against the Rock Island Bridge. Chadwick was an attorney in these cases.[16] Judging from the evidence presented at the trial, it is possible that Webster and the Pinkerton operatives had little to do with the evidence collected against the two men that stood accused. Most of the evidence presented against them in court came from Cyprus P. Bradley, who claimed he had been approached by Bissell and Chadwick to burn down the bridge, and Bradley

Davenport, 1858. North side of Second Street between Brady Street and Perry Street (Putnam Museum, of History and Natural Science, Davenport, Iowa).

went straight to the Rock Island Railroad superintendent to inform him of the plot. However, evidence was presented in the trial that showed that Pinkerton operatives were watching Bissell by 1859. What led them to suspect Bissell or what evidence they collected against him was not presented. Regardless of who collected the evidence, Pinkerton operatives took over when it was time for arrests.[17]

In Chicago, just over two years after Webster arrived in Davenport, warrants were issued for the arrest of Josiah Bissell and Walter Chadwick for conspiring to burn down the Rock Island Bridge. On Tuesday, August 7, 1860, Pinkerton operative Paul H. Dennis arrested Bissell at the Richmond House, a hotel in Chicago, and took him to the North-Western Police Agency's office, where he was held until the following day. While Bissell was being picked up in Chicago, Tim Webster made his move to arrest Walter Chadwick in Rock Island. Webster found an inventive way to get Chadwick to Cook County, where the warrant was issued.

Still posing as bridge superintendent J. R. Reed, Webster invited Chadwick to meet him at the train depot, telling Chadwick that he had some papers that he would like him to see. When Chadwick arrived, Webster told him that he had mistakenly left the papers on the train. The two men boarded the train and, by the time that Chadwick saw that the paper Webster wanted to show him was a warrant for his arrest, the train was already on its way to Chicago.[18]

Bissell was tried first. The trial of Josiah W. Bissell began on December 11, 1860, in Chicago. District Attorney Carlos Haven prosecuted the case with the assistance of Joseph Knox and Burton C. Cook. Bissell was represented by William McAllister of the law firm Walker, Van Arman, and Dexter.[19]

The defense claimed that Bissell was being set up. McAllister said that it was because Bissell was working for the St. Louis Chamber of Commerce to oppose the bridge and because he was an important witness in suits already pending against the bridge that it was in the best interest of the Rock Island Railroad Company to get him out of the way. This resulted, he said, in a conspiracy to have Bissell sent to prison. McAllister implicated Walter Chadwick in the conspiracy and claimed that this was why District Attorney Haven wanted separate trials for Bissell and Chadwick. Chadwick, McAllister claimed, was on the prosecution's side and they would make sure he went free. As evidence to this McAllister pointed to the fact that prosecuting attorney Knox had paid Chadwick's bail. A simpler explanation for this is that they were trying to work out a plea agreement with Chadwick. A few days following the arrests, Chadwick gave a statement in which he acknowledged his part in the plot but claimed that Bissell was the mastermind behind it.[20]

The first witness called was bridge watchman J. C. Flint. Flint testified to finding combustible matter, including powdered sulfur, oakum, lath bottles wrapped in cotton batting, and other items in the arches of the bridge and along the tracks on the morning of June 5. Flint also saw Bissell on the bridge that morning.[21]

He was followed by Cyprus P. Bradley, a former Cook County sheriff that Allan Pinkerton had once served as a deputy under. Bradley now owned a small private detective agency.[22] He stated that he was hired by Bissell in 1857 to serve notices to those whose depositions were needed for the cases against the bridge. Bradley then testified to a meeting he had with Bissell on April 13, 1860. He met Bissell in the parlor of the Richmond House. Bradley testified, that Bissell "prefaced by asking if he could talk to me confidentially. I said he could." Bradley continued, "He then asked if I wished to make $5,000 or $10,000. I said I did." Bissell told Bradley that "he was employed by the St. Louis Chamber of Commerce to have the bridge removed as a nuisance." Bissell said "that he had one judgment in Iowa against the bridge," which was being appealed. Because the process was too slow, he wanted a portion of the bridge destroyed. Bradley testified that Bissell said he would guarantee him $5,000 if he would do it and said he might even be able to get him $10,000 after the bridge was destroyed. Bissell also told Bradley "that an attempt had been made before to burn it, but the parties got frightened after they got the material on the bridge."

Bissell told Bradley that "he would furnish the material and one man." An "eminent chemist" he knew in St. Louis would make a substance which would ignite spontaneously when thrown on the bridge. Bradley asked Bissell if the bridge was being watched, and Bissell responded that "Pinkerton had fifteen or sixteen men watching it all the time," so getting the material on the bridge, he said, would be difficult. Bradley testified, "I told him I could manage to bring in a watchman on the bridge in my interest to let us on and burn it, but that it would take some money for expenses, to go down and examine." Bissell promised to send Bradley money for this.

At a second meeting each man agreed to find one other person to carry out the plot. Bradley told Bissell that the man he would get was Whitney Frank. Following the meeting Bradley immediately went to the office of Rock Island Railroad Superintendent John F. Tracy and informed him of Bissell's offer.[23]

At this point in his testimony Bradley identified letters between himself, Bissell, and Chadwick regarding the plan. He then testified to another meeting with Bissell that took place on June 12, 1860. According to Bradley, Bissell told him that he had raised $2,500 of the money for the job, "and when the job was done it could be made up to $10,000." Bissell then told Bradley that he would send for co-conspirator Walter Chadwick to come and meet with him the following day. Bradley then set it up so that the meeting could be witnessed by others. Bradley testified that he rented a room "in Matthews' Block, corner of Washington and State Street." He described the room's set up:

> The room was double, with folding doors, and a door from the hall into each room; I threw a partition across of matched boards, covered the boards with cloth and papered the whole room, cut away spaces near the top at the transom of the folding doors; a platform on the other side allowed three persons to sit and look down through holes in the paper as large as pen handles, and see and hear all that took place in the other room.

Bradley met Bissell by the Lake Michigan shore. It was here that Bissell introduced Bradley to Chadwick. Bradley stated, "Chadwick and I then went south and turned into Wabash Avenue and went to the room described." Waiting in the room was Frank, whom Bradley introduced to Chadwick. Also in the room were the hidden witnesses. Bradley questioned Chadwick about the reliability of the man who was supposed to help him and then asked him why the previous attempt had failed. Chadwick "said the parties heard the watchman coming, got scared and slid down the ropes into a boat." The conversation turned back to the plans for the upcoming attempt. Chadwick said the flammable materials would be shipped to Rock Island. Bradley continued, "Chadwick drew for me a plan of the bridge, showing me how, as he said, one span could be burned and the company be enjoined from repairing it; this would be as good as its removal." Bradley identified more letters which backed up his story.[24]

Cyprus Bradley testified to yet another meeting with Chadwick on the same day. Following that meeting, Bradley said, "I saw Mr. Bissell next 7th Aug., 1860." After this testimony court adjourned for the day.[25]

Back on the stand the next day, Bradley talked about the August 7 meeting with Bissell at the Matthews building. This meeting, like the June 13 meeting, was witnessed by hidden persons. When he entered he saw both Whitney Frank and Josiah Bissell there. Bissell asked Bradley if he received the package sent to him, which contained the materials to be used to destroy the bridge. Bradley said that he then explained his plan to get the materials onto the bridge, and showed him a shirt and belt with bottles attached that he would use.

Bradley testified, "I told him I must have money to pay off the man on the bridge. He asked how much. I told him $1000. Don't know if I said 'engineer on the tug' or 'man on the bridge.' He said he would go to Rock Island that night and deposit $1000 with a merchant named Dart—John Dart, I think, or with Mr. Chadwick, and this $1000 should be paid." By this time there was already a warrant out for Bissell so Bradley had him watched. That evening Bradley found Bissell at the Richmond House and went in to give him a message. Bradley left and informed Pinkerton operative Paul Dennis, who had the warrant for Bissell's arrest, where Bissell was.[26]

On cross-examination, Bradley stated that he first met Josiah Bissell about April 1, 1857, in Chicago, when Bissell came to his office. Bradley said Bissell hired him to serve notices dealing with the bridge cases. In response to another question, he added that he told Bissell, "in '59 perhaps, that Pinkerton and his men were following him round."[27]

A later witness, John P. Chapin, testified to being one of the men in the hidden room that witnessed the meetings between Bradley and Chadwick on June 13 and Bradley and Bissell on August 7. Chapin's recollection of the conversations in the room was similar to Bradley's. The next two witnesses, George W. Gage and William H. Bradley, gave similar testimony.[28]

When Rock Island Railroad superintendent John F. Tracy was questioned the following day, he said that getting the room where the meetings could be overheard was his idea. On cross-examination McAllister did his best to make the plan sound like a set up. Tracy defended his plan, saying, "Believing them to have intentions of destroying our bridge, it was, if we had plenty of evidence; wanted plenty of evidence, because if they were guilty we wished to punish them. I believed what Bradley told me. I got others to go there to hear what they had to say."[29]

There is no report of any testimony Timothy Webster may have given for the prosecution.

The defense began their case by calling St. Louis Chamber of Commerce President Derrick A. January to the stand.[30] January stated that Bissell was hired to collect evidence for cases pending against the Rock Island Bridge and explained what this entailed. January added that Bissell "was in no way authorized to do anything whatever to burn or otherwise destroy the bridge."[31] Much of the defense's brief rebuttal was not reported. This could be because their case hinged on how the bridge was described in the indictment, thus producing testimony that the newspapers did not consider important.

The case concluded on Saturday, December 15, with a verdict of not guilty. The jury based their decision on a technicality. They ruled that the location of the bridge was inaccurately described in the indictment.[32]

The case did not end with this verdict, however. More indictments were brought against Bissell and Chadwick for their alleged involvement in the conspiracy, but in the end, following then Colonel Bissell's Civil War service, all the indictments were dismissed.[33]

While neither Josiah Bissell nor Walter Chadwick were ever convicted of conspiring to burn down the Rock Island Bridge, it is difficult to believe that they were not involved in such a conspiracy. Considering the number of witnesses produced, either Bissell and Chadwick had formulated the plot to destroy the bridge or, as was suggested by the defense, the evidence was manufactured as part of a plan to get Bissell out of the way. The problem with the latter theory is that Bissell was a very small part of the cases against the bridge and was replaceable. It was the affidavits he obtained that were important, not him. It is difficult to see much of a benefit for the railroad interests by eliminating Bissell from the equation. Also, for the set up to be true, it would mean that not only did Bradley, the other witnesses to the meetings, and John Tracy lie, but so did Walter Chadwick, leaving Josiah Bissell as the only honest man. It would be interesting to know what evidence the Pinkerton operatives had collected that led them to suspect Bissell in 1859.

The battle over the bridge, which included St. Louis versus Chicago, north versus south, and the steamboat industry versus the railroad industry, continued, but was soon overshadowed by war. The fate of the Rock Island Bridge was finally settled on January 30, 1863, when the United States Supreme Court reversed a lower court's decision and allowed the bridge to stand.[34] The decision allowed the railroads to reshape the nation.

6

Plot to Assassinate the President-elect

The close of the 1850s was a troubled time for the United States. The issue of slavery was hotly contested. As the debate shifted to whether newly admitted states would be free or slave, the North and South grew further apart.

The debate grew to violent proportions with the Kansas Nebraska Act of 1854. The act allowed the territories to decide the issue of slavery in their borders for themselves. This left both sides of the debate dissatisfied. Those who were pro-slavery saw any restrictions to slavery as hurting their cause, and those who were against slavery were opposed to the act because it did not ban slavery in the territories. The result of the compromise was that both those for and against slavery moved into the territories to weigh the vote in their side's favor. This, of course, led to bloodshed.[1]

In the fall of 1859, John Brown, an abolitionist whom Allan Pinkerton had raised money for just seven months previous, made his now famous attempt to end slavery. On October 16, Brown, with a group of followers, attacked a federal armory in Harpers Ferry, Virginia. The purpose of the attack was to seize the weapons in the armory and start a slave insurrection. Unfortunately for Brown and his group, local militia stopped them from leaving. Soon, U.S. Marines led by Robert E. Lee arrived. Brown eventually surrendered. Abolitionists, including Allan Pinkerton, raised money for Brown's defense, but it did no good. Brown was found guilty of treason and hanged on December 2, 1859.[2]

On the morning of his execution Brown wrote, "I John Brown am now quite *certain* that the crimes of this *guilty, land: will* never be purged *away;* but with Blood. I had *as I now think: vainly* flattered myself that without *very much* bloodshed; it might be done."[3]

What Brown's raid did accomplish was to drive an even larger gap between the free and slave states, and to add to the distrust southerners had of northerners. In the South the raid on Harpers Ferry was seen as a preview of things to come if they remained in the Union. To many abolitionists John Brown became a hero and, on December 2, a martyr.[4]

The Republican Party, which was formed in 1854 in response to the slavery advocates, did its best to condemn and distance itself from Brown. Republicans, who were opposed to slavery's extension into the territories, worried that Brown's raid could hurt them at the polls.[5] It didn't matter since the Republican Party received help from an unlikely source in 1860: the Democrats. The issue of slavery had torn apart the Democratic Party.

Democratic Senator Stephen A. Douglas believed that each territory should have the right to decide the slavery issue for itself, which went against the southern radicals' belief that slavery should be allowed in the new territories, period. When Douglas received the Democratic nomination, the party split. The southern Democrats nominated John C. Breckinridge for president. The split votes allowed Republican nominee Abraham Lincoln to win the November 6, 1860, election with only 39.9 percent of the vote.[6]

The South feared the worst. South Carolina took drastic action. The state announced that it was seceding from the United States of America. Before Lincoln even took office six other states—Mississippi, Florida, Alabama, Georgia, Louisiana, and Texas—followed South Carolina. They formed the Confederate States of America. After Lincoln was inaugurated as the president of the United States, four more states—Virginia, Arkansas, North Carolina, and Tennessee—left the U.S. and joined the Confederacy. Because there was a regional split on the issue of secession in Virginia, the portion of the state that favored staying with the Union split from Virginia and became West Virginia. West Virginia was officially admitted to the Union in 1863.[7]

This was the political climate after Abraham Lincoln won the election. It was before Lincoln's inauguration, during this time of national unrest, that Allan Pinkerton was contacted by Samuel Felton, president of the Philadelphia, Wilmington and Baltimore Railroad, about secessionist threats to destroy bridges and railroad tracks connecting New York City to Washington, D.C. The threats were coming from Maryland, whose population was split on the issue of secession.[8]

Pinkerton replied that he would bring six operatives with him and personally supervise the investigation (he said that two or three operatives would have been enough had the case not been so time sensitive).[9] Felton agreed to Pinkerton's plan and Allan Pinkerton took a group of operatives with him to Philadelphia, where Pinkerton met with representatives of the railroad. Pinkerton then went to Baltimore with operatives Harry W. Davies, Kate Warne, and a third who used the alias Charles D. C. Williams. Two other operatives, Hattie Lewis and Timothy Webster, posing as a married couple, went to Perrymansville, Maryland.[10]

In an 1882 letter, Allan Pinkerton described Webster at this time:

> He was about 45 years of age [he turned thirty-eight on March 22, 1860], 5 feet 9 inches in height, weighed about 155 lbs, was well built, had clean shaven face with the exception of a moustache; rather inclined to be a little free and easy in his conversation and manners; he wore his hat a little to one side but back on forehead; his features were regular, and his complexion was rather dark. He wore a coat a little longer than the one represented on the cut [referring to a proposed illustration for *The Spy of the Rebellion*].[11]

Unfortunately little is known of Hattie Lewis, with whom Webster would team up frequently.

In Baltimore, Pinkerton, using the alias John H. Hutcheson, rented an office and posed as a stockbroker. In adjoining rooms on the same floor were the offices of a stockbroker named James H. Luckett, who was a dedicated secessionist. Luckett was a member of a convention that was discussing the possibility of Maryland seceding from the Union.[12]

Allan Pinkerton became friendly with Luckett and soon convinced him that he was dedicated to the southern cause. From Luckett, Pinkerton learned of a secret secessionist organization in Baltimore. Pinkerton reported a conversation about the organization he had with James Luckett, where Luckett said "they were *exceedingly cautious* as to who

Timothy Webster, 1860 (reprinted from *Timothy Webster: Spy of the Rebellion*, by Robert A. Pinkerton and William A. Pinkerton).

they talked with" because "they found that the Government had spies amongst them, and that since then they had been *very* careful." Luckett added that he wasn't a member of "the secret organization, for there were but very few, who could be admitted, but he knew many who were."[13]

The organization Luckett referred to was most likely the local branch of the Knights of the Golden Circle, a secret society that had been formed with the goal of creating a slaveholding nation that included the southern United States, the West Indies, Mexico, and parts of Central America. The society shifted to fighting for southern independence with the election of Abraham Lincoln as the U.S. president.[14]

Luckett went on to tell Pinkerton of a member of that organization, Cipriano Ferrandini. Ferrandini, who Luckett mistakenly thought was Italian (he was Corsican), "was the leading man," and "a true friend to the South" who "was ready to lose his life for their cause." Ferrandini, he said, "had a plan fixed to prevent Lincoln from passing through Baltimore, and would certainly see that Lincoln never should go to Washington," and added "that every Southern Rights man had confidence in Ferrandina [*sic*], and that before Lincoln should pass through Baltimore he (Ferrandina) would kill him: that Ferrandina had not many friends that knew his purpose, but was a particular friend of his (Lucketts [*sic*])."[15]

Cipriano Ferrandini, a thirty-eight-year-old hairdresser, was born on the French island of Corsica.[16] Corsica was populated by many people of Italian descent and Italian was one of the island's official languages. This accounts for Luckett's belief that Ferrandini was Italian. The "captain" title was likely a reference to Ferrandini's rank in the Knights of the Golden Circle, but may have instead referred to his rank in a militia called the Constitutional Guards.[17]

That evening Pinkerton met Luckett at Barr's Saloon on South Street, where Luckett had promised to introduce him to Ferrandini. Pinkerton reported,

> After supper I went to Barr's Saloon, and found Mr. Luckett and several other gentleman there. He asked me to drink and introduced me to Captain Ferrandina [*sic*], and Captain [William H. H.] Turner. He eulogized me very highly as a neighbor of his, and told Ferrandina that I was the gentleman who had given the Twenty five Dollars, he (Luckett) had given to Ferrandina.
>
> The conversation at once got into Politics, and Ferrandina who is a fine looking, intelligent appearing person, became very excited.... He has lived South for many years and is thoroughly imbued with the idea that the South

must rule: that they (Southerners) have been outraged in their rights by the election of Lincoln, and [are] freely justified resorting to any means to prevent Lincoln from taking his seat, and as he spoke his eyes fairly glared and glistened, and his whole frame quivered, but he was fully conscious of all he was doing. He is a man well calculated for controlling and directing the ardent minded — he is an enthusiast, and believes that, to use his own words, "Murder of any kind is justifiable and right to save the rights of the Southern people." In all his views he was ably seconded by Captain Turner.[18]

William H. H. Turner was a Baltimore Circuit Court clerk.[19] Pinkerton reported that Ferrandini continued with the message that Lincoln would never be president and that Ferrandini was willing to give his life for Lincoln's, his country, and the rights of the South. Turning to Turner, Ferrandini said, "We shall all die together, we shall show the North that we fear them not — every Captain will on that day prove himself a hero. The first shot fired, the main Traitor (Lincoln) dead, and all Maryland will be with us, and the South shall be free, and the North must then be ours." Turning to Pinkerton, he added, "If I alone must do it, I shall — Lincoln shall die in this city." Ferrandini and Turner soon left to attend a "secret meeting."[20]

Operative Harry Davies learned about Ferrandini independent of Pinkerton through a secessionist named Otis K. Hillard.[21] While becoming friendly with Hillard in an effort to learn all he could, Davies accompanied Hillard to saloons, billiard halls, and Annette Travis's brothel, where Hillard spent much of his time. O. K. Hillard and his friends spent most days drinking consistently. He once greeted Davies, who was trying to blend in, with the telling statement, "You look sober — what is the matter with you?"[22]

Davies's report of February 19 went into detail about a group who called themselves the National Volunteers. Hillard told him, "Ever since I went to Washington I am very careful in what I say. There are Government spies here all the time, (in Baltimore) even now.... We are all more careful (meaning the National Volunteers) — twenty times more careful than we were previously.... Do not think my friend that it is a want of confidence in you that makes me so cautious— it is because I have to be. I do not remember to have spoken to a person out of our Company, and the first thing I knew I was at Washington before that Committee." Hillard referred to a House of Representatives committee investigating groups in Washington that allegedly were hostile to the government. Hillard was questioned before them on February 6.[23] Hillard continued, "We have taken a solemn oath, which is to obey the orders of our Captain, without asking any questions, and in no case, or under any circumstances reveal any orders received by us, or entrusted to us, or anything that is confidential." Davies asked Hillard what the first object of the organization was and Hillard replied, "It was first organized to prevent the passage of Lincoln with the troops through Baltimore."[24]

In Perrymansville (now Perryman), a town about thirty miles northeast of Baltimore, Timothy Webster joined a group of Maryland secessionists in a militia cavalry. Pinkerton later said that Webster's reports showed "the manner in which the first Military organization of Maryland Secessionists was formed, and the promises repeatedly made by Governor Hicks [Maryland Governor Thomas H. Hicks] of arms being furnished to them."[25] Copies of only two of Webster's reports have survived and the information in these is minimal. Judging from the company he kept in Perrymansville, it is probable he provided information similar to that of Davies and Pinkerton. On February 17, 1861, Webster reported that after "a game of Tenpins," he and two others, whose names were Springer and Taylor, went together to eat. Springer and Taylor began talking about the route that Lincoln would take to Washington. When Taylor suggested that Lincoln might use "the Central Road," Springer responded that he "had better not come over this road with any Military," and that if they did attempt to take military over the road, "Lincoln would never get to Washington."

Webster reported on what Springer thought might happen to Lincoln in Baltimore:

> Springer talked some about Lincoln, and said that when Lincoln arrived in Baltimore, they would try to get him out to speak, and if he did come out, he (Springer) would not be surprised if they killed him; that there was in Baltimore about One Thousand men well organized, and ready for anything. I asked if the leaders were good men. Springer said they had the very best men in Baltimore, and that nearly all the Custom House Officers were in the Organization. I could not learn from him any of their names.[26]

The sum of the information gathered prompted Allan Pinkerton to act. There were several men planning to assassinate Lincoln. Pinkerton knew that if just one of these men followed through with an attempt on Lincoln's life, the president-elect would be in danger.

Abraham Lincoln had left his home in Springfield, Illinois, on February 11, 1861, and began his journey to Washington for his inauguration as the sixteenth president of the United States. Lincoln spoke to crowds in Indianapolis, Toledo, Columbus, Cincinnati, Cleveland, Pittsburgh,

Buffalo, Albany, New York, Trenton, Philadelphia, and Harrisburg along the way.[27] Allan Pinkerton sent a telegram to Norman Judd, a friend of Lincoln who was part of the presidential entourage. Later in New York, Pinkerton operative Kate Warne delivered a note from Pinkerton to Judd warning of the danger Lincoln faced.[28]

Pinkerton followed that by personally bringing the information to the presidential party when they were in Philadelphia. There he met with Samuel Felton and then with Norman Judd. After explaining his concerns and his plans to keep the president-elect safe, he met with Abraham Lincoln.[29] Pinkerton reported,

> I alluded to the expressions of Hillard and Ferrandina [*sic*]; that they were ready to give their lives for the welfare of their Country, as also that their country was South of Mason's and Dixon's line; that they were ready and willing to die to rid their Country of a tyrant as they considered Lincoln to be.
>
> I said that I did not desire to be understood as saying that there were any large number of men engaged in this attempt — but that on the contrary I thought there were very few — probably not exceeding from fifteen to twenty who would be really brave enough to make the attempt, — but that I thought Hillard was a fair sample of this class — a young man of good family, character and reputation — honorable, gallant and chivalrous, but thoroughly devoted to Southern rights, and who looked upon the North as being aggressors upon the rights of that section and upon every Northern man as an Abolitionist, and he (Mr. Lincoln) as the embodiment of all those evils, in whose death the South would be largely the gainers.[30]

Abraham Lincoln, circa 1861–1865 (Reproduction number: LC-DIG-ppmsca-19205, Library of Congress Prints and Photographs Division).

The detective warned Lincoln of how difficult it would be to protect him and how easy it would be for an assassin to kill him in the large crowds expected at Baltimore. Lincoln sat, quietly thinking, after

Pinkerton described the threat. Judd broke the silence by explaining the plan they had come up with to take Lincoln to Washington that night instead of following the public itinerary. Lincoln would not agree with the arrangement. He said he had commitments in Harrisburg the next day that he would not break. He said that after the engagements he was open to any plan they worked out.[31]

Judd and Pinkerton worked through the night to develop a plan to take Lincoln safely through Baltimore to Washington. Joining Pinkerton

Norman B. Judd, circa 1860–65 (Control number NWDNS-111-B-2563, National Archives and Records Administration, Still Picture Records Section).

and Judd for the meeting were Henry Sanford of the American Telegraph Company and George C. Franciscus of the Pennsylvania Railroad. Both were needed to carry out the plan: Franciscus to set up transportation and Sanford for communication and to cut the telegraph so word of Lincoln's early departure could not be sent ahead.[32]

The next morning Lincoln received information about the plots to assassinate him from a source independent of Pinkerton, General Winfield Scott. This confirmation from a different source convinced Lincoln that the plots were real.[33]

That evening Lincoln attended a banquet held by Pennsylvania Governor Andrew G. Curtin. Lincoln, faking sickness, bowed out early. According to Pinkerton's report, Lincoln "wore a brown Kossuth Hat" and had "an overcoat thrown loosely over his shoulders" for a disguise. He left for the train station on what Pinkerton described as a "chilly but not cold" night. Lincoln, along with Ward Lamon, was greeted at the station by Pinkerton. Already in the sleeping car was the twenty-seven or twenty-eight-year-old detective Kate Warne. Lincoln entered the sleeping car unrecognized and was soon on his way, through Baltimore, to Washington.[34] Warne reported, "Mr. P.— introduced me to Mr Lincoln. He talked very friendly for some time.... Mr P— Did not sleep, nor did Mr. Lincoln. The excitement seemed to keep us all awake."[35] The group arrived safely in Washington at six o'clock in the morning.

A coded message was sent to report the success of the journey. In the code Allan Pinkerton was "Plums," Abraham Lincoln was "Nuts," and Washington, D.C., was "Barley." The message read, "Plums has Nuts— arri'd at Barley — all right."[36]

Though Lincoln was mocked for sneaking into Washington by newspaper reporters who didn't have the facts, the secret journey seems not only reasonable, but absolutely necessary when considering all of the plots that existed against Lincoln. Although some have questioned if there really was a plot, the fact that a warning also came from General Winfield Scott, who had no connection to Pinkerton, seems to confirm the validity of the threats. Activist Dorothea Dix also warned Lincoln of assassination threats.[37] The evidence clearly shows that, while there may not have been a singular, well-organized plot, there were enough real threats from groups and individuals that precautions had to be taken.

Had Allan Pinkerton and his operatives not uncovered the plots against Lincoln, there is a real chance that Lincoln never would have lived to be sworn in as president. All it would have taken was for one of those conspirators to follow through on his plans. The country found out four years later how easy it is for a determined man to assassinate a president. Perhaps, had Lincoln never been warned about the plots, it would have been Cipriano Ferrandini in 1861 and not John Wilkes Booth in 1865 who killed him. Those extra four years of life would prove to be vital for the nation.

7

Work in Maryland
Continued

Lincoln's safe arrival did not mean the end of the detective force's work. Their next task was to learn if the secessionists posed further danger. The day after Lincoln's clandestine journey the operatives returned to Maryland to assess the situation.

There was anger at Lincoln's nighttime passage among the secessionists. Pinkerton reported that when he met Luckett at the depot at about 5:00 P.M., Luckett took Pinkerton to one side to complain about Lincoln's "damnable" passage through Baltimore. Pinkerton reported,

> He said that he was collecting money for the *friends* in Baltimore, and they would yet make the attempt to assassinate Lincoln; that if it had not been for d — d spies somewhere, Lincoln never could have passed through Baltimore; that the men were all ready to have done the job, and were in their places, and would have murdered the d — d Abolitionist had it not been that they were cheated. He said that Captain Ferrandina [*sic*] had had about Twenty picked men with good revolvers and Knives[;] that their calculation was to get up a row in the crowd with rotten eggs, and brick-bats, and that while the Police (some of whom understood the game) would be attending to this, that Captain Ferrandina [*sic*] and his men should attack the carriage with Lincoln and shoot every one in it, and trust to mixing up in the crowd to make their escape — but that if any of the members were taken the others were to rescue him at all cost....
>
> Mr. Luckett was very much excited and swore very hard against the d — d spies who had betrayed them, remarking that they would yet find them out, and when found they should meet the fate which Lincoln had for the present escaped.[1]

A few days before Lincoln's secret journey, on February 20, the operative going by the alias Charles Williams joined the secessionist militia the National Volunteers. Two other spies, New York policeman Tom Sampson and Ely De Voe, had previously joined the group.[2] The Pinkerton operative reported that he had a conversation with the men and learned that one, who called himself Thompson (Sampson's alias), claimed to be an Englishman who had been in the country since he was sixteen months old and had recently come to Baltimore from Alabama while traveling with his friend who had business in Baltimore. The friend said his name was Davis (De Voe's alias).

That evening Williams met the two at the Melodeon Concert Hall, where they had some casual conversation, mostly about a farm Thompson owned in Iowa. Upon hearing about his owning land in the North, Williams asked if he was for the South. Thompson replied that he was, but that "he was for peace, and hoped that the Union would be preserved." Williams added that "there was something peculiar about their movements" that Sherrington, another member of the National Volunteers, "did not like." Sherrington told Williams "to be careful of them, for he believed they were two d — d spies."[3]

Williams reported this to Pinkerton on the 25th of February, two days after Pinkerton had arrived with Lincoln in Washington. From the description of the two men Allan Pinkerton not only theorized that they were members of the New York Police force, but also correctly concluded that Thompson was Tom Sampson. Pinkerton was told the men were known to be government spies and that they were to be killed in Washington "if opportunity offered." Pinkerton set out a plan to warn the spies.[4]

When New York Chief of Police George W. Walling wrote his memoir twenty-six years later, he asked officer Sampson to relate his experiences as a spy. Sampson told about the experiences he and De Voe had posing as southern sympathizers and as members of the National Volunteers. Sampson said, "For a time things went on smoothly. De Voe and I became members of a military company that met regularly in a kind of barracks." He described their "presiding officer" and "military instructor," Captain Hays, as "a picturesque Texan ... with great flashing eyes and long floating hair, topped with a huge white sombrero." Sampson recalled that, because they had no firearms, the group that sometimes numbered forty men were drilled using laths.[5]

Sampson, who turned thirty-four in 1861, soon realized that he and De Voe were suspected of being spies.[6] He said that he had been asked "searching questions" about "Davis" (De Voe). De Voe's wife had sent him a letter. Though it was addressed to De Voe's alias, it had a New York postmark, which aroused suspicion. Sampson recalled that he "was at once asked many questions in regard to the letter — where it came from and what it was about." He explained it as well as he could, but knew it was time to leave the National Volunteers. He explained the danger they faced: "The 'Volunteers' were loud in their threats against traitors. The desperadoes of the company were in the majority. All carried revolvers, and De Voe and I stood a first-rate chance of being killed on sight. There was even a detail whose duty it was to 'do away' with suspected persons."[7]

The men left for Washington quickly, leaving everything behind and taking on new wardrobes for disguise. Sampson wrote one detail of his change of clothes, "I remember that I had worn a heavy cloth cap with a band of fur around it. I gave it away, and donned a soft slouch hat." The men went to Willard's Hotel and registered under their aliases Thompson and Davis. Then they went to their hotel room to discuss their situation.[8]

After a while the men left their rooms to look over the main hall in the hotel. In the lobby were several of the National Volunteers. They were examining the hotel register. Sampson recalled, "I cursed my stupidity in not having thought to change my alias." Sampson watched as one of the men "turned and whispered to his associates," and then they all walked out. The New York detectives didn't know what to do. Sampson hoped they wouldn't be spotted in the crowded room. De Voe leaned on a cigar stand while Sampson looked toward the billiard room and became separated from De Voe. Sampson felt fear as he tried to think of way out of the city. It was at that moment "when a man in a long overcoat lounged along and got his back directly toward" Sampson. Suddenly, "in a very low tone" so Sampson could just make out the words, the man spoke.

"For God's sake, Tom, come out of this," he said. Sampson was startled, but kept his composure enough to realize he shouldn't move or let on to others that the man was speaking to him.[9]

Both men stood still. With his back still to the stranger, Sampson replied, "I do not recognize you." Sampson remembered, "The man's hand just faintly moved behind him, as though bidding me to follow." Though he did not know if the man was actually trying to help him, or just get him alone so he could murder him, when the stranger walked out of the hotel, Sampson followed. He remembered, "I followed very close to him, my steps almost locking his. I carried a self-cocking pistol, and I knew how to use it. I made up my mind that at the first suspicious movement I would shoot."[10] Out on Pennsylvania Avenue, still in a quiet voice, the unidentified man said, "My God! Where is Wash. Walling?"

"What Wash. Walling?" Sampson asked.

"Why, Tom, Captain Walling," was the reply. Frightened by this mention of the New York City Chief of Police, Sampson gave no reply. As they walked, Sampson was still unable to get a view of the stranger's face. He described the man, "My companion had on a great, rough coat, with the collar turned up to his nose. A heavy cap was drawn over his eyes." Sampson feared the worst, and kept his hand on a pistol he carried as they walked.

Then the man spoke again, "Tom, for God's sake tell me who is with you, and where is your fur cap?" Sampson recalled his reaction to the question. "This made me start. The man knew I had exchanged my cap for a soft hat. He must have followed me from Baltimore. I could stand the suspense no longer. I caught him suddenly by the arm, spun him around with my left hand, while with my right I still gripped the pistol. The violence of the movement flung open his coat and shifted his cap, so that his face was revealed. He made no movement but looked calmly at me. Then slowly, very slowly, his face came back to me."

"Is that you, Tim?" Sampson cried out.

"You did not know Tim Webster, Tom?" he calmly replied.

Sampson was overjoyed to see this old friend. When writing about this incident, he remembered of Webster, "Now Tim was one of Captain Walling's and my best friends. He had been on the force with us in former years and I knew him to be a man of exceptional honesty and courage."

Relieved, Sampson told Webster how close he was to shooting him. "You will never know, Tim, how near you came to being killed. For the last five minutes my finger has been on the trigger of my pistol."[11]

Webster was in no mood for small talk. "It was not a question of killing me, Tom," he said rapidly, "but it is to save you from death that I have followed you. Your life is not worth a cent. I swear to you there are twenty men after you this very instant. Even now I expect we are being watched. I may not be suspected, for I am with them, but they shan't kill my old friend if I can help it. But you clear out of this just as fast as you can, Tom; it is more serious than you think. The chances are you will not get through safely unless you use every precaution. Quickness of movement is everything now." Webster added, "Tom, it's so close a shave that at this moment if there's anything particular you'd like to say to your wife you'd better say it to me for her."

"But, Tim," Sampson replied, "I can't leave De Voe in the lurch."

"He will have to take care of himself. You're a dead man if you go back after him."

Sampson said he insisted that they go back for De Voe, and that Webster reluctantly agreed to help. They went back to Willard's Hotel "by a back way" and, on the way, Webster told Sampson that in his role as a secessionist, he had been given the assignment to kill him and De Voe.

They left Willard's with De Voe. Webster then gave them instructions. "If you go to the railroad depot you will both be dead men," he told them. "You will have to walk around Washington some fifteen miles and take the train there. I will start with you and put you on the track. It is your only chance of escape, for every other exit is guarded."[12]

Tim Webster led them out of the city and left them near a barn. Sampson and De Voe slept in the barn. Early the next morning they boarded a train to Baltimore. Their luck didn't improve. On the train, according to Sampson's memory, were six of the National Volunteers. Sampson and De Voe decided they needed to get off the train and jumped off the platform before reaching Baltimore. De Voe sprained his ankle and Sampson sustained minor injuries from the jump. They were able to make their way to the depot and were soon on a train headed north. Sampson recalled, "We should have been murdered but for the good head and great heart of Tim Webster, the bravest, coolest man, I think, that ever lived."[13]

The gratitude of Sampson toward Webster was well deserved. Webster not only saved the lives of the two detectives, but in the process risked blowing his cover and losing his own life.

The day after helping Sampson and De Voe out of town, Webster, in Baltimore, told Pinkerton what had happened. Pinkerton reported,

At 10.30. A.M. T. W. returned from Washington, D.C., and made a Verbal report in relation to Detective Tom Sampson, and Ely De Voe, who

Thomas Sampson in later years (Reprinted from *Recollections of a New York Chief of Police*, by George W. Walling).

were the parties known as Thompson and Davis, late of Sherwood Hotel. They were both very much frightened at the receipt of the news by T. W. and left their Hotel without paying the bill or getting their baggage — in short they made a precipitate retreat, thanking T. W. for his information.

T. W. had also called on N. B. Judd in his room at Willards [*sic*] Hotel. Judd was very much pleased to see T. W. and laughed very heartily at the New York Detectives being discovered.[14]

Webster's report covering that same day is his last surviving report dealing with operations in Perrymansville.

Tuesday 26th, February 1861.

I had breakfast, after which I went to the Depot and took the 7.40. A.M. Train for Baltimore.

On arriving at Baltimore I went to the Office, saw A. P — and reported to him. We then walked up town, A. P — all the time giving me my instructions. He requested me to leave Perrymansville on Wednesday, or Thursday, and laid the plan by which I was to draw off. A. P.— also told me that I was to go with one of his men (Williams) in the afternoon and get acquainted with some of the leading men of the Military Company's [*sic*] that were recruiting for South Carolina service. Williams was to meet me at the White Beer Brewery, and introduce me to Sherrington, after which we would go to the Drill

Willard's Hotel, circa 1890s (CHS 02282, Historical Society of Washington, D.C.).

room and get an introduction to Col. Haskill. Williams then went to look for Sherrington, while Mr. P—went and "spotted" the White Beer Brewery to me.

I then left A. P—and went to Springer's Store. I found Mr. Forward in, but Springer had gone out to collect some bills. Forward, and I, had a glass of beer—whilst we were Drinking he told me that the boys felt mighty sore about Lincoln's giving them the slip: that if Lincoln had gone through when he was expected, he would have been shot, and then Baltimore would have been the battle-field but now he thought Charleston would be. I said, that was just what I thought. I then bade him good bye and went to the White Beer Saloon, where I took a seat and called for a glass of beer.[15]

About a half hour later Williams entered the saloon with Sherrington. They ordered beers and, after receiving them, approached Webster, as Williams called out, "My God, Webster, when did you come up here?" He introduced Sherrington to Webster, and told Sherrington that Tim "was of the right stripe." They ordered more drinks and began talking politics. Webster said he thought Baltimore was going to be the battlefield until "old Abe had got safe to Washington."

Sherrington replied, "By God, he would not if the boys had got their eyes on him." Sherrington said they were prepared to shoot Lincoln, and offered to show Webster the types of weapons they carried. Webster took him up on the offer and went with Sherrington to a store on Baltimore Street. The store clerk showed them some pistols that Sherrington said "were the kind the boys carried" and added that he was going to get one. Sherrington said it "was the best Pistol that was made." Webster reported, "I went into the back-room and tried one, and found it very good."

The operative's report continued, "We then went to a Saloon and got a Drink, and from the Saloon went to Sherwoods [sic] where we got some Oysters, and another Drink. There were several persons in the place talking about shooting 'Old Abe.' some said that they did not believe Lincoln would have been hurt, and others again said that they knew a d—d sight better." They went from there to the "drill room" where they conversed some more and had another drink.

Webster then reported to Pinkerton. After leaving Pinkerton's office he went to the Howard House to meet up with Pinkerton operative Hattie Lewis.[16] Because they posed as husband and wife they surely lived together in Perrymansville, as evidence shows they did later in Baltimore.[17] Lewis and Webster went to Springer's store. They arrived and talked to Springer, who told them that he would be in Perrymansville in the morning. That would be Webster and Lewis's next stop, also. The operatives took the 5:10 P.M. train for Perrymansville. They arrived at 6:30, had dinner, and then split up and Webster went to visit a man he called Captain Keen. Operative Webster reported that he "found Mr. Ellis and five or six others at the Store, talking about Lincoln's passage through Baltimore." They were talking "pretty hard about it," and directed much of their anger at the railroad company personnel, whom they were convinced were in on the plan to protect Lincoln. Webster reported,

Inauguration of President Abraham Lincoln at the Capitol, March 4, 1861 (Reproduction number: LC-USZ62–48564, Library of Congress Prints and Photographs Division).

Washington, D.C., looking northwest from the Capitol roof, June 27, 1861 (Reproduction number: LC-USZ62–78348, Library of Congress Prints and Photographs Division).

James Micheal (Captain Keens [*sic*] brother-in-law) said that when you come to look at it, it was plain enough to see that the Company must have known all about it, and, that was why they had so many men at the Bridges, and changing the Telegraph operatives. Mr. Ellis, a member of the Rangers, proposed to pull up the Rail-Road track and stop the travel South; that it was the only thing left to bring them Northerners to their senses. James Micheal thought to make the work complete they should besides tearing up the Rail-Road track, sink, or burn the boat at Havre-de-Grace, so they could not cross the River. Captain Keen wanted to bet that before three weeks had passed, that Maryland would be out of the Union, and then he would like to see them run the trains over this Road, or any other in the State. They talked on in this strain for some time, after which we all went over to Taylors [*sic*] Saloon. At 10.00. P.M. I went to my room, wrote my report and then went to bed.[18]

Webster's operations in Perrymansville would soon conclude. What he was quietly a part of in Maryland may have shaped the history of the United States. Had that small group of detectives not uncovered the danger Lincoln faced, from multiple groups and individuals, the history and development of the United States might have been vastly different.

8

A Spy in Memphis

In his inaugural address Abraham Lincoln pledged to keep the Union together and said he hoped to do it peacefully. A peaceful resolution was not to be. The Confederacy demanded that U.S. troops evacuate Fort Sumter, which sat on a man-made island in Charleston Harbor. The United States refused to abandon the fort, so newly named Confederate President Jefferson Davis ordered an attack. On April 12, 1861, the opening shots of the American Civil War sounded.[1]

On April 21 Allan Pinkerton wrote to President Lincoln to offer the services of his agency to the United States.

Chicago April 21st 1861

To His Excellense [sic]
A Lincoln Prest of the U. S

Dear Sir

When I saw you last I said that if the time should ever come that I could be of service to you I was ready. If that time has come I am on hand.

I have in my Force from Sixteen to Eighteen persons on whose courage. Skill & Devotion to their Country I can rely. If they with myself at the head can be at service in the way of obtaining information of the movements of the Traitors, or Safely conveying your letters or dispatches, or that class of Secret Service which is the most dangerous. I am at your command.

In the present disturbed state of Affairs I dare not trust this to the mail, so send by one of My Force who was with me at Baltimore — You may safely trust him with Any Message for me — Written or Verbal — I fully guarantee his fidelity. He will act as you direct, and return here with your answer[.]

Secrecy is the great lever I propose to operate with — Hence the necessity of this movement (If you contemplate it) being kept *Strictly Private*, and that should you desire another interview with the Bearer that you should so arrange it as that he will not be noticed.

The Bearer will hand you A Copy of A Telegraph Cipher which you may use if you desire to Telegraph me.

My Force comprises both Sexes— All of Good Character — And well Skilled in their Business.

> Respectfully yours
> *Allan Pinkerton*[2]

The operative Pinkerton trusted with this letter was Timothy Webster. Pinkerton later wrote that the letter and cipher were sewn into the lining of Webster's coat. Included in the cipher were code names for each operative. The code name for Webster was "Peaches."

Pinkerton wrote about the man he chose to carry the letter and code in *The Spy of the Rebellion.*

He was a tall, broad-shouldered, good-looking man of about forty years [he was thirty-nine] of age. In height he was about five feet ten inches; his brown hair, which was brushed carelessly back from a broad, high forehead, surmounted a face of a character to at once attract attention.

There was such a decided mixture of sternness and amiability, of innate force and gentle feelings, of frankness and resolution stamped upon his features, that he instinctively impressed the beholder at a glance.

The deep gray eyes could twinkle and sparkle with good humor, or they would grow dark and menacing, and seem to flash under the influence of anger. The mouth, almost concealed by the heavy brown mustaches which he wore, and the square, firm chin evinced a firmness that was unmistakable. His nose, large and well-formed, and the prominent cheek bones all seemed in perfect harmony with the bold spirit which leaped from the eyes, and the strong will that lurked about the set lips. In figure, he was rather stout, but his shoulders were so broad, his feet and hands so shapely, and the lithe limbs so well formed, that he did not appear of as full habit as he really was.... I felt that I could implicitly rely upon him in any emergency in which he might be placed, and to perform any service for which he might be selected.

This man was Timothy Webster, a faithful officer, a true friend, and an ardent patriot.

I had known this man for years. He had been in my employ for a long time [five years], and had been engaged upon operations of a varied and diverse nature, consequently I knew precisely what his capabilities were, and how entirely he could be trusted. Though not a man of great enlightenment, he was gifted with a large amount of natural shrewdness, which enabled him to successfully meet any emergency which might arise. From his association with people in the various walks of life, he had acquired that habit of easy adaptation which made him appear, and feel, perfectly at home in almost any society, whether in the drawing-room or the tavern, in the marts of trade, or laboring at the plow.

From my knowledge of Timothy Webster, and my confidence in his wis-

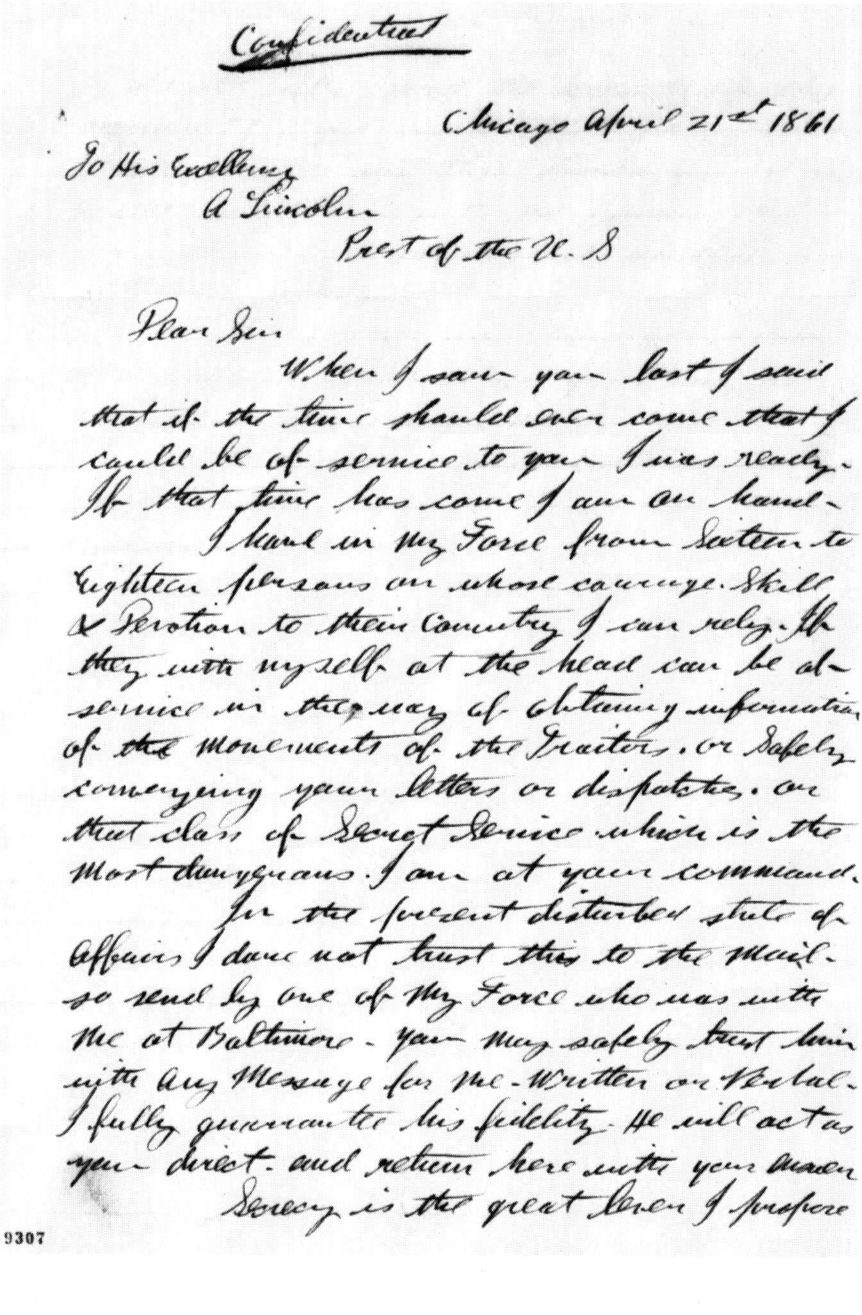

Confidential

Chicago April 21st 1861

To His Excellency
A Lincoln
Prest of the U. S

Dear Sir

When I saw you last I said
that if the time should ever come that I
could be of service to you I was ready.
If that time has come I am on hand.

I have in my Force from Sixteen to
Eighteen persons on whose courage, Skill
& Devotion to their Country I can rely. If
they, with myself at the head can be at
service in the way of Obtaining information
of the Movements of the Traitors. or Safely
conveying your letters or dispatches. or
that class of Secret Service which is the
Most dangerous. I am at your command.

In the present disturbed state of
Affairs I dare not trust this to the Mail.
so send by one of my Force who was with
me at Baltimore. You may safely trust him
with any Message for me. Written or Verbal.
I fully guarantee his fidelity. He will act as
you direct. and return here with your answer

Secrecy is the great lever I propose

9307

70

9308

Opposite and above: Letter that Timothy Webster delivered to Abraham Lincoln (Abraham Lincoln Papers, General Correspondence, Library of Congress Manuscript Division).

dom and reliability, I had chosen him to be the bearer of the dispatches to Mr. Lincoln.[3]

Accompanying Pinkerton's letter to Lincoln was a letter from Lincoln's friend Norman B. Judd, written on Pinkerton stationary.

Dear Lincoln,

You know my confidence in Pinkerton and his men. He has a force thoroughly reliable and sagacious of about sixteen men and *women*.... I believe that no force can be used to so good [an] advantage in obtaining information. His men can live in Richmond and elsewhere with perfect safety. I know the bearer well and he is trustworthy.[4]

Lincoln invited Pinkerton to Washington to discuss what Pinkerton's agency could do for his country. Pinkerton left with no offer from Lincoln. On his way back to Chicago, while in Philadelphia, Pinkerton received mail forwarded from his office. Included was a request for his services from George B. McClellan.

McClellan, who became acquainted with Pinkerton when McClellan was chief engineer of the Illinois Central Railroad, was now the major general of the Department of Ohio, which, in addition to Ohio, included Indiana and Illinois. Lincoln was so impressed with the thirty-four-year-old red haired general that he appointed him major-general in the regular army and made him second in command of the entire U.S. military behind General Winfield Scott.[5]

McClellan asked Allan Pinkerton to set up a secret service for the Department of Ohio. Pinkerton accepted and, under the alias Major E. J. Allen, established headquarters in Cincinnati, Ohio.[6]

Wartime espionage was a relatively new concept; therefore, Pinkerton had no blueprint for establishing the Secret Service and gathering military data. Considering this, Pinkerton and his men did a commendable job of obtaining information. The analysis of the information and Confederate troop numbers reported, however, left much to be desired, as will be seen.

As Pinkerton quickly assembled the Secret Service he relied heavily on Timothy Webster who, of all the operatives, would supply Pinkerton with the most detailed and accurate reports.

Webster, according Allan Pinkerton's highly inaccurate book *The Spy of the Rebellion*, stopped off at Pittsburgh on his way to Cincinnati. In Pittsburgh, Webster was said to have narrowly escaped being lynched as a suspected Southern spy.[7] There is no other record of this event. It may or may not have happened.

Soon Pinkerton had operatives (including himself) spread out south of Ohio gathering information. Of immediate concern to General McClellan were Kentucky and Tennessee. Kentucky, which borders Ohio to the south, was technically neutral in the war. Its neutrality was a position few expected to last, so McClellan (and others in Washington) wanted to get a sense of whether Kentucky could become hostile. McClellan was also preparing to move if the Confederates violated Kentucky's neutrality. General Gideon Pillow positioned his troops along Tennessee's northern (Kentucky's southern) border. Finding out what Pillow had in Tennessee was another important objective, not only because of the possibility of a conflict over Kentucky, but because McClellan believed Cincinnati would be a very tempting target for the Confederacy. McClellan considered defense of Cincinnati top priority. He wrote to General-in-Chief Winfield Scott, "I will consider it my duty to take all possible measures for the protection of Cincinnati & the line of the Ohio, from the Great Miami to Wheeling; I will obtain all the information possible in regard to ground opposite Cincinnati on the Ky side," which led to both Webster and Pinkerton spending time in Kentucky. McClellan also wanted information to plan a possible offensive against Nashville, Ten-

George Brinton McClellan, 1861, photograph by Mathew Brady (Reproduction number: LC-DIG-ppmsca-19389, Library of Congress Prints and Photographs Division).

Cincinnati, 1866 (Prints and Photograph Department, Cincinnati Museum Center — Cincinnati Historical Society).

nessee. For this he not only needed to learn the defenses around Nashville, but everything that stood between him and the city.

For all of these reasons sentiment on the war in Kentucky and military data from Tennessee was considered vital. Webster was sent to both states.[8] In *The Spy of the Rebellion*, Pinkerton wrote,

> The general informed me that he would like observations made within the rebel lines, and I resolved to at once send some scouts into the disaffected region lying south of us, for the purpose of obtaining information concerning the numbers, equipments, movements and intentions of the enemy, as well as to ascertain the general feeling of the Southern people in regard to the war. I fully realized the delicacy of this business, and the necessity of conducting it with the greatest care, caution and secrecy. None but good, true, reliable men could be detailed for such service, and knowing this, I made my selections accordingly; my thoughts reverting first of all to Timothy Webster.[9]

Tim Webster went to work immediately. His earliest surviving report from this time period doesn't begin until July 23, 1861, but Pinkerton account books show he was at work by at least May 13. A July 2 entry in the account book noting that Webster received $50.00 in Memphis is the only primary source record of Webster's location before July 23. According to Pinkerton in *The Spy of the Rebellion*, Webster was sent to Memphis, with instructions to stop at Bowling Green, Kentucky, and Clarksville, Tennessee, along the way.[10]

In Pinkerton's heavily fictitious *The Spy of the Rebellion*, one man he wrote about was John Scobell, an ex-slave-turned-spy. Over the years numerous books have told of Scobell and his work for the Union. However, a little modern day detective work shows that John Scobell was an invention of Allan Pinkerton's imagination. *The Spy of the Rebellion* contains the first ever mention of him. All subsequent references to Scobell can be traced back to this source. Scobell does not appear in Pinkerton's reports to McClellan, nor does he appear in the account books or any other contemporary records.

Another falsehood that began with this book was the use of the name Hattie Lawton for Hattie Lewis. Because surviving reports and account books use only her initials, H. H. L., historians have had to reluctantly accept Lawton as her last name, even though no other records of a Hattie Lawton that could have possibly been her have been found. To further complicate questions about her name is the fact that when he wrote his memoirs in 1888, Pryce Lewis remembered her as Hattie Lewis. I recently discovered a letter from Allan Pinkerton to Joseph B. Beale written in 1882 confirming that her name was Hattie Lewis.[11]

The missing bulk of Pinkerton's National Detective Agency records before 1871 sometimes makes it impossible to know what is fact and what is fiction in Pinkerton's books. In some cases Pinkerton's accounts conflict completely with known facts. In other instances they are accurate down to the last detail. With this in mind, when an Allan Pinkerton authored book is the main source for an event described here, it will always be mentioned and analyzed for its accuracy. That being said, the account of Webster's journey to Memphis fully matches Pinkerton's objectives and corresponds with the Pinkerton account book.

The account book shows Webster receiving $200.00 for expenses on May 13.[12] According to *The Spy of the Rebellion*, Webster left Cincinnati on May 13 and headed south. He stayed the night in Louisville, Kentucky. The next day he went to Bowling Green, Kentucky, where he stayed for a day or two, and from there he went to Clarksville, Tennessee. Pinkerton wrote of Webster as a spy, "He made friends of all he met, and cleverly ingratiated himself into the good graces of those whom he believed might be of service to him." His reminiscence of Tim Webster continued,

He partook of soldiers' fare in the rebel camp, shook hands warmly with raw recruits, joked and laughed with petty officers, became familiar with colonels and captains, and talked profoundly with brigadier-generals. He was apparently an enthusiastic and determined rebel, and in a few cunningly-worded sentences he would rouse the stagnant blood of his hearers till it fairly boiled with virtuous indignation against Yankees in general, and "Abe Linkin" in particular.

Webster's talent in sustaining a *role* of this kind amounted to positive genius, and it was this that forced me to admire the man as sincerely as I prized his services. Naturally, he was of a quiet, reserved disposition, seldom speaking unless spoken to, and never betraying emotion or excitement under any pressure of circumstances. His face always wore that calm, imperturbable expression denoting a well-balanced mind and a thorough self-control, while the immobile countenance and close-set lips showed that he was naturally as inscrutable as the Sphinx. Many of his associates were of the opinion that he was cold and unfeeling, but *I* knew there could be no greater mistake than this; *I* knew that a manlier, nobler heart never existed than that which beat within the broad breast of Timothy Webster; and I knew that, reserved and modest as he was, he was never wanting in courtesy, never derelict in his duty, never behind his fellows in acts of kindness and mercy.

It was when he was detailed for such operations as the one in question that his disposition underwent a complete metamorphosis. Then his reserve vanished, and he became the chatty, entertaining boon companion, the hero of the card-table, the storyteller of the bar-room, or the lion of the social gathering, as the exigencies of the case might require. He could go into a strange place and in one day surround himself with warm friends, who would end by telling him all he desired to know. In a life-time of varied detective experience, I have never met one who could more readily and agreeably adapt himself to circumstances.[13]

Pinkerton added that Webster found people willing to share what they knew about the South's plans and defenses.[14] Soon Webster was being told about troop numbers, troop locations, and weapons.

Webster soon left Clarksville for Memphis. Pinkerton wrote that in Memphis, Webster became aware of a "vigilance committee" that was watching and arresting strangers for fear that they might be spies. Webster soon discovered that he was being followed. Despite passing himself off as a native Kentuckian who was raised in Baltimore and making friends that included high-ranking officers in the Confederate military, one man continued to follow Webster.[15] Later reports confirm the acquaintances Pinkerton said Webster made. The reports also confirm that the detective used no alias.

Pinkerton wrote about an incident that took place at a Confederate camp — Camp Rector — near Mound City. Webster had been shown around by a Dr. Burton and some Confederate officers. The men decided to go into a tent to escape the hot summer sun. While sitting around a table and conversing, "their conversation was interrupted by a shadow falling across the strip of sunlight that streamed in through the opening of the tent." Standing in the entrance was the man who had been watching Webster. As the men looked up and saw him, he turned and walked away. The conversation turned to the man. It was said that he must be looking for a "Northern man."[16]

Webster returned to Memphis that night and told his friends that he was going to leave for Chattanooga. Webster kept an eye out for the man from the safety committee, whom Pinkerton described like this: "This man was a dark-complexioned, sharp-visaged, long-haired individual, clad in civilian's garb, and wearing a broad-brimmed hat."[17]

In *The Spy of the Rebellion*, Pinkerton wrote that Webster thought he had escaped his pursuer. After spending the night at the Worsham Hotel, Webster arrived at the train depot early the next morning hoping to get out of town unnoticed. He didn't see the man as he boarded the train, which was packed with soldiers. At Grand Junction, Webster changed cars and boarded the train headed north to Jackson, Tennessee. As the train headed for Jackson, Webster saw the man who had been following him. This man was with another.

When the train stopped at Jackson, Webster stepped out onto the platform, and the men following him did the same. Webster approached the conductor, who was near, and, in a voice loud enough to be heard by those following him, asked the conductor how long before the train to Humboldt would be leaving. After being told it would be in about twenty minutes, Webster asked the conductor if he knew of any hotels in Humboldt. The conductor recommended a place close to the depot.

When he boarded the train for Humboldt his shadows did the same. They sat in the same car. When the train was on its way a woman approached Webster and asked if she could occupy a portion of the seat. After sitting down she began to speak to Webster in a quiet voice while never turning her head toward him. She asked if he was going to Humboldt. He replied that he was. She next asked if he was a Northern man, and when he acted surprised at the question she told him that, while sitting in the rear portion of the car, she overheard two men who she believed were talking about him. They had planned to go to the same hotel as he did and if he attempted to go north would arrest him and take him back to Memphis, where they would "deal" with him as they would any Northern spy.[18] After giving Webster the message the woman stood up and walked off.

As the train approached the depot Webster exited the back of the car. The men who had been following him saw him do this and left the car at the front. Upon exiting the car Webster quickly hid behind a pile of baggage.

Webster was able to stay out of their sight and board the train to Louisville. When he was on his way he removed his rebel hat and replaced it with a less conspicuous one. Tim Webster arrived safely in Cincinnati and reported to Pinkerton.[19] Without contemporary documentation the truth of this will never be known.

Webster's next trip south is documented by his handwritten reports. His report of Tuesday, July 23 began, "About 5^{oc} P.M. I left Cincinnati for Memphis by the Ohio & Mississippi R.R. I arrived at Louisville & put up at the National Hotel there[.]" Webster spent the next day traveling by rail. On July 25 he arrived at Humboldt, Tennessee, where the train was ordered to stop because General Leonidas E. Polk had taken charge of the road.

Webster used the time in Humboldt to socialize with Confederate officers. Webster reported that he "Drank & talked with officers" from Union City. From them he obtained troop numbers and weapons information. In the evening the train's conductor received permission to continue. Webster reported: "I arrived at Memphis about 8^{oc} P.M."[20]

Memphis, Tennessee, a city of just over 22,000 people in 1861, was a key location for trade between the North and South. Two key elements of Memphis's economy were cotton and slavery.[21] Webster likely checked into Worsham House after arriving in Memphis.

Webster soon made friends, including a Confederate colonel named Seely, who showed him around Memphis on Friday the 26th. Webster reported that Memphis "was all up in arms" with men under General Pillow leaving, in their own words, to "clean out the Dutch in St. Louis before a Month." Webster also took note of notices posted at the hotel stating that no one was allowed to leave Memphis without a passport from a Mr. Morgan on Main Street.[22]

The next morning Webster went to Mound city "with Col. Seely, Hill (Clerk at the Worsham) & others." That evening the operative "was around town with Bob [Rowley], Seely & others." Webster reported that the "whole

Memphis, Tennessee, circa 1895, view of Front Street (courtesy of Memphis and Shelby County Room, Memphis Public Library and Information Center).

conversation" that night was about how the southern army "had Cleaned the 'Yankees'" out of Bull Run and Manassas and how the troops under General Pillow, General William J. Hardee, and General Benjamin McCulloch "would clean the Dutch out in Missouri."[23]

Webster spent the next day "around Town ... with Dr. [Roger B.] Scott of Texas, late of Virginia & others." The others included a Lieutenant Connor. Webster obtained troop numbers from Richard D. Baugh, a former mayor of Memphis, the following day, and the day after that Webster received letters of introduction to various men in Virginia and Tennessee.[24]

On the 31st Webster reported that he saw Baugh early in the morning and obtained more information from him. Then he boarded a morning train headed for Chattanooga. His observations for the day included seeing Missouri Governor Claiborne F. Jackson at Grand Junction. Webster arrived in Knoxville the following day.[25]

Over the next three days Webster picked up more information about the number of troops and arms at two camps near Knoxville and reported trains of armed men headed toward Richmond.

Webster returned to Memphis. He left that city for the North on Sunday, August 4. The operative spent Monday in Nashville and received more troop numbers. He left Nashville at 3:30 A.M. on Tuesday morning and went to Louisville. Kentucky's neutrality in the conflict made passage from the South to the North easier than it otherwise would have been. Webster's next stop was New Albany, Indiana. From there he took a train to Cincinnati.[26] The contacts he was able to make and information he gathered made the mission a huge success on his part, although, because McClellan wasn't threatened by an advance on Cincinnati, and because McClellan's next move would take him to Virginia, not Nashville, the mission was of little importance to the course of the war. However, George McClellan was assigned to a new division that would soon be called "The Army of the Potomac," and his new concerns were the defense of Washington, D.C., and planning an offensive against Richmond, so while Webster's reports of troops in Tennessee were of little value to the general, his reports of troops headed east were of vital importance.

On August 8 McClellan wrote to Winfield Scott, "I have also to-day received a telegram from a reliable agent just from Knoxville Tenn. that large reinforcements are still passing through there to Richmond." Unfortunately, this added to McClellan's mistaken belief that there were "at least 100,000 men" in that region. Once he had that figure set in his mind he believed it to be fact, so reports of more troops headed to Richmond only increased what McClellan believed was there. In reality there were fewer than 45,000 men in and around Richmond at the time.[27]

With the detailed reports Webster submitted, the question of how accurate Webster's reports were must be addressed. General George McClellan has taken much criticism for hesitancy and inaction. Part of this blame has been focused on Allan Pinkerton for reporting inflated Confederate troop numbers. The question is, who was at fault for the inflated numbers?

The fault did not lie with Timothy Webster. Though not perfect, his reports were fairly accurate. Historian and Civil War espionage expert Edwin C. Fishel, who called Webster "the star performer on Pinkerton's detective force," wrote in *The Secret War for the Union: The Untold Story of Military Intelligence in the Civil War* that "From the relative accuracy of the data Webster collected, it appears that he was a skillful interviewer,

The first page of Tim Webster's August 7, 1861, report (Records of Pinkerton's National Detective Agency, Box 25, Folder 4, Library of Congress. Photograph by author).

The last page of Tim Webster's August 7, 1861, report (Records of Pinkerton's National Detective Agency, Box 25, Folder 4, Library of Congress. Photograph by author).

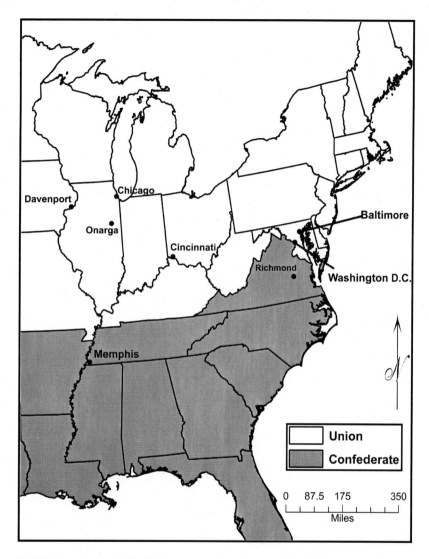

The Union states and Confederate states in the second half of 1861. While West Virginia wasn't yet a state in 1861, it is included here because this section had already broken from Virginia on the secession issue (map by Michelle Davis).

able to circumvent a good many of the obstacles presented by the resistance, mistaken knowledge, or gasconade of his various Southern subjects."[28] In some cases his numbers were high, but not extremely so.

Despite the accuracy of Webster's reports, the final data presented to McClellan and the data McClellan reported to President Lincoln inflated the troop numbers. These numbers vastly overestimated Confederate troop totals, sometimes more than doubling Rebel strength. In one instance in April 1862, when General McClellan began a campaign intended to take the Confederate Capital of Richmond, the estimate Pinkerton gave McClellan was that there were 180,000 troops guarding the city. The actual number was approximately 85,000.[29] Occasional mathematical errors in Pinkerton's reports to McClellan compounded the problem.[30]

While Allan Pinkerton's lack of military intelligence experience showed, the major problem with Pinkerton's reports to McClellan was not because of Pinkerton, but because of McClellan. Several comments in the reports show not only that McClellan was aware of the inflated data, but that he had in fact requested it. The logic behind this was twofold. First, it was assumed that the intelligence coming in from the operatives and southern refugees would never be complete, so the numbers were increased to account for the uncounted troops. The trouble was, the numbers Pinkerton received were, if anything, already too high, so increasing the number made the problem worse. The second reason behind the inflated numbers was that McClellan never wanted to get caught off guard by encountering more troops than he expected. Considering the even higher troop estimates that McClellan gave Lincoln, a possible third rationale by McClellan may have been to justify his requests for more troops. Still, the fact that McClellan included the high estimates in letters to his wife showed he likely believed them.[31] In the final analysis it appears the troop numbers were inflated because McClellan thought the uncounted troops existed, thus leading Pinkerton to believe it because of his trust in the general.

Allan Pinkerton, 1861 (photograph taken at the Mathew Brady Studio; Records of Pinkerton's National Detective Agency, Box 4, Folder 6, Library of Congress).

9

Operations in Baltimore

Timothy Webster's surviving reports do not pick up again until August 22. By this time Pinkerton had moved his headquarters to a house on I Street in Washington to follow General McClellan who, on July 27, was assigned to command a division made up of forces that had been defeated at the Battle of Bull Run under General Irvin McDowell combined with the forces defending Washington. This made McClellan's priority the defense of the capital, which made Baltimore important. As McClellan explained to Secretary of War Simon Cameron, "It is well understood that although the ultimate design of the enemy is to possess himself of the City of Washington, his first efforts will probably be directed towards Baltimore, with the intention of cutting our line of communications and supplies as well as to arouse an insurrection in Maryland."[1] Allan Pinkerton remembered, "By direction of General McClellan, I sent several of my best operatives to Baltimore, chief among whom was Timothy Webster, with whom the others were to co-operate whenever their assistance were required by him. The principal object in this was to enable Webster to associate with the secessionists of that city, and by becoming familiar and popular with them, to pave his way for an early trip into the rebel lines."[2] The proposed trip behind enemy lines, which would ultimately take Webster to the Confederate capital, was necessary to gather data for McClellan's planned offensive to take Richmond. General McClellan believed that by taking Richmond then marching south, the war would be ended. With Richmond the primary target, McClellan needed to know what stood between him and the Confederate capital city.[3]

Webster was sent immediately to work, making Baltimore his home base. The details of what Webster did between the 7th and 22nd are unknown. Pinkerton's account book shows Webster received money in Baltimore during this time.[4] In all probability he began renewing old Maryland acquaintances while learning the general feeling toward secession in Baltimore, learning what danger secessionists in the city might pose, and laying the groundwork for later trips into the Confederacy. Webster and Hattie Lewis, who was still posing as his wife, made their home at Miller's Hotel.

In *The Spy of the Rebellion*, Allan Pinkerton wrote that Webster "was directed to represent himself as a gentleman of means and leisure." To enable him to play this role properly, Pinkerton gave him "a span of fine horses and a carriage." Webster immediately went to work socializing with the secessionists of the city. Pinkerton wrote that, through the numerous acquaintances he already had in the city, "He was introduced into the houses of many warm sympathizers with the South.... Through all, he was apparently an earnest and consistent advocate of Southern rights, never overdoing the matter by any exhibition of strained excitement or loud avowals, but always conversing on the subject with an air of calm conviction, using the strongest arguments he could invent in support of his pretended views."[5]

Tim Webster's report for Thursday, August 22, begins "About 9^{oc} A.M. I left for Washington City. I arrived & reported to Mr P. at No. 404 E. Street [Pinkerton's Washington home] & at about 2–30 P.M. I left for Baltimore again[.]" He arrived in Baltimore at about 4:30 and went to Miller's Hotel, where John Earl, a secessionist staying there, told Webster that three or four men had been at Miller's asking for him. Webster stayed at the hotel drinking and talking to Sam Sloan until about 11:00 P.M. Webster reported that he "was laying pipe to get in with" Sloan.[6]

At 8:00 A.M. the next day Webster, on his way downtown, stopped "at Merrill's No 239 Baltimore Street[.]" He went in to discuss some rifles he and his secessionist associates were interested in. Webster told Merrill that they thought the rifles should be had for less than the $40 Merrill was asking.

To this Merrill responded, "Mr. Webster, walk in the office, I want to talk with you." They went in the office and Merrill said, "Mr. Webster, I can not take one cent less than forty dollars for if there comes a reaction here I can get fifty dollars for them with out a word." Webster asked him if he thought the Southern army would be in Baltimore soon. Merrill said he "would not be surprised" if they were there in two weeks.

Playing his role as secessionist, Webster opined that "we were agoing to clean out Western Virginia before we came to Maryland."

Merrill said, "That is my plan. Keep a few men around Alexander [Alexandria] to keep Lincoln's army in a fever and then the main body of our army cross over above Harpers Ferry and come in to Baltimore then

Baltimore Street, Baltimore, circa late 1860s or early 1870s (photograph by William Moody Chase. Author's Collection).

all the arms that I have got would come in play." Webster asked him if many of the citizens of Baltimore were armed. Merrill answered, "I sold a great many rifles and guns on the 19th of April [day of a riot caused by secessionists] and I suppose that we could race in and right around Baltimore from six to seven-thousand stand of arms."

"And men to use them?" Webster asked.

"Yes indeed and more men than that."

"Well Mr. Merrill, if we make up our minds to take the rifles we can get them at a minute's notice?"

"Yes," answered Merrill. Webster asked how many rifles he had and Merrill said about three hundred. Webster then added that they may want some Bowie knives. To this Merrill responded, "I have not got many but I can get them by having a few days' notice."

"Very well," Webster said. "I will call again." Webster left and went to Allen's Eating Saloon, where he ran into some acquaintances, including Alexander Slayden. Webster asked them to have a drink and then went with Slayden "to the Sun office corner."

On their walk, Slayden told Webster that "there was from 5 to 6000 stand of arms in Baltimore."

Webster replied, "I am damn glad to hear that but what are you agoing to do for a leader now [that] Kane [Marshal George P. Kane] is locked up?"

Slayden said, "Oh, we have leaders enough."

It was about noon when Webster returned to Miller's Hotel for lunch. He saw Sloan, who introduced him to "D. R. Stiltz, Photography artice [sic] corner Saratoga & Charles Street No 56 North Charles Street." Stiltz and Sloan talked about a trip that Stiltz was taking that coming Monday, and Sloan warned him that he must be careful.

Stiltz asked, "Well, how will I work it, Sam?"[7]

Sloan told Stiltz that he would give him a letter of introduction to Charles Butler, who owned a "China or Crockery" store in Washington. Sloan told Stiltz, "he is a strong union man and you must talk union like hell."

Stiltz said, "I understand that Sam." Sloan then wrote the letter of introduction, read it to Stiltz, and told him, "you give him this letter and talk union and he will get you a passport to visit the camps."

Webster went upstairs to his residence and wrote to Pinkerton to send him operative John Scully. Wrote Webster, "I wanted to spot Stiltz to Sculey [sic] so he could be piped in Washington." He sent Hattie Lewis with the dispatch. Webster then went to the horse racetrack with Sam Sloan. Webster reported, "I got my horses & we left for the track about 3 Miles East of Town. There we met 10 or 15 we knew[.]" On the way to the track, Webster asked Sloan if Stiltz was going South after he came back from Washington. Sloan said he was, that his plan was to go to Manassas and Richmond. Webster said he would have a hard time getting there now. Sloan expected a route south to open and said that he ran "a good many things through by the way of Harpers Ferry before that Route was cut off." When they returned from the track, in Miller's Hotel Yard, Sloan showed Webster a wagon he had with a false bottom to be used for smuggling.[8]

In *The Spy of the Rebellion*, Pinkerton added, "In compliance with the request of many of his Southern friends, he and John Scully ... went to a photograph gallery one day and had their pictures taken, holding a large Confederate flag between them, while Webster wore the rebel hat ... presented to him in Memphis."[9] No copies of the photograph, if it was really taken, have been found. The fact that Webster's reports show that he not only sent for John Scully, but also met photographer Daniel R. Stiltz the same day, make it possible that they were photographed.

Pinkerton added, "During all this time Webster was gathering information from every quarter concerning the secret plots and movements of the disloyal citizens, and promptly conveying it to me, and for this purpose he made frequent trips to Washington for verbal instructions, and to report in person the success of his operations." According to Pinkerton, Webster sometimes made trips to Washington with his secessionist friends, which allowed Webster to "increase his acquaintance with the traitorous element of Washington, and finally was enabled to unmask several guilty ones whose loyalty had never been impeached or suspected."[10] Pinkerton was involved with the arrests of suspected traitors in Washington. Given the location of Webster's operations, it is likely the above statement is true.

At this time Webster began to let people know that he planned to go to Virginia and offered to be of service to the secessionists by carrying messages to their friends and relatives. This was more than a pretense. The skilled detective lived the part he was playing and, over the next few months, Webster brought many messages, both written and verbal, across enemy lines. This enabled him not only to keep his cover, but to gain trust among the Southerners and meet people he never would have come in contact with otherwise. As Webster let people know of his plans, Pinkerton said that Webster also let them know that "he desired to sell his horses and carriage before leaving." According to Pinkerton, another one of his operatives was sent down to "buy" the horses and carriage so they could be returned to Pinkerton in Washington.[11]

Allan Pinkerton wrote in *The Spy of the Rebellion* that Webster, with John Scully accompanying him, started south on September 26. Carrying a pass issued by the Baltimore provost-marshal, the spies took the steamboat *Mary Washington* down the Chesapeake to Fairhaven. From Fairhaven, by land, they went to the town of Friendship. From there they traveled to Prince Frederick, Benedict, and Charlotte Hall, with Webster delivering many messages, both written and verbal, along the way. The messenger cover enabled the spies to become friendly with secessionists at every stop and receive letters of introduction to other secessionists on their route. Allan Pinkerton wrote, "Through this medium they secured attention and hospitality wherever they stopped, and had the advantage of valuable advice and assistance in the matter of pursuing their journey safely." From Charlotte Hall, Webster and Scully walked twenty miles to Leonardtown. At Leonardtown, they met up with operative William Scott, and continued south with him.

The men were "frequently cautioned to be very careful, as there were Union soldiers stationed all along the river." They were told that "people whose hearts were with the South were not permitted to express their sentiments with impunity." They went as far south as Allen's Fresh, Maryland, and then returned, which indicates that this journey's purpose was simply to lay the groundwork for later trips to Virginia. Pinkerton finished his account of this mission: "When Webster re-appeared on the streets of Baltimore, after completing this trip, he was more than ever lionized by his numerous friends who were in the secret of his Southern journey.... By endangering his life in the Southern cause ... he had made himself a hero in the eyes of the traitors who were attached to him."[12]

While Pinkerton's account seems to be an accurate depiction of Webster's mission, what Pinkerton wrote next is less likely a true account of events. He claimed that from Sam Sloan and others, Webster soon learned of a recently formed organization to oppose the U.S. government known as the Knights of Liberty. Sloan told Webster, "Some of the best in town are among our members." They wanted Webster to join. Webster took the oath at a secret midnight meeting.

Webster soon learned that the group planned an attack on Washington, D.C. According to Pinkerton's book, U.S. soldiers broke up one of the midnight meetings and arrested many in attendance while letting Tim Webster "escape."[13]

It's an exciting story. It's a shame that it doesn't appear to be true. It is true that in September, under the direction of Allan Pinkerton, several secessionists were arrested in separate locations in Baltimore. Those arrested included politicians such as George William Brown, Baltimore's mayor. Timothy Webster's main contacts were left alone.[14] It is possible that the men arrested at this time were members of a pro–Southern group, such as the Knights of the Golden Circle. Whether Webster became a member of such a group is not known, but it does seem likely. There are records of Webster being called captain by secessionists, which was probably a reference to his rank in some such organization. Though Webster's membership in a secret society may have led to the arrests, the breakup of a secret meeting seems to be pure fiction. With the number of inconsequential arrests that Allan Pinkerton reported to McClellan, it is extremely unlikely that this raid would not be included in his reports. There is no mention of it, nor is there any contemporary record of this event.

Luckily for history, the guesswork ends here. The rest of Timothy Webster's work for the Union is documented in detailed reports that Allan Pinkerton wrote up for George McClellan and that were backed up and added to by other sources. The first of Pinkerton's reports documents Webster's trip to the Confederate capital.

10

Tim Webster in Richmond

Timothy Webster left Baltimore on October 14 with fellow operative William Scott. Webster and Scott traveled down the eastern shore of Virginia. The pair turned west and passed through Accomack County and into North Hampton County. They arrived at the North Hampton County seat of Eastville on October 22, where Scott and Webster parted.[1]

Webster stayed in Eastville for three days while waiting for transportation across the Chesapeake Bay to the Virginia mainland from a man named Marshall. Marshall had experience running federal blockades in his sloop (a type of sailboat). He had recently been forced to abandon the sloop to avoid capture and now used what was described as a canoe to bring people to Virginia. Webster described Marshall's canoe as "31 feet long and 5ft. 3 inches wide, carrying three sails."[2]

On Friday, October 25th, Marshall loaded his canoe with twelve passengers, including Webster, for passage to Virginia. Eight of the passengers were going to Richmond to enlist in the Confederate Army and Navy. It was a windy evening when the canoe left from Cherrystone Lighthouse and began the voyage across Chesapeake Bay. Marshall placed Tim Webster on lookout. About half way across the bay Webster spotted a light in the darkness. He informed Marshall, who replied, "She is a gun boat with a light on her bows. Let her come. She can't catch us for, with our present headway, no boat on the view can catch us."

It took three hours on this windy October night to cross Chesapeake Bay. As they approached their destination, Gloucester Point, they were greeted by a Confederate sentinel, who, after questioning who they were, let them pass.[3]

Marshall took the passengers to a shanty he had, which was located in the Confederate camp at Gloucester Point. The next morning Webster and ten others received a pass to go to Richmond from Colonel Charles

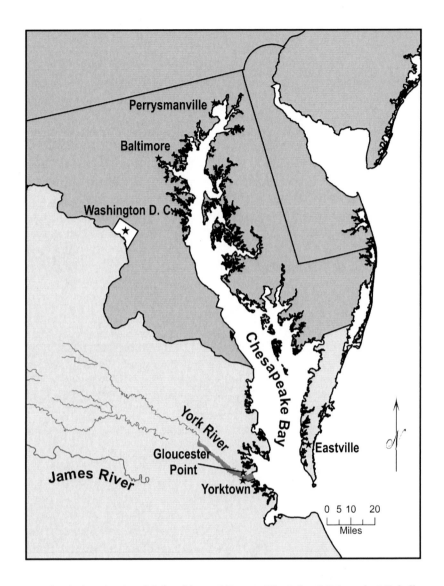

Maryland, the District of Columbia, and Eastern Virginia, 1861 (map by Michelle Davis).

A. Crump, commander of the Gloucester Point camp. Webster reported on forces at Gloucester Point and said that General John B. Magruder was the commander of the forces that occupied the peninsula.[4]

It was about noon when Webster, with the other passengers from the previous night, crossed the York River to Yorktown in a small boat. Of

Yorktown, Webster noted that the landing was in front of a hill about twenty-five feet high. On top of the hill and in front of the town were six to eight mounted guns. Webster also reported that Magruder's headquarters were at Yorktown.

From Yorktown the travelers crossed the peninsula to Grove Wharf, where they could take a boat to Richmond via the James River. The men learned that no boat would be leaving for Richmond until Monday (it was Saturday), but were lucky enough to find a nearby farmhouse at which to stay. That Sunday, Webster learned more about the defenses in the area, the number of troops, their arms, and supplies.

On Monday morning Tim Webster boarded a steam packet for Richmond. The boat arrived that evening.[5] Webster's arrival in Richmond was reported in the Richmond *Dispatch* under the headline "Maryland Refugees." It read,

> A number of Baltimoreans have recently arrived in this city by a very circuitous and dangerous route, occupying two weeks in the accomplishment of the journey. They had been marked by the Federals as men who sympathized with the Southern movement, and but for their timely escape would doubtless have been arrested ere this. The party consists of John F. C. Offutt, J. Pierson Wight, S. D. Fletcher, Capt. Timothy Webster, Wm. Cooper, James Cooper, Anthony P. Ross, Joseph Lowenbach, Lewis Lowubach [*sic*], Lewis Smith, Capt. Joseph Scott, and James Ford.[6]

"Captain" likely referred to Webster's rank in a pro-southern organization. In Richmond, Webster checked into the Spotswood Hotel (sometimes called Spotswood House).[7]

Spotswood guests included members of the Confederate legislature.[8] Staying there put Webster in a central location — the opposite side of the block the Spotswood was on bordered Capitol Square — and close to important people for his stay in Richmond, a city whose 1860 population of 37,910 had doubled since becoming the capital of the Confederate States of America.[9]

Tim Webster spent his first full day in Richmond delivering letters. He also laid the groundwork for a meeting with Confederate Secretary of War Judah P. Benjamin, but the meeting, for now, did not come to pass.[10]

On October 31 Webster, with William Campbell, to whom Webster had a letter of introduction, visited the batteries that were on the hills around Richmond to defend the city.[11] Campbell afterwards took Webster to the Ordnance Department, where the operative met many of those who

Spotswood Hotel (Accession No. 1998.69.3, Virginia Historical Society).

ran the department and learned much about the Confederate weapons supply.

In the evening Campbell and Webster went to visit John B. Jones, a clerk and pass adjutant to General John H. Winder that Webster had met earlier in the day.[12] Jones gave them a pass to Manassas so Webster could deliver a letter he had for a John Bowen.

Campbell and Webster left Richmond for Manassas by train at 7:40 the next morning. On the way the Union spy picked up more troop information. They arrived at Manassas about 5:00 P.M. and found out that the

95

Richmond, 1862 (Control number: NWDNS-111-B-35, National Archives and Records Administration, Still Picture Records Section).

man they had come to see, Bowen, was sick with typhoid fever and had been taken to Richmond that day. This wasn't bad news for Webster. The trip still made it possible for Webster to visit Manassas and pick up information.[13]

An acquaintance of Campbell's arranged for them to stay the night with the quartermaster at the camp under Colonel William Smith. Webster reported that the camp was about a mile south of Manassas Junction.[14]

Campbell introduced Webster to Colonel Smith, who invited them to have supper with him. They declined, having previously eaten at Manassas. That evening Webster questioned the quartermaster about the number of batteries and troops around Manassas Junction. Webster was told that there were "10 or 12" regiments at Manassas Junction that were "well armed but dam'd [sic] badly off for winter Clothing." The quartermaster went on to say "that there was not half the sickness in the Army, then, that there was two months previous; that the measles had pretty much disappeared, and what sickness there was, now, was Typhus Fever."

That night brought "a terrible storm, of rain and wind," which blew nearly every tent in the camp down. Because the rain was still falling hard the next day and "there being no comfortable place to stay," Campbell and Webster went to Warrenton, the seat of Fauquier County, Virginia.[15] After checking into a hotel Campbell introduced Webster to Charles Bragg, the mayor of Warrenton.[16] Timothy Webster asked Bragg about obtaining a pass to visit the 1st Maryland Regiment, stationed at Centreville, because he had letters for some of the regiment. The mayor said "it would be very difficult to obtain a pass," but that he would introduce Webster to the local provost marshal and "see what could be done." Bragg made the introduction the following day and the operative received a pass. A man named Dempsey, who was an acquaintance of Campbell's, also received a pass to Centreville.

Webster then obtained a horse and buggy and, with Dempsey, went to Centreville. They arrived at 4:00 P.M.[17] Allan Pinkerton later reported Webster's findings to George McClellan.

> Shortly after crossing the stone bridge [at Bull Run] aforesaid and about half a mile east of the bridge he came to the first camps which, together with those *further* on, *around, and in Centerville* [*sic*] *numbered 49 Regiments* of Infantry which he counted, together with 12 Field Batteries, Eight of which had Six, and four of which had Eight guns; that the greatest number of these guns was Brass; That he came near to one of these batteries and found that four out of six of the guns were rifled [had grooves cut into the interior of the barrel, causing the bullets to spin] ... That he saw some scattering Cavalry but no great number in one body....[18]

This is just one example of the detail which came from Webster, Pinkerton's most skilled operative.

Timothy Webster arrived at the 1st Maryland's camp "about Sundown" to deliver the letters. Because of the arrival of the letters there was an order "to allow a light to be kept up, in one of the tents, *all night,* to enable the men to read their letters and write others to be taken back" by Webster.

While at the camp the detective asked a captain "where all their cavalary [*sic*] was, about which he had heard so much?" The captain told Webster that "they were Scattered all along the line" from Winchester to General Theophilus H. Holmes's command at Brook Station. Webster learned more through further questioning, showing his skill to get answers without blowing his cover.[19]

Webster observed soldiers drilling the next day as he and Dempsey made their way from the camp to the town of Centreville. He also reported on the defenses of Centreville. He described the town like this: "Centerville [*sic*] is on a piece of ground higher than its surroundings for a considerable distance from the town; that the whole of Centerville, proper, is made up from about fifteen buildings."[20]

While in Centreville Webster visited the provost marshal to ask for a pass to return to Warrenton. He received the pass and went to Warrenton that day. The following day, Tuesday, November 5, he and Campbell left for Richmond.

On the way to Richmond the operative met a lieutenant from whom he learned about four regiments of infantry and militia between Winchester and Martinsburg and thirteen regiments of infantry in Leesburg, as well as learning about their equipment and commanders.[21]

Webster checked back into the Spotswood Hotel in Richmond. On Wednesday the 6, Webster, with J. H. Price, a merchant from Warrenton, went to the office of Provost Marshal Jones to obtain a pass to go north. Price wished to travel to Baltimore for goods. The two received the passes to go to Maryland with the provision that they receive the consent of General Theophilus Holmes. Webster and Price began their journey by taking a train to Fredericksburg, where they spent the night.

The following day Webster delivered a letter to a man named Hazzard, who was the chief clerk in the Commissary Department in Fredericksburg.[22] Hazzard then went with Webster to see Montgomery Slaughter, the mayor of Fredericksburg, to request help in Webster's effort to obtain General Holmes's permission to pass into Maryland.[23] After Hazzard introduced the men, Webster told the mayor his purpose for wanting to go to Maryland was not only to bring over letters from southerners, of which he had many, but also to go back to assist northerners who wished to come south and to bring back goods.

Montgomery gave Webster a pass and on the back of it wrote a request that Webster be allowed to meet with General Holmes. Before Webster left to go to General Holmes's headquarters, Hazzard asked him to return later to pick up two letters Hazzard had for his mother-in-law in Baltimore. Webster then went to the headquarters of General Holmes at Brook Station. He arrived at sundown. Webster learned the general was not there and might not return for several days. The operative was also told that "it was doubtful" that the general would give Webster a pass to cross into Maryland.[24]

Webster returned to Hazzard's house and the two men walked into town, where Webster picked up more troop information from Captain Parker, who was an aide to General Holmes. Parker introduced Webster to William H. Coffin, a surgeon on General Magruder's staff. Coffin also worked to help Webster get his pass.

Even though the Yankee spy was making all the right connections, he was unable to meet with Holmes and had to return to Richmond the next morning. In Richmond he received a pass to allow him to go to Accomack County and, with General Magruder's approval, on to Maryland.

On Saturday, November 9, Webster and Price took a train to West Point and from there took a sloop down the York River to Gloucester Point, where they stayed the night.[25]

On Sunday morning Webster met with Colonel Charles Crump and showed Crump his pass and note from Coffin. Crump said that since he had seen Webster before, Webster did not need to see General Magruder. Crump would give him the pass he needed and told him that he could go with Marshall the next time he crossed the Chesapeake Bay. The detective's observations around the camp that day included complaints from soldiers who wanted warmer clothing and overcoats.

Marshall arrived with a group of people on Monday the 11th. Webster asked Marshall if he was going back that night. Marshall said he was not. He was "worn out with running so constantly, night and day, for so long a time." Marshall went to visit his family, who lived seven miles from Gloucester Point. It was not reported when Marshall had intended to return, but whatever his plans were, they changed when Webster received a request from the Confederate Army.[26]

It was about 5:00 P.M. when Tim Webster learned that Colonel Crump had sent for him. When Webster arrived at Crump's headquarters the colonel told him that he had just received a dispatch from General Magruder for Colonel Charles Smith that needed to go out that night.[27] Crump said that if they accepted the mission, Webster and Price could cross the bay with Marshall and deliver the dispatch. They agreed to it, which meant that now Webster was working for the Confederacy as well as the Union, while only betraying the Confederates. The two men walked seven miles to get Marshall. They were in Marshall's canoe and entering Chesapeake Bay by 11:00 P.M.

The men traveled through heavy winds and rough waters. They reached the shore at about 4:30 A.M. From there they traveled on horseback and arrived at Smith's camp about 7:00 A.M. After delivering the dispatch Webster and Price went to Tully Wise's hotel in Eastville for breakfast.[28]

Considering their arduous travels, the appearance of the men must have been quite rough.

From Eastville, Webster and Price, with Tully Wise and his servant, traveled to Drummondtown (now Accomac), with Webster making more observations of Confederate forces along the way.

At Drummondtown, Webster was informed that he and Price would have to get permission of Colonel Smith if they intended to go north. Smith had ordered that no one was allowed to cross the lines after November 9 (it was now the 13th).[29]

Upon arriving at Smith's headquarters they learned that the colonel was not there. A major who knew Webster gave him a pass to go north. Either it was much easier to obtain passes than everybody made it sound or Webster was especially skilled at selling his cover and getting what he wanted. While it may have been partially the former, Webster did prove his skill in the field time and time again.

While at the camp Webster made observations of the troops there and gathered information from John Kane, a man whom Webster knew from Baltimore who was now a private in Smith's regiment. Webster and Price then went and found a man along the river who took them across on his boat, warning them, according to Pinkerton's report to McClellan, "to take to the woods as the Yankees were down about Shelltown." They followed the man's advice and "took to the woods" until they reached Rehobeth, Maryland. There they obtained a horse and wagon which took them to Princess Anne, and from Princess Anne they went to Salisbury, where they spent the night.

The two men left by train at 5:30 the next morning. They then went their separate ways. Price went to Chestertown. Webster went through Baltimore to Washington and reported to Allan Pinkerton.[30]

According to operative Pryce Lewis,

> Webster's usual plan was to bring the rebel mail bag himself to the office of the Provost Marshall [sic] at Washington where the letters, one by one, were steamed, opened and read and a careful record kept of the important ones. Then they were sealed up again.[31]

11

Timothy Webster
Returns to Richmond

While Webster had been gathering information in the heart of the Confederacy, there had been changes in the Union command. General Winfield Scott resigned as general-in-chief of the Union forces and President Lincoln named George McClellan as his replacement.[1] The move meant that Allan Pinkerton now reported to the commander of the entire Union army. Pinkerton continued to send McClellan reports of his operatives' movements as well as interviews with refugees, prisoners, and others with knowledge of Confederate troop numbers and locations.

In the meantime McClellan continued to fortify Washington while simultaneously planning for an offensive against Richmond. Because of his belief that the Confederates had a superior number of troops, he kept delaying for more time to train his forces and get more troops, bringing him much criticism for his inaction. Also, the reports of the Confederate defenses around Centreville and Manassas Junction caused the general to reconsider if his campaign to Richmond should go that direction. For the time this meant Webster was to continue what he was already doing. His next mission, however, would take him farther west so he could provide information to help McClellan plan his grand design of having all the armies assist the Army of the Potomac's Richmond strike. While troops in the east and south would cut off reinforcements, the Army of the Potomac would strike.[2] For this reason Webster would not only return to Virginia but also to Tennessee.

When Timothy Webster returned north from his previous mission he no doubt spent time delivering the letters he carried with him. While in Baltimore, according to *Spy of the Rebellion*, Webster visited Sam Sloan to bring him a letter and to secure Sloan's assistance in delivering others he had for Baltimore residents and to collect letters for his next trip south.

One day, Webster was informed by John Earl that a stranger "desired to send a draft for a large amount of money to Richmond," and insisted on giving the draft to Webster personally. Webster did not like the idea, so he asked Earl to get the draft from the man. The stranger would not agree to this. Webster finally agreed to meet the man and asked Earl to bring him to Miller's Hotel. Because he was suspicious of the stranger, Webster used the alias William Hart when dealing with him. This was the beginning of an operation that, according to *The Spy of the Rebellion*, concluded the next day.[3] There is no evidence whether Pinkerton's timeline is correct, and much of Pinkerton's account of this event appears to be fiction. But whether Pinkerton's recollections were correct or not, the fact is somebody, or many persons, were watching Webster. They were connected to the provost-marshal in Baltimore and believed that Webster was a southerner working for the Confederate cause.

The operation resulted in a raid on Miller's Hotel. Timothy Webster and John Earl were both arrested. Also taken into custody at this time was Webster's "wife" Hattie Lewis.[4] There is no record of how long she was detained.

Newspapers across the country ran almost identical stories of the raid. The New York *Times* reported that on Wednesday, November 20, "The Mail Arrangements of the Rebels Interfered with." The provost-marshal sent "a large" police force to Miller's Hotel and seized "the whole establishment and all its contents, including a large number of horses, the contents of the bar-room, safe and vault. The object of this movement is said to be to prostrate the mail arrangements of the rebel sympathizers here." It was reported that the proprietors of the hotel were not suspected, "but it is supposed that certain employees or lodgers have been receiving and transmitting letters forward to secessia. A number of letters were seized, but have not yet been examined. Two parties, WM. HART [Webster] and JOHN EARL, were arrested. The nature of the evidence against them is not known."[5]

According to Pinkerton, Webster was turned over to a lieutenant after his arrest. Webster attempted to tell the lieutenant who he was when they were alone, but the lieutenant refused to "talk with rebels" and soon Webster was turned over to another man who locked him in a cell.[6]

Pinkerton wrote, "In the afternoon another officer, accompanied by four men, came to his cell, and requested his appearance at the office." Webster was searched. On him were letters, a pass from Colonel Crump, and about seventy dollars.

As the items were being taken from him, Webster asked who the man was that arrested him. They told him the man was named McPhail.[7] James L. McPhail was a deputy provost-marshal of Baltimore.[8] Webster recognized the name.

Per Pinkerton's account, in response to hearing McPhail's name, Webster asked, "Well, will you be kind enough to send for Mr. McPhail, and ask him to telegraph to Major Allen, and inquire if Tim is all right?" The message was sent.[9]

It was about ten o'clock that night when the officer returned to Webster's cell. He told Webster that he had been ordered to take him to Fort McHenry, where many prisoners were kept. From the way he told Webster, the operative knew that his position was understood.[10]

Webster was loaded into a covered wagon in front of the station. Pinkerton wrote, "After they had started, the officer explained to Webster that it had been arranged, in order to prevent suspicion, that he should be allowed to jump from the wagon as it was driven along, and after a pretended pursuit, he would make his escape to his rebel friends with whom he should remain quietly for a few days."

Webster followed the plan and, when they were nearing Fort McHenry, jumped from the wagon and headed into the city. According to Pinkerton, Webster went directly to Sam Sloan's. Sloan was undoubtedly surprised to see Webster, who told him how he leapt from the wagon and made his escape from the "Yankees."[11]

The details of this story come from *The Spy of the Rebellion*. That Webster did escape is backed up by the November 22, 1861, edition of the newspaper the Baltimore *American and Commercial Advertiser*. The paper reported:

Escape of a State Prisoner.— It was rumored yesterday that the man Webster, who was arrested at the hotel of Messrs. McGee [Miller's Hotel proprietor Joseph H. McGee], upon the charge of being concerned in the regular transportation of letters between Baltimore and the Seceded States, had succeeded in making his escape. It is learned upon the best authority that during a late hour of night he was removed from the Western Police Station and placed in a carriage, and under the charge of a special detective officer driven towards Fort McHenry, he having been previously ordered to that post. But when the vehicle had arrived within a short distance of the main gate he gave a sudden bound from his seat, and before the officer could seize him was beyond his grasp. It is not known which direction he took, but he will scarcely be able to escape from the city. He is a citizen of Kentucky, but left there in the early part of April, and since that time has been residing in Baltimore.[12]

The report surely raised the Baltimore secessionists' opinion of Tim Webster. The operative soon returned to Washington to report to Allan Pinkerton.[13]

On Webster's next trip south he took with him a letter of introduction to General John H. Winder from a Doctor Herndon, who Webster, in his role as a southern sympathizer, helped in his effort to desert the Union Army and escape to Virginia. Most of the details of this mission south are unknown, but we do know that Webster made it to Richmond, where he met with General Winder. The operative returned with a verbal message from General Winder to his son, William, who was a captain in the Union Army.

General Winder wanted his son to come south. William Winder, when speaking with Webster, claimed that "his sympathies were with the South" and said that he would desert and go south if possible, but that he had a wife and son to support and his pay as a captain was all he had to support them with. William Winder told Webster that he had made his feeling clear to General McClellan, who he said had arranged for him to serve in California where he would not be called upon to raise arms against the South. This was the message Webster was to deliver to General Winder. Captain William Winder was watched for a time by Pinkerton spies, but soon sent to California by McClellan.[14]

Around the same time Webster was approached by Union Captain Joseph H. Maddox, who sought Webster's aid in a project he had worked out with a Confederate captain named Alexander, whereby Maddox sent information by signals across the Potomac. Webster reported this to Pinkerton and Maddox was arrested in 1862. He did not remain in custody for long. After his release he resumed spying for the South.[15]

During this time Allan Pinkerton lost his cover. Pinkerton had investigated the treatment of blacks in Washington jails. Along with their treatment, he investigated why they were there. Many escaped slaves were held under fugitive slave laws even though many helped the Union cause by providing information about the South. The results of Pinkerton's investigation were brought to the attention of the Senate by Senator Henry Wilson. The Washington *Star* attacked the report and Major "E. J. Allen."[16]

The *Star* charged, "The report in question is evidently being used to bring about the legal abolition of negro slavery in the District of Columbia." and stated that if the laws were changed,

> Instead of a free negro population of perhaps 14,000, in the current anomalous condition of the country the District of Columbia cannot fail to become at once the harbor for at least 50,000 negroes, practically freed as an incident of war. With such a population, without especial restraining laws, Washing-

ton will be rendered almost uninhabitable to the white man. The business of our white laboring population of both sexes will be utterly ruined by this influx of negroes, who will only work, as at the North, when they cannot otherwise manage to keep life in their bodies. The abolitionists of Congress who can see naught worthy of their sympathy in the condition of any class in any community but the negro class, will of course continue their tinkering experiments upon the local affairs of the District of Columbia, until they make it nothing less than a hell upon earth.[17]

Apparently black rights were a sore spot for the *Star*. The paper continued their attacks, and on December 13 reported that "'E. J. Allen' means 'Pinkerton,'" outing the detective. What effect this had on the safety of Pinkerton and his operatives is unknown. Pinkerton continued to use the alias E. J. Allen.

Timothy Webster's next journey south commenced on Christmas day. He traveled from Washington, intending to cross from Maryland into Virginia at Leonardtown, but found this impossible "because of the extra vigilance on the part of Federal troops." J.W.J. Morris, a hotel keeper and secessionist in Leonardtown, advised Webster to cross near the mouth of Cuckold Creek from a point called Cobb Neck which, he said, was about thirty miles away by wagon road.

The Union operative left Leonardtown on the 27th of December and arrived at Cobb Neck on Saturday the 28th.[18] Here Webster met up with fellow operative E. H. Stein. The next night Webster and Stein crossed into Virginia.[19] Webster and Stein paid $50 each to cross the Potomac. Also crossing at this time were two women and three children. Webster and Stein carried these passengers— and the passengers' baggage — on their backs through two feet of water to get to the canoe. Wet and cold, they sailed across the Potomac, which took more than three hours. They made their landing at a place called Washington's Farm, a few miles from the mouth of Monroe Creek. Because the buildings at the landing spot had been destroyed by Union boats, they had to sleep on the frozen ground that night.[20] This would have a lasting effect on Webster's health.

The next day, Monday, December 30, Webster, Stein, the women, and children started toward Richmond in an ox cart but, because of the poor condition of the road, only covered six miles. They found a house to stay at that night and borrowed transportation to travel to Hop-Yard Wharf on the Rappahannock River the following day. That night, New Year's Eve, they took a steamboat to Fredericksburg. It was here that Webster and Stein split up.[21]

Due to the rough travel, Webster was sick and spent the next day stuck in Fredericksburg. The thirty-nine-year-old's illness was likely the rheumatism he suffered from for the remainder of his life. The term rheumatism covers a range of medical problems usually associated with pain and stiffness in the muscles and joints. Webster left Fredericksburg the next day by train. On his way to Richmond, a captain of a Louisiana regiment stationed at Dumfries told the spy that his regiment had lost seventy-five men in six weeks. Many died, he said, because of the "change of climate." Webster arrived in Richmond the same day.[22]

While in Richmond, Webster received passes from Confederate Secretary of War Judah P. Benjamin to go to Nashville, but, before he could leave the rebel capital, Webster again became sick and stayed in the city until the 7th.

On the 7th, Webster left Richmond with William Campbell, who had a contract with the Confederate government to supply leather goods—including five-thousand knapsacks—for the troops. Campbell was on his way to obtain leather from tanneries in Knoxville, Chattanooga, and Nashville.

Webster reported that railroad was "in a bad condition from Richmond to Bowling Green," and that the trains' average speed was not over ten miles per hour. The next train Webster took carried six car loads of Confederate soldiers. The train brought Webster to Lynchburg that day.[23]

The operative reached Abingdon at 3 o'clock the following morning and, being too sick to travel, he stayed there for the day. His illness did not stop him from making observations of troops arriving in Abingdon.

Tim Webster, along with Campbell, left Abingdon the following day for Nashville, but he had to spend the night in Knoxville because the trains were not running at night for "fear of some injury being inflicted" by the Union. Webster made a detailed report on forces in and around Knoxville.

Webster left Knoxville for Nashville on Friday, January 10. He reported that he shared the train with one hundred and fifty soldiers who were on the way to Bowling Green. Webster also reported on forces around Chattanooga and Cleveland, Tennessee. The Union spy arrived at Nashville the next day. He made a detailed report of forces and fortifications in and around Nashville and of the soldiers guarding railroad bridges.

Webster also reported that near the Nashville and Bowling Green railroad depot "were *three very large* Ware houses now being used as *hospitals*, all of which were *filled with the sick*—apparently well cared for."[24]

In Nashville, Webster obtained a pass to Bowling Green. He left by train for Bowling Green on Sunday, January 12. The operative reported that the railroad "was in bad condition" and that the train ran not more than ten miles an hour. The train was about eighteen miles outside Nashville when it ran off the track and turned over. Though there were seven passenger cars and the large group of passengers included over three-hundred soldiers, only one man was hurt, according to Webster. The engine was destroyed. How Webster reached Bowling Green is not included in the reports to McClellan.

The day after the train accident, while in Bowling Green, Timothy Webster received a pass from the provost marshal of that city to visit the 1st Arkansas Regiment, which had its camp about three miles northwest of the city. He took a horse and buggy to the camp. The spy made a detailed report on the regiment, what he learned from officers about other regiments, and what he observed going to and from the camp. On his way back to town Webster was forced to stop many times to pull his wagon wheels out of the deep mud.[25]

Webster left Bowling Green the following day and began his journey to Manassas. He stayed that night in Knoxville. When traveling the next day, Webster learned of about five local Union supporters who were accused of burning bridges. The accused men, who were farmers and included a father and son, were hanged.

Webster spent the night in Lynchburg. He left for Manassas in the morning and arrived that evening. The next day Webster wanted to visit the 1st Maryland Regiment, which was stationed at Centreville, but because the roads were in "horrible" condition, he could not find transportation. Not letting this stop him, Webster walked seven miles to Centreville. The walk appears to have been worth the effort. Webster made a detailed report of fortifications around Centreville and of the poor morale among the troops due to lack of fighting and bad weather. Webster learned more about the troops the following day, but did not visit as much of the area as he would have liked because of the weather, bad roads, and his poor health.[26]

Tim left Manassas on Tuesday, January 21, by train for Richmond, where he arrived the same day. Webster met with Confederate Secretary of War Benjamin on Wednesday and from him acquired a pass to go through rebel lines. Even with Benjamin's signature Webster would still have to get his pass countersigned by the general of any division he needed to pass.[27]

Detective Webster left Richmond for Maryland on the 24th. He first

went to Fredericksburg, where his pass was countersigned by General
Theophilus Holmes. While there Webster ran into General Winder and
from him learned that his son had been sent to California by McClellan.
Webster also saw Dr. Herndon, who was now a medical director under

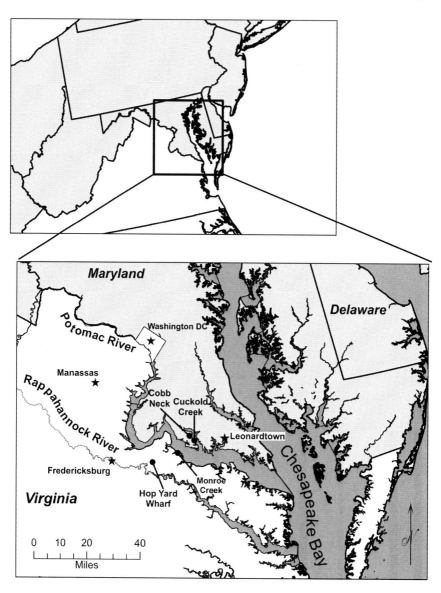

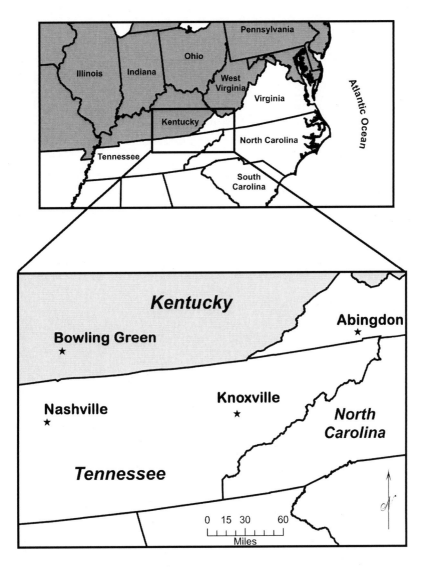

Opposite and above: Maps of key points from Webster's December 25, 1861 to January 30, 1862, mission. West Virginia, although not officially a state at this time, is included because it had split from Virginia to stay with the Union (maps by Michelle Davis).

General Holmes. Herndon told Webster that "*sickness* was *fearfully great*" in Holmes's division.

The operative left the next day and arrived at Monroe Creek the following night. The lieutenant in charge there let Webster use a boat with two men to take him across the Potomac to Cobb Neck. From there he headed to Washington by both foot and wagon, having to avoid Union troops along the way.[28]

Webster reported to Allan Pinkerton who, in turn, submitted two detailed reports to General McClellan. The reports—one eighteen pages and the other thirty-five—contained all the information from Webster's journey behind enemy lines.

12

Pinkerton's Blunder

Tim Webster, despite his recurring rheumatism, continued delivering letters and collecting letters for his return south. On his next journey south Webster was accompanied by operative Hattie Lewis, who posed as his wife. It is likely that she went with Webster to care for him in the event that his rheumatism became a problem.

The spies left for Richmond, while Webster, according to *The Spy of the Rebellion*, delivered some letters in Fredericksburg on the way. After Webster and Lewis left Washington all went silent.

It is probable the operatives' trip south was planned to be a short one, because it did not take long for Allan Pinkerton to suspect that something had happened to them. Perhaps Pinkerton felt guilty about sending an ailing man behind enemy lines. Whatever the reason, Pinkerton thought something was wrong and immediately put together a plan to find out what.

Allan Pinkerton decided to send two operatives to find Timothy Webster and Hattie Lewis. The men chosen for this assignment were John Scully and Pryce Lewis. Scully was a native of Ireland. He and his wife Julia had two young children at the time.[1] Pryce Lewis had been born in Wales in October 1834. The twenty-seven-year-old had worked for Pinkerton for nearly three years when he was chosen for this assignment.[2] In *The Spy of the Rebellion*, Pinkerton wrote about the selection of Scully and Lewis for this mission. He remembered that both men had "been engaged upon various investigations" and had "rendered good service" since the start of the war. Pinkerton wrote about his meeting with the spies.

> Requesting their presence in my private office, I broached the matter to them, and submitted the question of their undertaking this task to their own election. Upon operations of this kind, where there was danger to be incurred, where a man literally took his life into his own hands, and where death might be the result of detection, I invariably placed the question upon

its merits, before the person selected for the mission, and then allowed him to decide for himself, whether he would voluntarily undertake its accomplishment.

I did this for various reasons. In the first place, I felt very loath to peremptorily order a man upon an enterprize [sic] where there was every possibility of danger, for in the event of fatal result, I should be disposed to reproach myself for thus endangering the lives of those under my command. It is true, that under their terms of service, and by virtue of the authority vested in me, I had the undoubted right to issue such order; but I always preferred that my men should voluntarily, and without urging, signify their willingness to undertake hazardous missions. Again, I have invariably found, that the ready and cheerful officer performs the most acceptable service, and that the absence of fear or hesitation are sure passports to success; while on the other hand, should there be timidity or unwillingness, or a disposition to avoid danger, success is rarely, if ever, attained.

It is but just, however, to state that during my entire connection with the secret service of the government, I never found any of my men disinclined to undertake an operation that was delegated to them; but on the contrary, I always experienced the utmost cheerfulness and ready support from those who so valiantly served under my orders. Nor was I disappointed in the present instance. On presenting the case, with all its attendant dangers, to Price [sic] Lewis and John Scully, both of them signified, without the slightest hesitation, their voluntary desire to go to Richmond, and to make the inquiries, which were considered of so much importance by both General McClellan and myself.[3]

In his memoir, dictated in 1888, Pryce Lewis remembered the meeting with Pinkerton, and the decision to go to Richmond, differently. He said he was called into Pinkerton's office, and could immediately tell it was for something important.

"Mr. Lewis," Pinkerton said to him, "have you any objections to going to Richmond?"

"Yes," Lewis claimed he promptly replied. "I have played the part of a spy for the last time. If my services are not wanted here in Washington, I will take a musket, join the army, and go to the front."

"I don't want you to play the part of a spy," Pinkerton told him.

"What is it, then? What do you want me to go for?"

"I simply want you to carry a letter to Tim Webster who is now in Richmond and we can't hear from him. I haven't heard from him in some time and I think he is sick."

"This looks very much like playing the spy," Lewis stated.

"Well, I can't see it in that way."

"There is no use in discussing it. It would be folly for me to go to Richmond under any circumstances," Lewis claimed he said.

"Why?" Pinkerton asked.

"I believe I am better known in Richmond as a detective, though I have never been there, than I am in Washington."

"How is that?"

"Good heavens, Mr. Pinkerton! Think of the people I have assisted in arresting who have gone through the lines." Lewis proceeded to name them, including the family of Jackson and Elizabeth Morton, who had known him as a government operative and now resided in the South. Pinkerton, according to Lewis, said he knew where each of them had gone. None of them, he assured Lewis, were in Richmond. Lewis recalled, "I had implicit faith in what he said and this emphatic assurance made me waver. Finally I said that I didn't like the mission, but would undertake it if I was sure that I would not be recognized.... I remembered every word of this conversation for I had much occasion to go over it again and again in my mind. I recalled his every look and gesture, his intonation of each word."[4]

Lewis went to say that, when informed that Scully would accompany him, he told Pinkerton, "Then, I will not go—positively."

"Why?" Pinkerton asked.

"Because I have had experience enough taking any one with me—as in West Virginia, for example," Lewis remembered saying. "I can take the responsibility of going alone anywhere, but I don't want company that I must be responsible for, too. It's dangerous, because one man can tell a story and stick to it. Two will be sure to differ."

"Mr. Lewis," Pinkerton said, "It may take you a long time to work your way by yourself to Richmond. You will have to lay out in the woods at night; you will be lonesome and need company. Besides, I want Scully to come back at once with the information Webster will give you, while you go on further South, working your way to Chattanooga, ascertaining the conditions of the railroads and of the rolling stock and picking up what information you can. Then you can return to Washington the best way you can. Webster will give Scully directions how to get back promptly."

Lewis, who had claimed that he no longer wanted to be a spy, suddenly had a change of heart. He wrote of his reaction to Pinkerton's request,

I thought this was extending the range of his first request immensely, as that had been simply to deliver a letter to Webster, but I made no objections now.

For I felt it was necessary for some one to go in order to relieve McClellan's anxiety and permit a forward movement, and I felt rather proud of the mission, only I would have preferred to go alone.

Against Scully, personally, I had no prejudice, though I did not feel intimately acquainted with him. He was an Irishman of fair complexion and nearly as tall as myself. There was nothing noticeable in his appearance. He was honest and zealous or he would not have been in Pinkerton's service.[5]

Lewis's memoir has a self-serving ring to it. If what he wrote was true, then Allan Pinkerton made a major mistake not listening to Lewis, but, considering the events that would unfold in Richmond, Lewis's account may be an attempt to pass off the blame or the result of guilt for a mission gone horribly wrong. Many of Pinkerton's writings have the same self-serving feel. Whether they are trying to convince themselves or others, both men try to pass off the blame for mistakes made.

Whatever went into the decision and the operatives' feelings about it, the fact is that Pryce Lewis and John Scully went to find Timothy Webster and Hattie Lewis. They left the United States capital in mid–February in the company of operative William H. Scott, who helped them cross enemy lines. Scott was selected for this because of his acquaintances near the border.[6]

Lewis and Scully, posing respectively as English and Irish immigrants who were neutral in the conflict and hoping to profit in the contraband trade, reached Richmond in late February. After finding the Spotswood Hotel full, the two operatives registered at the Exchange Hotel.[7]

The day after arriving in

Pryce Lewis posing as an English lord for a mission in 1861 (Mss. 6, Box 2, Folder 10, photograph 10, Pryce Lewis Collection, St. Lawrence University Archives, Owen D. Young Library).

Richmond they began their search for Webster and Lewis. The operatives went to the office of the editor of the Richmond *Dispatch*, where Webster often delivered letters. Here they learned that Webster and Lewis were at the Monumental Hotel. Webster was confined to his bed with rheumatism.[8]

Lewis remembered that he and Scully went to the Monumental Hotel, "which was a second rate house," at about four o'clock. They found Webster in bed. Hattie Lewis was in the room taking care of him and they had a visitor who was only identified as Price (possibly J. H. Price).

Monumental Hotel, Richmond, in the post Civil War 19th century, when the structure was known as the St. Claire Hotel. The photograph is taken from Capitol Square. The view is of the 9th Street side. The fence to the left is surrounding the George Washington Equestrian Monument, which was already in Capitol Square during Webster's time in Richmond (Accession No. 1998.69.7 [this image has been taken from the background of a photograph of Capitol Square and the George Washington Equestrian Monument] Virginia Historical Society).

Pryce Lewis remembered that Webster was staying in "a long, narrow room." The bed he occupied was to the right of the door. Lewis walked to Webster's bedside and they "shook hands as old friends." Then Webster shook hands with Scully and introduced them to Price, whom Lewis described as a "young man." Lewis wrote,

> Everything was natural and informal in our meeting. The real expression in Webster's face, as far as I could judge beneath the apparent one, was that of utter astonishment. I said to him, "I have a letter for you," (It was the blind letter warning him not to come north via Leonardtown), and I delivered it.
> Scully and Miss Lewis with Price withdrew to the window and I sat down beside the bed. Webster made a beckoning motion and I stooped over.

Lewis claimed that Webster, "in a low tone," asked, "Lewis, why in hell did the 'Old Man' send Scully here?" Lewis responded, "Captain, I don't know. I opposed it, but my objections were over-ruled."

Said Webster, "I will send to the editor of the *Dispatch* and have a mail made up and send Scully with it to Washington." Lewis said that it was after that statement that he told Webster that while Scully was returning to Washington he was to go to Chattanooga to gather intelligence for McClellan, who was being pushed to act. As the others came back to the conversation, Webster told Lewis that he "had been laid up suffering from rheumatism for some time." He told Lewis and Scully that Price was a friend from Baltimore and then they all talked. The operatives visited for "hour or more." Near the end of the visit Price invited Scully and Lewis to the theater that night. After making arrangements, the spies returned to their hotel.[9]

Lewis said that Scully visited Webster the following morning and Lewis visited later that day. What makes Lewis's visit important is who was there at the time. Confederate Captain Samuel McCubbin, General Winder's chief detective, was paying Webster a friendly visit.[10]

Lewis recalled that when he arrived at Webster's room he found him "propped up in bed talking to a visitor." Webster welcomed Lewis and introduced him to the visitor — Captain McCubbin. Lewis remembered, "Captain McCubbin informed me that he occupied the room adjoining that of Webster. We had a pleasant chat upon indifferent subjects. Webster possessed the manners of a refined gentleman and, though an invalid and suffering from acute rheumatism, appeared to enjoy our company."

During the conversation McCubbin asked Lewis, "I understand you and your friend came across the Potomac."

"Yes," he replied.

"Have you reported to the military governor, General Winder?" McCubbin asked.

Lewis said he did not know that was necessary and added that they reported themselves to a Major Beals, who he said told them they were free to be in Richmond. Then he went on to explain that he had come to Richmond to warn Webster not to return north by way of Leonardtown because "the Yankees were on the lookout for him."

"Very good," said McCubbin, "but probably Major Beals did not know that an order has been issued requiring all who have crossed the Potomac to report to General Winder's office on their arrival here. I am chief of detectives, attached to General Winder's headquarters, and know it is necessary for you to report. If you and your friend will come to General Winder's headquarters at about four o'clock, I will meet you there and introduce you to the General."

Lewis thanked McCubbin and then left to get Scully so they could make it to Winder's headquarters by the agreed upon time. Lewis remembered his thoughts as he left the Monumental Hotel: "I went away admiring the nerve of Tim Webster in his ingratiating himself into the very citadel of the enemy. The truth was that he had gained the entire confidence of the leading officials in the Confederate capital and was no more suspected of being a spy than Jeff Davis himself."[11]

Then, in his memoir, Lewis continued with his claims that he had known all along that Scully should not have been sent with him. He wrote that when he told Scully of his conversation with McCubbin, Scully appeared "agitated and alarmed."

Then, ready to leave, Lewis said to Scully, "Now, we have no time to lose, we must go and report at once. You have our story at your tongue's end, I suppose, so that there will be no discrepancy if we should be separately examined."

"I have forgotten all about it," Scully responded.

Lewis remembered that he "must have turned pale at first" and then was "angry." "Good God!" he exclaimed, "Supposing Winder suspects and examines us separately. It seems you are bound to hang us both anyway. That is the danger of sending two together, just as I told Pinkerton. Now, let us go over the story again."

They went over the story again and when finished Scully said, "I will remember it now."[12] Then the pair went to Winder's headquarters on Main Street where they found Captain McCubbin standing outside. Lewis said he introduced Scully to McCubbin and the captain took them inside. After a short wait they were brought to the general's office. Winder greeted them, according to Lewis, with "I am very glad to meet any friends of Captain Webster's. He is a noble fellow, a most valuable man to us."

Lewis told General Winder that Webster's friends were worried about him, and Lewis said he brought a letter warning Webster not to come north via Leonardtown because United States detectives were watching for him.[13] Winder responded, "Gentlemen, I thank you heartily. Webster must not go north again. He is too valuable a man. We cannot afford to lose him." Winder then began talking about the North and asking Lewis and Scully about "the administration at Washington." Winder denounced Secretary of State William Seward, who he said "was most to blame for what he called the 'war on the South.'" He said that Lincoln was merely figurehead. Lewis recalled,

> During our conversation a citizen came in and asked the general for a pass or permit of some kind. The general said to us, ["]Excuse me," and, turning to his desk, began writing. While writing he suddenly raised his pen, wheeled around to us and inquired, "Gentlemen, is there one or two n's in 'cannot'?" I answered, generally two, unless it is abbreviated." He smiled and turned back to his writing. I remember this trivial incident as clearly as if it had occurred today, which shows to some degree how alert all my faculties were.

When the man left they resumed their conversation. Lewis said to Winder, "General, we are strangers here and would like something from you to show that we have reported here and are all right, so to avoid interference from the guards."

"Oh Sir!" Winder said, "You are all right. You require no pass or permit. If any one interferes with you, just tell them that you reported to me; but no one will trouble you." As they left Winder added, "Call and see me whenever you feel like it."[14]

John H. Winder (Museum of the Confederacy, Richmond, Virginia).

118

That evening Lewis and Scully went to visit Webster together. According to *The Spy of the Rebellion*, shortly after they arrived at Webster's room, a detective under General Winder showed up and asked Lewis and Scully what parts of England and Ireland they were from. This was all the information he desired. Upon the southern detective's exit, Webster told Lewis and Scully they must leave, saying the detective would never have come to ask such a trivial question unless something was wrong.[15]

Whether this incident actually happened or is a figment of Pinkerton's imagination or faulty memory is unknown. Lewis makes no mention of it in his memoir. Otherwise, Pinkerton and Lewis's accounts of that evening basically agree. If it did take place, Lewis and Scully made a fatal mistake not leaving immediately.

Lewis recalled that after supper he and Scully went to visit Webster. They hoped to make arrangements to leave Richmond. When they arrived at Webster's hotel, they found that he was being visited by Price. Price asked Lewis and Scully to go to the theater with him, which they agreed to do when he returned from supper.

When they were finally alone with Webster, Lewis told Webster that he was ready to leave the next day. Webster said that the mail was being made up for Scully so he could leave as soon as possible.[16]

Lewis said that they had been speaking to Webster for about fifteen minutes when there was a knock at the door. Webster invited whomever was knocking in. Two men entered. One was George Clackner, one of Winder's detectives. The other was Chase Morton.[17]

William Chase Morton was the son of Jackson and Elizabeth Morton. Jackson Morton had, a few years previous, been a senator from the state of Florida. The family resided in Washington, D.C., when the war began. Elizabeth Morton had been suspected of being a Southern sympathizer who had been sending information to rebel leaders. The case went to Allan Pinkerton, who made the mistake of sending operatives who also worked as spies to search the Mortons' property. The men sent were William H. Scott, John Scully, and Pryce Lewis. They found nothing incriminating in the family's home. Shortly after the search the Mortons relocated to Richmond, Virginia, which, by a horrible coincidence, brought Chase Morton into contact with two of the men he had earlier witnessed searching his family's home.[18] It is probable that a member of the Morton family had seen Lewis and/or Scully earlier that day and reported it. This brought Clackner and Chase Morton to Webster's room in search of the men.

Lewis and Scully immediately recognized Chase Morton when he entered the room. Lewis acted casual, but Scully, according to Lewis, panicked at the sight of young Morton and walked right out of the room without saying a word. All indications are that Webster did not know Morton, nor did he understand why Scully bolted from the room.

Webster and Clackner began to talk "like old acquaintances." As far as Tim Webster knew, it appeared as if Clackner was just coming to visit him. Lewis later wrote that he joined Webster and Clackner's conversation "with an occasional remark." Morton was not introduced and from all reports added little or nothing to the conversation. Pryce Lewis soon said his goodbyes and left the room.[19]

Lewis found Scully waiting at the top of the stairs. At that point the door of Webster's room opened and Clackner and Morton came out. According to Lewis's memoir, Clackner came up to him and asked, "Is your name Lewis?"

"Yes," Lewis answered.

Then he turned to Scully and asked, "Is your name Scully?"

"Yes," Scully said.

"Well, General Winder wishes to see you both."

"We saw the General this afternoon," Lewis said.

"Well, he wishes to see you again."

"All right," Lewis said and they descended the stairs and to the hotel's barroom. There they found McCubbin and "four or five" other detectives.

"Captain," Lewis asked McCubbin, "What does this mean?"

"Lewis, I don't know," he replied. "The General wants to see you about something and I suppose you can make it all right with him."

"Oh, yes, at least I suppose so." They all had a drink "in a perfectly friendly way" then went down Main Street to Winder's office. Lewis recalled, "We walked directly in, all of us, and went into a lighted room at the end of the main hall where we took seats to await General Winder who was absent. Here the detectives began to question me, Clackner taking the lead. I answered in monosyllables. I could perceive from their questions that they thought I was from New York, while the story that Scully and I agreed to stick to was that I had been in this country but sixteen months, and in answer to their question I stated this."[20]

Lewis and Scully were questioned further, but did not betray their cover. Then Chase Morton, who thus far had been quiet, turned to Lewis and said, "Mr. Lewis, don't you recognize me?" "No, I do not," Lewis exclaimed, acting as if he was surprised by the question. "Good heavens! Don't you remember examining my father's papers in Washington?"

"No, sir," Lewis insisted. "I never saw you before that I know of. Why, my dear sir, I was never in Washington but one night and a day in my life. I have often heard of cases of mistaken identity and this is evidently one of them."[21] Apparently Lewis did not think this strong protest was suspicious. He recalled, "My coolness took him quite aback for a moment."

Morton finally responded, "It is impossible that I can be mistaken," then pointed at Scully and said, "and that man, too, he was in that case."

Lewis wrote,

> Some little time elapsed before the General was announced. I saw him coming down the long hall in full uniform, with cocked hat and all, very stiff and military. He entered and came to where I sat. I arose and he extended his hand.
>
> "How are you, Mr. Lewis, and how is Secretary Seward?"
>
> "General," I replied, "I don't understand you. I don't know what all this means. I never saw Secretary Seward in my life."
>
> Then he paid me a back-handed compliment. "Mr. Lewis," he said, "There is no doubt you are a smart man. If you were not, they would not send you on this mission. But we are smart enough for you this time. I suspected you all along." (I thought to myself, "What an old fibber he is! He never suspected me at all.") He added, "I hope, Mr. Lewis, you can prove your innocence. You shall have a fair trial and every opportunity to prove it." He spoke very politely and with some feeling.
>
> "General, this is certainly a case of mistaken identity," I replied, and I repeated what I had already said about having been in Washington but once. I spoke at some length, vigorously maintaining my innocence of the unjust suspicions.
>
> When I concluded, the General turned to young Morton and asked him if it were possible that he could be mistaken. He replied again, "I cannot be mistaken. These are the two gentlemen who examined my father's papers in Washington."[22]

The General then sent two or three detectives to retrieve Lewis and Scully's baggage. When they returned Lewis and Scully gave them the keys for the bags and Lewis "called their attention to the pocket at the side containing revolvers." Lewis recalled that they "examined the valises thoroughly, spreading out our clothing, ripping out the lining of the trousers and feeling along all the seams." They then went through the clothes that Lewis and Scully were wearing.

Following this, Winder, McCubbin, and one other man went into an adjoining room. Lewis claimed he heard the men whispering. They were calling names off a list, he said. Lewis claims he distinctly overheard two of the names. They were both members of Pinkerton's force. Lewis did not hear if he or Scully were on this list. Pryce Lewis remembered, "At length they came out of the little room and the General, seating himself at his desk, made out a commitment consigning us to Henrico County Jail."[23] This happened on Friday, February 28. The Richmond *Dispatch* predicted that Lewis and Scully would hang.[24]

On their way to jail, according to Lewis, they stopped by a bar and had a drink with the officers who were taking them to jail. When they arrived at their destination they found that the jailer had left, so Lewis and Scully were put up in the guardhouse for the night.[25]

Clackner took the prisoners from the guardhouse the next morning. On their way through town they made a stop. Pryce Lewis recalled that Clackner said, "See here, Lewis, you are an Englishman. If you like we can go to a place where we will find some old London Tom gin."

"Very well," Lewis replied.

Clackner took them to a second floor bar on Main Street. The bartender was in the billiard hall when they entered and came walking toward the men. Lewis was shocked to see a man he recognized. The bartender was Pinkerton operative E. H. Stein. Lewis wrote, "I have always believed from something in Clackner's manner, in the way in which he watched us as we spoke to the bartender, that this meeting was brought about purposely (Stein probably being under some suspicion) to see if we knew each other. But he could determine nothing from the manner of our meeting."[26] Stein wasted no time getting out of Richmond. He returned to Washington and reported Lewis and Scully's situation to Pinkerton.[27]

After leaving the bar, Clackner took Lewis and Scully to Henrico Jail.[28]

No record exists showing that Webster was suspected of being a spy during this time. Some have since speculated that he was under suspicion and, although this is possible, it is likely the Confederates who arrested Lewis and Scully knew and trusted Webster so much that the thought of him being a Yankee spy never crossed their minds.

Webster, according to *The Spy of the Rebellion*, learned of the arrests of Lewis and Scully first from Hattie Lewis and then from Captain McCubbin, who came to get the letter the suspected spies had delivered to Webster.[29]

While Webster was confined to his bed, Pryce Lewis and John Scully were locked in an upstairs room of the two-story Henrico Jail with six other prisoners. After a few days a visitor was brought to see the accused spies. It was the eldest son in the Morton family. Morton identified both Lewis and Scully, but the spies denied recognizing him.[30]

Their stay in jail continued. Lewis said that Scully was depressed and "made no effort to adapt" to the circumstances. John Scully was soon taken from Henrico Jail to another location. It is probable that the Confederates saw that Scully was weak and believed they could get a confession out of him.

In Scully's absence Lewis became involved with a group of prisoners who were planning an escape. The building they were confined in consisted of two floors, with two cells on each floor. The locks on the cell doors could be easily picked with a knife blade, but two more doors secured the main entrance of the jail. The inner door was made of thick iron bars and fastened with a secure lock. The outer door was a wooden door fastened with an ordinary padlock. The prisoners believed if they could get to the outer door that the padlock could be picked.[31] The challenge was the inner door.

The plan they decided on was to saw through one of the bars so they could squeeze between them. They used knives and a file as saws and worked at it whenever they were alone. They mixed a piece of soap with ashes which resulted in a color similar to the bar. The soap would be rubbed over the saw marks whenever they heard anyone coming. This successfully hid their work. It took two weeks to saw through the entire bar.

To get through the outer door, it was decided that they needed to conceal someone outside during their daily recess. This person would hide until night, when he could pick the padlock on the outer door. The prisoner chosen for this was O. C. Stanton. During the recess, Stanton was hidden in a pile of ashes in the corner of the yard. Another prisoner changed the straw in his bed, dumping the old straw on top of Stanton. This allowed him to have his head in the straw — instead of in the ashes — so he could breathe. A broomstick wrapped in blankets was placed in the corner of Stanton's cell to cover the possibility that the prisoners were counted.[32]

Things began as planned when the prisoners were locked back in their cells with the guards not taking notice of the missing Stanton. Then a problem presented itself. It was a possibility that should have occurred to the prisoners, since it had likely happened many times before, resulting in the ash pile. The jailer saw the new straw in the corner and went over to light it on fire. Luckily for Stanton, a light drizzle kept him from successfully igniting the straw.

Night came and Stanton opened the outer doors, which was made easy because they were left unlocked that night. Then they ran into a problem. The prisoners found that the hole they had made in the bars was not big enough to slip through. After some time they were able to pick the lock of the inner door and were on their way. The ten prisoners scaled a

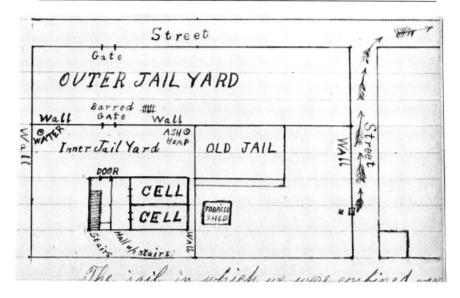

Map of Henrico Jail by Pryce Lewis (Mss. 6, Box 2, Folder 10, photograph 6, Pryce Lewis Collection, St. Lawrence University Archives, Owen D. Young Library).

wall to the yard of the old jail and then scaled a second wall to escape to the streets of Richmond.[33]

The escapees needed to get out of Richmond fast. If they were seen out after the 10:00 P.M. curfew they would likely be arrested. They moved quickly and were out of the city in about a half hour.

Their journey to the North was through the woods in the cold winter. Having to cross through swamps and streams and deal with cold rain made it even more torturous for the men. They traveled by night and rested (although getting much rest proved impossible) by day.

Two of the escapees separated from the group and were the first to be caught. The other eight were rounded up shortly after. They were in custody less than a week after their escape. The men were returned to the jail and put in shackles.[34]

While Lewis had been on the lam, John Scully was court-martialed. He was identified as a spy by every member of the Morton family. His defense, according to Lewis's memoir, was that he had at one time worked for the United States government but, being a foreigner who became "disgusted" with the government, quit. Pinkerton, in *The Spy of the Rebellion*, wrote that Scully claimed to be a secessionist and even called Timothy

Webster as a witness on his behalf. The records of the court-martial no longer exist, and there is no other known account of Scully's defense. Whatever the defense, the fact is that Scully was found guilty and sent back to jail to await his sentence.[35]

Pryce Lewis appeared before the court next. He was given counsel and began work on his defense. Before the trial began he was transferred to Castle Godwin.[36] Castle Godwin, which was a Negro prison known as Lumpkin's Jail before the war, served as a prison for suspected spies, political prisoners, and women.[37]

Lewis, who was not shackled in Castle Godwin, soon learned of an escape plan by other prisoners. He eagerly joined them. The plan was simply to dig a hole through the brick wall of the jail. Lewis wrote that "case knives and pocket knives" were used, with "each prisoner taking a turn until he was tired." Unfortunately, while one of the men was digging through the brick, an officer suddenly burst in, laid his hand on the man's shoulder, and asked, "What are you doing?"

"Trying to get out," answered the prisoner.[38]

The prisoners involved in the escape attempt were moved to a different cell, which Lewis described as "a truly horrible place." The following morning his trial began.[39]

Lewis remembered that the trial lasted "three or four days" and that the main witnesses against him were members of the Morton family. A verdict did not immediately follow the trial.[40]

After a few days passed, Pryce Lewis was taken to the cell of John Scully. Scully was ill and Lewis was brought there to take care of him. Lewis observed of Scully, "I knew he was suffering more from mental anxiety than bodily pain. It was plain to perceive that he had given up all hope and his despondency distressed me."[41]

The following morning Lewis learned that he was found guilty. He and Scully were sentenced to hang in two days. While Scully, according to Lewis, was "moaning and crying," Lewis wrote to the British Council in Richmond for assistance. This was a smart move, since both Lewis and Scully had been born in Great Britain (which at the time included both Scully's birthplace of Ireland and Lewis's birthplace of Wales). The Confederate government was hoping to gain English recognition, so it was reasonable to think that they would attempt to avoid executing British subjects and possibly angering the British government.

In the meantime, the Roman Catholic John Scully asked to see a priest. Father Augustine L. McMullen visited the condemned man and promised to visit again the following day — one day before the scheduled execution — to hear Scully's confession and administer last rites.[42] Lewis, who was raised a Baptist, but had quit the church, desired no such visit from what he called an "enemy" minister.[43]

Father McMullen, according the Lewis's memoir, was late the following day. Scully worried that the Confederates would not let McMullen come see him and "broke down again and cried so loud that he could be heard in the next rooms." Lewis said that he did his best to console Scully, but it did no good. McMullen did eventually show. Lewis was taken to another room so McMullen and Scully could be alone.[44]

After McMullen left, Scully's mood greatly improved. Lewis remembered, "Scully was dressed up in his best clothes, sitting on a bench with his back toward me reading a book. As he turned about I was startled by the pallor of his face and its cool self-possession, without a trace of anxiety. He was completely transformed. I would not have known him had I met him in the streets."[45]

Following a visit from John Frederick Cridland, the acting British counsel in Richmond, who offered the men little hope that he could do anything to delay the execution,[46] Scully made a revelation to Lewis. Scully said that he asked Father McMullen to go to General Winder and inform him that, if he would receive leniency, he would tell all he knew. Winder soon arrived and took Scully's statement.[47] That it was Scully who confessed at this time is confirmed by Pinkerton's report to McClellan[48] as well as other sources.

Later in the day Lewis witnessed, with much shock, the result of Scully's confession. He watched from his window cell as a carriage pulled up to the prison. From the carriage emerged Timothy Webster and Hattie Lewis, both under arrest. In his effort to save himself, John Scully had sacrificed everybody else.

Lewis described Webster as "very pale and ill" and remembered that he had to be helped from the carriage.[49] According to *The Spy of the Rebellion*, Webster's health had improved to the point where he was able to get out of bed and be moved to the home of William Campbell before his arrest. Through it all, Hattie Lewis remained at Webster's side.[50]

It was in Campbell's house, according to Pinkerton, that Webster and Lewis were arrested by Philip Cashmeyer. After each was questioned by General Winder, they were confined in separate cells in Castle Godwin.[51] This happened on Thursday, April 3. The Confederates still believed that Lewis was Webster's wife.[52]

13

April 1862

Pryce Lewis recalled that on the morning of April 4, the day he was to be executed, he was informed that the execution had been postponed for two weeks by order of Confederate President Jefferson Davis. Lewis claimed that during the stay of execution, Scully told him that he had made a full confession and that both he and Father McMullen urged Lewis to do the same.[1] It is beyond question that Father McMullen played a role in leading Scully to confess to help himself, and, based on what is known, it seems likely that the priest did also urge Lewis to confess.

Lewis finally gave in and, to save his own neck, talked. He claimed that he only confessed to the fact that he worked for Pinkerton and did not implicate Timothy Webster or anyone else.[2] Many have believed Lewis's claim that he did not confess; however, it seems doubtful the Confederate government would commute Lewis's sentence without his giving up information about others. They already convicted him of being a spy, so just admitting to that fact wasn't likely to be enough for the Confederates to show him mercy. Pinkerton later claimed that once Lewis learned that Scully had told all, he knew the damage to Tim Webster and Hattie Lewis had been done and it wouldn't hurt them anymore if he confessed and saved himself.[3] This story agrees with speculation that ran in the Richmond *Dispatch* on April 5, 1862. The *Dispatch* confirms that Jefferson Davis granted a stay of execution and that Lewis and Scully had approached the local British counsel for help. The paper continues by speculating that the most likely reason for the stay was that the prisoners had confessed and implicated others.[4] One final piece of evidence that supports the supposition that Pryce Lewis admitted that Webster was a spy is his admission that he was called as a witness during Webster's trial.[5] The Confederates wouldn't have called Lewis to testify unless his testimony helped establish Webster's guilt.

The trial of Timothy Webster took two to three weeks.[6] What information was presented against Webster besides Scully's and Lewis's confessions is not known for sure. According to the Richmond *Dispatch*, the charges against Webster were that he "lurked about the armies and fortifications of the Confederate States in and near Richmond," and did the same in Memphis in July 1861. It is likely the evidence used against Webster in the trial included testimony about the places Webster visited and the people he knew, showing what types of information he was able to obtain that could be damaging to the Confederacy. In his memoir, Pryce Lewis claimed that information had come from Baltimore that Webster was a spy.[7] This claim, of course, may have simply been an attempt to shift the blame away from himself.

Lewis had another memory from Webster's trial.

> I was taken to the Court House to testify. I was first conducted into a small room where there were a number of persons, all, I supposed, strangers to me, and therefore when one of them — a rather tall, well-dressed man — looked at me and nodded, I did not suppose he was bowing to me and so did not return the bow. I did not recognize him. This I deeply regretted afterward for this tall man was Tim Webster and I might have passed a few words with him. He was so changed that I did not know him and, when a few minutes later in the Court Room I saw who he was, it was too late to speak with him. I felt that he thought I had purposely refused to recognize him, and from this I suffered keenly, ever after, whenever I thought of him.[8]

Lewis added that Webster wore a mustache at this time.[9]

Pryce Lewis and John Scully repeated their confessions in front of Webster at the trial. What passed through the ailing man's mind as his fellow operatives testified against him can only be imagined.

Webster was found guilty of the charge of "lurking about the armies & fortifications of the Confederate States" in Richmond while he was "at that time an alien enemy and in the service and employment of the United States." He was found not guilty of the charge of doing the same in Memphis. Tim Webster was sentenced to hang.[10] Hattie Lewis escaped death but would remain in Confederate custody.

Allan Pinkerton first heard about the arrests of Lewis and Scully from Richmond newspapers. He remembered, "For a moment I sat almost stupefied, and unable to move. My blood seemed to freeze in my veins — my heart stood still — I was speechless.[11] The first official surviving record showing that Pinkerton knew of the arrests of his spies was an April 20, 1862, report of the operations of operative E. H. Stein.[12]

Pinkerton, who was at McClellan's camp at Yorktown when he received the news of Webster's sentence, went back to Washington to meet with the president and cabinet members, including Secretary of War Edwin Stanton, regarding Webster's position.[13] According to Pinkerton, Secretary Stanton expressed in strong terms his willingness to help Webster, but was less inclined to help Lewis and Scully who, he said, had "betrayed their companion to save their own lives."[14]

The Confederate government was contacted and leniency for Webster was requested. It was pointed out that not only had the United States government not executed spies, but, in most cases, suspected rebel spies were released after only a short confinement. The message also contained a warning: hang Timothy Webster and Confederate spies will face the same punishment. Pinkerton claimed that Hattie Lewis met with Varina Davis, Jeff Davis's wife, to plead for Webster's life, but the president's wife declined to interfere in matters of state.[15] Jefferson Davis showed no sympathy to the prisoner. The execution would go forward.

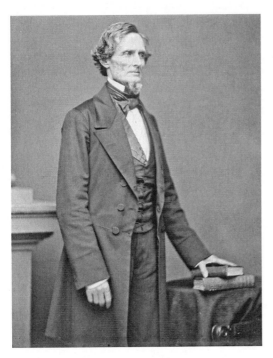

Jefferson Davis, circa 1860, photograph by Mathew Brady (Variant Control Number: NWDNS-111-B-4146, National Archives and Records Administration, Still Picture Records Section).

With little hope of a reprieve, Webster had one final request. He asked to be executed by a firing squad, like a solider, not to be hanged like a common criminal. This request was denied.[16]

The final week of Timothy Webster's life began with his fortieth birthday. A fellow prisoner remembered him at this time, "He was greatly suffering from rheumatic pains in his limbs at that time and was compelled to use crutches."[17] He was in a small cell with Hattie Lewis as his only friend. He also had occasional meetings with Episcopal Reverend Dr. George Woodbridge.

Tim Webster spent his last night on Earth writing messages for Lewis to give to the family he would leave behind. His thoughts were surely with his wife and children that night.

Webster was taken from his cell before six o'clock on the morning of April 29. Hattie Lewis did not accompany him. They had their final good-bye in the cell. It must have been an emotional one.

The gallows were built in the old Richmond fairgrounds which were part of Camp Lee. Webster was brought to the camp and held in a small room, where he was met by Reverend Woodbridge, who stayed with the condemned man about an hour. Reverend Moses D. Hoge, a Presbyterian who would be with Webster on the scaffold, also spent time with him. At about ten minutes past eleven the United States patriot was taken to the scaffold. Still in poor health, he had to be helped up the stairs.

His hands were tied behind his back, his legs tied together, and the rope was placed around his neck by executioner John Caphart, a "heavy set" man with a long white beard, "hard" facial features, and gray eyes that were described as "cold and cruel." Reverend Hoge said a prayer and then a black hood was placed over Webster's head. The trap was sprung, but it did not end there for the brave man. The knot on the noose slipped and Webster crashed to the ground beneath. Sick, hands and feet tied, and with a hood over his head, he was picked up and brought back to the scaffold.

The trap was set once more. "I suffer a double death," Webster calmly said. The rope was again placed around his neck. This time it was tied so tight that it was too short. "Oh, you are going to choke me this time?" Those were Timothy Webster's last words. The trap was sprung. Tim Webster died quickly.[18]

130

14

Post-Mortem

The body of Timothy Webster was cut down after hanging for a half hour. According to the Richmond *Examiner*, some of General Winder's detectives cut the rope used to hang Webster into pieces for souvenirs.[1]

Allan Pinkerton later wrote that Hattie Lewis had bought — no doubt with Pinkerton's money — a metallic coffin for Webster. A request was sent to General Winder to have Webster's body sent north. Like every request made to Winder dealing with Webster's execution, this was denied. It was next requested that Webster's body be kept in a vault in Richmond until the end of the war. This was also denied.[2]

As the denial of these requests show, the disdain of the South, and General Winder in particular, toward Tim Webster lasted beyond the spy's death. The petty behavior by Winder and going all the way up to Confederate President Jefferson Davis was a tribute to Webster's skill as a spy. He had fooled high ranking officials in the Confederate government and acted as a courier for General Winder and others in the military. He even transported official military correspondence. The rebels had been embarrassed by the Union operative, so they made sure they had their revenge.

The Richmond papers showed the same vindictiveness. Both the *Dispatch* and the *Examiner* carried detailed reports of the execution, and both slandered Timothy Webster. While much of the coverage of the execution is identical, the reports diverge when attacking Webster. Perhaps their attacks would have been more believable if they had compared notes, but, as it stands, what they wrote appears to be nothing more than lies designed to injure the reputation of a Northerner who deceived them all.

The *Examiner*, in its so-called coverage of the execution, reported that Webster was in "tears, moaning, and crying out" before his hanging. The paper also said that Webster was disappointed in the size of the crowd that turned out for his execution. The *Examiner* continued, "It was evident that he had prepared a dying speech, from the effect of the delivery of which he expected to desire great satisfaction. He complained repeatedly

131

and bitterly that his last pleasure had been denied him. As that fatal hour grew near he wept constantly."

The report went on the paint a villainous portrait of Webster on the scaffold. "His eyes were his most striking feature. They were of a cold disagreeable stone grey color. His other features were strongly marked, having a long nose, high cheek bones, and a rather butting brow."

And the paper ended with one final shot, "As far as the citizens are concerned no execution has ever taken place here that produced so little excitement. On the trees and high places overlooking the camp and commanding a view of the gallows there may have been as many as two hundred persons.... On the day on which it was thought Scully and Lewis were to have been hung the road leading to the camp was crowded with people."[3]

The Richmond *Dispatch* did not show any more class. In that paper, it was reported that, before his execution, Webster "asked the clergyman to read the Psalm of David, invoking vengeance on his enemies." The paper reported that when Reverend Hoge refused, "Webster grew indignant, causing the clergyman to take an early departure," even though there was no truth in this statement.[4]

Writers for the *Dispatch* further showed their spite when the paper ran a story in December 1862 about Lewis and Scully possibly being released and sent to the North. The report read, "It will be remembered that it was principally on the testimony of a man named Webster that they were found guilty."[5] Of course, the *Dispatch* had reported that it was Lewis and Scully who testified against Webster, and not the other way around, when the events actually happened. But why let the facts get in the way when there was an opportunity to malign an enemy? The story went on to call Webster "the biggest rascal of the three," and reported that he was an agent working for both governments and sold secrets to both.[6] It mattered not that this was untrue.

The reaction of the Northern press to Timothy Webster's execution had a common theme: If the Confederacy is going to execute Union spies, the North needs to do the same to southern spies. For the year following Webster's execution the American government did not respond to these calls for revenge. In 1862, following Webster's execution, the Confederacy executed eight other suspected spies. The Union did not begin executing Confederate spies until 1863.[7]

The other Pinkerton spies arrested in early 1862 remained in custody for a time. Hattie Lewis, who took care of Timothy Webster until the end, was released and returned north in December 1862.[8] Nothing is known about the remainder of her life.

Pryce Lewis and John Scully remained in Confederate confinement until September 1863, when they were freed and went north.[9]

John Scully continued to work for Pinkerton's National Detective Agency for a short time after the war. He worked as a police officer after that. By 1876 he was working as a clerk in Chicago's City Collector's office. John and his wife Julia had five children. John Scully died on December 14, 1902, after accidentally falling and striking his head on a street corner.[10]

After his release, Pryce Lewis went to work as a bailiff and detective at the Old Capitol Prison in Washington. Following the war, Lewis and former Pinkerton detective William H. Scott opened a detective agency in Chicago, which they later moved to New York City. After Scott's death, Lewis went to work as a detective for the Equitable Life Assurance Society.

In Lewis's twilight years, the former Union spy was unable to receive a government pension because he was not a U.S. citizen. Lewis was a widower who had one deceased son and a daughter he had no contact with. Broke and alone, Pryce Lewis took an elevator to the top floor of New York City's World Building and jumped from the dome atop the building. The three-hundred and sixty-five foot plunge ended when Lewis landed on a car. It was December 7, 1911. Pryce Lewis was seventy-seven years old.[11]

Allan Pinkerton continued on as Major E. J. Allen for General George McClellan. While Webster was bedridden in Richmond and Pryce Lewis and John Scully were in custody, on March 12, 1861, General George B. McClellan decided to begin his campaign against Richmond from Fort Monroe, which sat on the southern end of the Virginia Peninsula. The advance from Fort Monroe to the initial target of Yorktown began on April 4, one day after Tim Webster's arrest. The Union took Yorktown and slowly marched to just outside Richmond. That's where they stalled. Delays, some due to overestimated Confederate strength, proved costly, and the Peninsula Campaign ended with a series of battles that forced McClellan to retreat his forces. Following the failed campaign, McClellan, with Pinkerton's help, continued to overestimate enemy troop numbers. This caused the general to proceed with great caution when going after the enemy. General McClellan received much criticism for his inaction. This led to his removal as commander of the Army of the Potomac on November 7, 1862.[12]

Following McClellan's dismissal Allan Pinkerton resigned from the Army of the Potomac. Pinkerton and his operatives still worked for the United States government, but on a different front — they investigated fraud and criminal claims for the remainder of the war.[13]

Allan Pinkerton returned to Chicago after the war and Pinkerton's National Detective Agency flourished, opening branches across the county and gaining national fame. Their most notable positive fame was for their pursuit of the West's most famous outlaws, while their work as labor spies and strikebreakers brought intense criticism. Criticism from labor aside, Pinkerton's National Detective Agency was a key crime fighting force during the second half of the nineteenth century and what Pinkerton created left an important and lasting impression on law enforcement. One example of this was the agency's Rogues Gallery, used for cataloging and spreading information (and mug shots) of wanted men, which was the basis for the

Left to right: Allan Pinkerton, President Abraham Lincoln, and General John A. McClernand at Antietam, 1862 in a photograph by Alexander Gardner (Record Group 111. ARG Identifier: 530414. Local Identifier: 111-B-6348, National Archives and Records Administration, Still Picture Records Section).

A Richmond, Virginia, street after Union forces took control of the city in 1865 (ARG Identifier: 524883. Local Identifier: 111-B-465, National Archives and Records Administration, Still Picture Records Section).

FBI's Criminal Identification Bureau. Allan Pinkerton died in 1884. He was sixty-four.[14]

The American Civil War continued for three more years after Webster's execution. The unlucky spy was one of over 600,000 deaths. He was one of many who died for their country.

Timothy Webster left behind a wife and two (or three, depending on when

Charlotte Webster in December 1885 (courtesy of Lucille Campbell).

Onarga in the early 1900s (courtesy of Cheryl Rabe).

Eva died) children. His only son, Timothy, a Union soldier, died from wounds received in battle on July 4, 1864. Timothy Webster's widow, Charlotte, never remarried. She died on December 1, 1907, in Evergreen, California.[15]

In the final analysis, Timothy Webster made little difference in the outcome of the war with his work as a Union spy, although his skill and the accuracy and detail of the information he collected suggest he may have made a significant impact had his career not been cut short. Tim Webster's most important contribution to the United States came before the war began with his role in uncovering the plots to assassinate president-elect Abraham Lincoln in 1861. What these spies found may have saved Lincoln's life and changed the course of history. For that we owe Timothy Webster, Hattie Lewis, Allan Pinkerton, Charles D. C. Williams, Harry W. Davies, William H. Scott, and Kate Warne our gratitude.

Tim Webster, like so may of the men who died during the war between the states, had loved ones who mourned his passing. The tragedy in Webster's case was that it could have been so easily avoided. He was a sick man who could have been kept in custody, just like Hattie Lewis, Pryce Lewis, and John Scully had been. If Scully and then Lewis had not turned on him to save themselves, he may never have been arrested in the first place. But it was the Confederates who chose to execute him. It was a decision that did not have to be made.

Six years after the war, in 1871, Allan Pinkerton sent George Bangs to Richmond to find Webster's body and bring it back to Illinois. Bangs arrived in Richmond on April 27 and located Webster's body on the 29th. His remains were then sent to Illinois.[16]

Finding Webster's body was important for Allan Pinkerton, who praised Webster like no other detective on his force. Though he later defended his actions during the war, Pinkerton surely regretted sending Scully and Lewis to Richmond.

Timothy Webster was laid to rest in Onarga, Illinois, between his father, Timothy Webster, and his son, Timothy Webster III. The inscription on Webster's tombstone reads, "I die for my country." The man who was once, along with other New York City policemen,

The headstone for the graves of Timothy Webster and his son, both casualties of the Civil War (photograph by author, 2008).

attacked by the city aldermen simply because he was foreign-born, had given all he could for the United States of America.

Appendix I

Timothy Webster's Testimony in Front of the New York City Board of Aldermen, 1855

New York Herald, May 3, 1855 (Excerpt)

Mr. Timothy Webster, lieutenant of police, made his appearance at the conclusion of the foregoing testimony, and was sworn by Ald. Briggs, but he proved as refractory as Mr. McKellar.

Ald. B., administering the oath — You do solemnly swear that you will answer all questions—

Lt. W.— I solemnly swear that the evidence I shall give will be the truth, the whole truth, and nothing but the truth, so help me God.

Ald. B.— Put your hand on the book. Now, you do solemnly swear that the evidence you will give shall be the truth.

Lt. W., after repeating the oath — Now, I decline answering any questions put by this committee.

Ald. B.— What is your name?

No answer.

The Clerk — Give us your name, can't you?

No answer.

The Clerk — Timothy Webster — is that your name?

Lt. W.— That is the name on the subpoena I received.

Ald. B.— Have you ever answered any questions put to you in the station house in regard to your nativity, &c.?

Lt. W.— I refuse to answer.

Ald. B.— What country are you a native of?

Lt. W.— I positively decline to answer any question this committee puts to me. I wish that to be distinctly understood.

Ald. B.— Have you been posted up by Mr. McKellar, outside?

No answer. Alderman B. leaves the room and the witness indulges himself with a piece of tobacco.

New York Times, May 3, 1855 (Excerpt)

Timothy Webster was called. He declined to take the oath that Alderman Briggs offered him, but would swear the usual oath. After much hesitancy, much deliberation, much walking of the Chairman into the next room, much whispering on the part of spectators, and much wondering what would come of such contumacy, witness was sworn after his own fashion.

Alderman Briggs—What is your name?

Witness—I decline answering.

But being urged, he handed over the subpoena which had compelled his attendance; as it was endorsed "Timothy Webster," the conclusion was reached that the witness was of the Webster breed, and his particular name "Timothy;" moreover it was whispered around the Board that he was Lieutenant of the Twenty-second Ward, but it was not given in evidence.

Alderman Briggs—Have you ever answered any questions touching your nativity?

Witness—I refuse to answer.

Alderman Briggs—What country are you a native of?

Witness—I positively decline to answer.

Alderman Briggs—Have you just been posted outside by Mr. McKellar?

The witness took a chew of tobocco [*sic*], but continued refusing.

New York Times, May 21, 1855 (Excerpt)

The questions to Timothy Webster were two—"Have you ever answered in the Station-house any questions as to your nativity?" He (counsel) would like to know what that had to do with the public business? Then, "What country are you a native of?" If a Committee of the Common Council could inquire as to the nativity of a man, why not about his religion also? Some honest, sincere and intelligent men in this country, as we knew [*sic*], thought that some religious test or qualification ought to be prescribed for holding public office. But the law did not permit any such thing; decency did not justify it, and he hoped a Court of Justice would never sanction it, nor anything like it, in any way whatever. Webster's name, however, had not a very transatlantic sound, and the probability was that he would have answered that he was born in this country.

New York Times, September 8, 1855 (Excerpt)

WEBSTER UP — WEBSTER IS VERY STUBBORN.

Timothy Webster, the last of the contumacious three, was then called and made his appearance, but he demurred to the oath tendered him by the Clerk of the Committee, Mr. Selmes. I came here, said he, of my own free will.

Briggs—Well, we did not want you brought here by half a dozen policemen.

Webster —I don't think you would have had any right to fetch me here as a witness.

Briggs—Well, that is not the question now; you are here? that's enough.

Webster —(sarcastically)— Will the honorable Chairman allow me the same privilege that he took himself?

WANTED A LAWYER.

I should like to have counsel in this matter.

Briggs— Oh, we cannot allow a witness to leave the stand. You need not say anything criminating yourself or anything of that kind. We want plain facts.

Webster — Yes, Sir, I know that.

Briggs— Any honest man ought to be ready to tell the truth without the aid of counsel, and that is all that is required.

Webster — All I want is that you shall proceed legally, and not usurp powers that do not belong to you.

DEFIANCE.

Briggs— I do not intend to deal hardly with you.

Webster — I do not intend that you shall, if I know it.

Briggs— If there is anyone present you want to consult, you can do it.

Webster — I will refer to your associate, Alderman Tucker.

THE OATH.

The witness then took the oath, declaring that he intended to be governed entirely by the decision of Judge Daly, and the resolution referred to therein.

Briggs— What is your full name?

Webster — I never deny it; my full name is Timothy Webster.

Briggs— How long have you been attached to the Police Department?

Webster — Does Alderman Tucker say that is embraced in the decision of Judge Daly?

Briggs— I ask the question.

Webster — I have a right to refer to your colleague, I believe.

Briggs— Well, we will give you all the line you are entitled to, and a little more.

Webster — I do not ask for more.

JUDGE DALY UP AGAIN.

Tucker —(After consulting the decision)— This is not one of the questions enumerated by Judge Daly, which he decided upon as having been asked you before.

Briggs— What has that to do with it?

Tucker — It is my opinion that the Judge, in his decision, allows us to ask any questions.

Webster — That is your opinion, but not the decision of the Judge.

Tucker — That is my opinion of the Judge's decision.

Webster — I do not so read it.

Briggs— We decide that you are bound to answer all questions relating to the subject now pending before the Committee.

Webster — I have no desire to prevent you from claiming anything you choose.

Briggs— What answer do you make to the question?

Webster — If you will ask me any of the questions enumerated in this decision, I will answer them fairly.

He Don't Refuse.

Briggs— Then you refuse to answer my question?

Webster —(again referring to the decision)— I do not see it here.

Briggs— What class of office do you hold in the Police Department?

Webster — Is that in the decision, Alderman Tucker, or in the resolution?

Tucker — It is not among the questions asked you before.

Briggs— What answer do you make to the last question?

Webster — I abide by the decision of Judge Daly.

Briggs— Were you ever attached to the Chief's office?

Hangs His Banner on the Outer Wall.

Webster —(holding up the decision)— This is what I am governed by.

Briggs— Are you a citizen of the United States and of the State of New York?

Webster —(laughing)— Judge Daly refers to that point strictly, and I abide strictly by his decision.

Briggs— Perhaps you know more than the Judge does himself, but that has to be settled some other time. When were you naturalized, by whom, and in what Court? [A Long Pause] Do you decline answering that question?

Webster — I abide by the decision.

Briggs— I understand you to refuse to answer the question.

He Speaks Plain English.

Webster — I cannot help what construction you put upon what I say. I speak the plain English language.

Briggs— Well, Mr. Webster, that will do for to day, Sir. We shall require to call you some other day, I suppose.

Curtain Falls — Committee Goes Home.

New York Herald, September 8, 1855 (Excerpt)

On taking the oath, Mr. Webster made the reservation that he should answer all questions embraced within the resolution of the Board of Aldermen and the decision of Judge Daly — such as he had been legally furnished with. There was, consequently, some difficulty in regulating the form of oath to his taste.

Alderman Briggs— Do you refuse taking the oath?

Witness— I came here to testify, and I am ready to do it — will the Hon. Chairman allow me the same privilege he has taken himself?

Alderman Briggs— Certainly.

Witness— Then I want to consult counsel as you have done.

Alderman Briggs— You have only to answer as an honest man.

Witness— I only want legal advice, so that you shall not over ride me.

Alderman Briggs— Do you refuse to take the oath?

Witness— Read it again.

Alderman Briggs read the oath.

Witness— To satisfy you I'll take that oath, but I intend to be governed by the resolution and decision altogether.

Witness having been accordingly sworn, sat down, with the decision and resolution before him.

Ald. Briggs— What is your full name?

Witness— I will never deny that — my full name is Timothy Webster, sir.

Q. How long have you been attached to the police department?

A pause.

Alderman Briggs— What answer do you give to that question?

Witness— Does your associate (Ald. Tucker) say that that is embraced in the resolution and decision? I intend to be governed by them.

Ald. Tucker (to witness)— It is not enumerated in the questions, but it is my opinion that the Judge goes on and gives us the power to examine witnesses on the matters referred to the committee.

Witness— Yes, sir, that is your opinion; but I do not read it as such.

Ald. Briggs— We claim that you are bound to answer all questions on the subject.

Witness— I have no objection that you shall claim what you think proper.

Ald. Briggs— Then you decline to answer this question?

Witness (referring to the pamphlet)— I do not see it here.

Ald. Briggs— It has nothing to do with that book.

Q. What class of office do you hold in the police department?

Witness— Is that in the decision and resolution, Alderman Tucker?

Alderman Tucker — It is not answering the question asked you before.

(Mr. McKellar being seen here leaning on the back of one of the reporters' chairs, Alderman Briggs asked him whether he was acting as counsel, and requested him to take a seat. Mr. McKellar gracefully declined the request, and denied acting as counsel. He was merely speaking to a gentleman.)

Witness— (having had time to reflect.)— I abide by the decision of Judge Daly.

Q. Was you ever attached to the Chief's office?

Witness— (heaving a sigh.)— It is not in the decision which I am governed by.

Q. Are you a citizen of the United States, or of the State of New York?

Witness— Judge Daly refers to that part strictly. I abide strictly by his decision.

Alderman Briggs— Perhaps you know more than the Judge does himself. That has got to be settled another time.

Q. When were you naturalized, and by whom, and in what court?

Witness (resignedly)— I abide by the decision of Judge Daly.

Alderman Briggs— Then I understand you to refuse answering the question.

Witness— I do not know what construction you may place on what I say. I speak the plain English language.

Alderman Briggs (giving it up as a bad job)— Well, Mr. Webster, that will do for to-day. We will require you another day, I suppose. There being no other witnesses ready, we will adjourn the Committee to the next Wednesday, at 8 o'clock.

Appendix II
Timothy Webster's Reports
from Maryland, 1861

Tuesday 17th February 1861.

Captain Keen and some four or five others then came in, and got up a game of Ten-pins, we played until 1.45. p.m., when Springer, Taylor, and I went in to Dinner — They commenced talking about what route Lincoln would take to Washington. Springer said that he was going over the Philadelphia, Willmington [sic], and Baltimore Rail Road, and Taylor said "No," that Lincoln would go over the Central Road: that he (Lincoln) had better not come over this road with any Military — for if he did that Boat would never make another across the River. Springer replied that they had not better attempt to take any Military over this Road, for if they did Lincoln would never get to Washington.

Taylor got the Horse and Buggy ready, when Springer and I, left for Aberdeen. We had got about two miles on our way, when we had to turn back on account of the bad roads. On the way Springer talked some about Lincoln, and said that when Lincoln arrived in Baltimore, they would try to get him out to speak, and if he did come out, he (Springer) would not be surprised if they killed him; that there was in Baltimore about One Thousand men well organized, and ready for anything. I asked if the leaders were good men. Springer said they had the very best men in Baltimore, and that nearly all the Custom House Officers were in the Organization. I could not learn from him any of their names.

Tuesday 26th, February 1861.

I had breakfast, after which I went to the Depot and took the 7.40. A.M. Train for Baltimore.

On arriving at Baltimore I went to the Office, saw A. P — and reported to him. We then walked up town, A. P — all the time giving me my instructions. He requested me to leave Perrymansville on Wednesday, or Thursday, and laid the plan by which I was to draw off. A. P.— also told me that I was to go with one of his men (Williams) in the afternoon and get acquainted with some of the leading men of the Military Company's [sic] that were recruiting for South Carolina service. Williams was to meet me at the White Beer Brewery, and introduce me to Sherrington, after which we would go to the Drill room and get an introduction to Col. Haskill. Williams then went to look for Sherrington, while Mr. P — went and "spotted" the White Beer Brewery to me.

I then left A. P — and went to Springer's Store. I found Mr. Forward in, but Springer had gone out to collect some bills. Forward, and I, had a glass of beer — whilst we were Drinking he told me that the boys felt mighty sore about Lincoln's giving them the slip: that if Lincoln had gone through when he was expected, he would have been shot, and then Baltimore would have been the battle-field but now he thought Charleston would be. I said, that was just what I thought. I then bade him good bye and went to the White Beer Saloon, where I took a seat and called for a glass of beer.

In about half an hour Williams and Sherrington came in, Williams called for two glasses of beer, and whilst drinking started up quite suddenly, came towards me and said "my God, Webster when did you come up here &c." He then introduced me to Sherrington, and told him that I was of the right stripe — we then had another glass of beer each, and began talking politics. I said I thought Baltimore was going to be the battle-field, but old Abe had got safe to Washington. Sherrington replied "By G — d, he would not if the boys had got their eyes on him, that they would have shot him for they had everything ready to do it with, and that if we would go up the street he would show us the kind of tools the boys carried here.

We then went to a Store on Baltimore Street, where he got the Clerk to show us some pistols. Sherrington said they were the kind that he was telling me about, and was the best Pistol that was made. I went into the back-room and tried one, and found it very good. Sherrington said that those were the kind the boys carried, and that he was going to get one.

We then went to a Saloon and got a Drink, and from the Saloon went to Sherwoods [*sic*] where we got some Oysters, and another Drink. There were several persons in the place talking about shooting "Old Abe." Some said that they did not believe Lincoln would have been hurt, and others again said that they knew a d — d sight better, for they were acquainted with men who belonged to the Organization who were ready for anything, and would just as leave shoot Lincoln as they would a rat. We then went to the Drill room, but found very few men there. We waited there some time, when a few more came, with whom Sherrington and Williams got into conversation. They learned from this last party that Col. Haskell would not be in Baltimore until Friday; that they expected him here to-day so as to make arrangement to go with him to Charleston. I said that that would just suit me. Sherrington replied that if I came there on Friday I could see him, and I promised that I would try to be there, so as to make arrangements to go with him to Charleston. We then took another drink and seperated [*sic*].

I then went to the Office, and reported to Mr. P —, after which I left for the Howard House, where I met H. H. L. —, and went with her to Mr. Springers [*sic*] Store. He told us that he would be in Perrymansville in the morning.

We then went to the Depot and took the 5.10. P.M. train for Perrymans, arriving there at 6.30. P.M. had supper, after which I called to see Captain Keen. I found Mr. Ellis and five or six others at the Store, talking about Lincoln's passage through Baltimore. Mr. Ellis said that they talked pretty hard about it in Baltimore, and believed just as we did here, that the Rail Road Company knew all about it several days before he passed through. James Micheal (Captain Keens [*sic*] brother-in-law) said that when you come to look at it, it was plain enough to see that the Company must have known all about it, and, that was why they had so many men at the Bridges, and changing the Telegraph operatives. Mr. Ellis a member of the Rangers proposed to pull up the Rail-Road track and stop the travel South; that it was the only thing left to bring them Northerners to their senses. James Micheal thought to make the work complete they should besides tearing up the Rail-Road track, sink, or burn the boat at Havre-de-Grace, so they could not cross the River. Captain Keen wanted to bet that before three weeks had passed, that Maryland would be out of the Union, and then he would like to see them run the trains over this Road, or any other in the State. They talked on in this strain for some time, after which we all went over to Taylors [sic] Saloon. At 10.00. P.M. I went to my room, wrote my report and then went to bed.

Source: Herndon-Weik Collection of Lincolniana, LN 2408, Volume 3, The Huntington Library, San Marino, California.

Appendix III

Timothy Webster's Reports from Kentucky and Tennessee, 1861

Report of T. Webster on Trip to Memphis & Knoxville August 7th 1861

Tuesday 23rd July

About 5ᵒᶜ P.M., I left Cincinnati for Memphis by the Ohio & Mississippi R.R. I arrived at Louisville & put up at the National Hotel there I saw Myers of Clarksville (clerk at the National)

Wednesday 24

About 9ᵒᶜ A.M. I took the train for — Memphis on the way I got in conversation with men from Louisville going to Camp Boone Ten. under Col. Tillman Near the State Line in Tennessee there is a camp of 200 men but few of them armed. At Camp Boone near Clarksville under Col. Tillman there is 1800 men all Kentuckians not armed. at Clarksville an officer from Fort Dover on the Comberland [*sic*] River — near the Ohio. He said there was 500 men well armed, & 4–32 pounders (Iron) to guard the River.

Saw also on the Cars 2 officers going to Fort Henry on the Tennessee River — 20 miles below the R.R. Crossing. they said they had 1500 men well armed and 4–32 pounders & expected 2 more all Iron, To guard the River

Thursday 25th

Arrived at Humbolt [*sic*] Conductor Received a despatch [*sic*] from R.R. officer to Stop the train till further orders. Conductor said Gen. Polk had taken charge of the Road & supt. wanted to know what it meant before the train went to Memphis &c. At Humbolt [*sic*] I Drank & talked with officers from Union City they said they 6000 men nearl [*sic*] all armed & 2–32 pounders (Iron) after Dinner Conductor got a despatch to come through to Memphis. I arrived at Memphis about 8ᵒᶜ P.M.

Friday 26th

I was around Town all day with Col. Seely, Engineer "Bob." Rowley & others. The Town (Memphis) was all up in arms men leaving & geting [*sic*] read [*sic*] to leave for Missouri under Gen. Pilow [*sic*], "to Clean out the Dutch in St Louis before a

Month." Printed orders posted at all the Hotels from Gen. Polk no one alowed [*sic*] to leave Memphis without a Passport from his Agent — Mr Morgan on Main Street

Saturday 27th

in the morning I went to Mound City with Col. Seely, Hill (Clerk at the Worsham) & others in the Evening I was around town with Bob, Seely & others the whole conversation was about how they the (southern army) had Cleaned the "Yankees" out at Bulls [*sic*] run & Manassas & how Pilow, Hardee & Ben. McCalough [*sic*] would Clean the Dutch out in Missouri, & about 3000 hand cuffs that they had taken from the "yankees" at Manassa [*sic*] which the Yankees were agoing to put on them when they took them prisoners & now as they had about 5000 Prisoners they believed it would be the best way to hand cuff them together & march them in front & make a Breast work of them & march right in to washington &c.

Sunday 28th

I was around Town all Day with Dr. Scott of Texas, late of Virginia & others we met Lieut. Connor of Virginia now station at Randolph (an old friend of Scotts [*sic*]) He said Dr. I have just got a letter from my Brother at Manassa. He then read the letter. It read thus, we Killed between 3 & 4000 Yankees I do not know how many wounded & taken prisoners but a great many more than we want to take care of. we took 60 peaces [*sic*] of artilery [*sic*], all of Shermans Battery & about 5000 stand of arms, & 3000 hand cuffs which the yanks were agoing to use on us. you must not be surprised if you hear of us being in Washington in 10 or 13 Days &c, & about the same number of our men killed. Connor told me that there was 4000 Men at Randolph when he left on Thurdsay (25th inst.) but he expected Pilow would take some to Missouri. the Batteries would all remain there. the field pieces would be taken to Missouri. The port at Fort Clearborn would be the stronges [*sic*] port on the River they would have from 35 to 36 guns there & from 1500 to 2000 men there was a 1000 men there no well armed

Monday 29th

I was around town all Day with Bob. Seely & others. Bob. introduced me to a Capt. from Randolph He told me that there was 3000 men at Randolph well armed Gen. Pilow had taken some men & field pieces from there. He said there was 1000 men at Fort Clearborn [*sic*] & 35 havey [*sic*] guns & if Pilow was beat in Missouri he would fall back on Fort Clearborn & make a stand there. He said one of the Gun Boats the Yankee was up the River looking out for the Cairo Boats. I was at the Joyosa the officers that were there was talking about the Manassa Batel [*sic*]. they all wanted to Rush to Washington & St. Louis Ex. Mayor Baugh to me there was 5500 men at union City, Part armed 3000 men at Randolph well armed.

Tuesday 30th

I was figuring all Day with Seely, Scott, & Rambaut & got letters of Introduction to men in Virginia Seely gave me one to Charles Stebbins, Cor of 8th Broad St. Richmon [*sic*] Va. one to Col. Wm Ritchie, Richmon, one to James T. Lewis Chattanooga Ten. one to Col. J. S. Calvert State Treasurer Richmon Va. Mr. Rambaut of the Worham [*sic*] House gave me one to Roger A. Pryer Petersburg Va. Mr Dr Rog. B. Scott gave me one to James C. Hunt, or Geo. Bagby Edt. Messenger Richmon Va. &

one to Col. Sam. Garland Lynchburg or Manassas Junction. after geting the above letters we took a walk around Town. in the Evening I got ready to leave for Knoxville

Wednesday 31st

I got at 6ᵒᶜ A.M. I saw Mayor Baugh he told me he came down from New Madred [*sic*] yesterday Morning that he went up with Gen. Pilow & that Pilow had 9000 men at New Madred all well armed several field pieces & some 32 pounders. the Missourians were coming in fast. Pilow would leave the Missourians in charge of the Batery [*sic*] with their shoot [*sic*] guns & Rifels [*sic*], & Pilow would march through Missouri with about 15000 Men. at 6–30 A.M. I took the train for Chattanooga. at Corinth I saw an officer he told me they had 1000 men all armed, had orders to march next Day. I saw Governor Jackson at Grand Junction going west At Juka Camp 1500 not armed all uniformed

Thursday 1st

At Loudon R.R. Bridge there is 200 men well armed & uniformed to gaurd [*sic*] the Bridge. arrived at Knoxville about 12ᵒᶜ M. in the afternoon I met a Baltimore by the name of Sly I went around with him he introduced me to Jim Brownlow & others. Bownlow [*sic*] told me his Father would have to stop his paper in a few Days for it was of no use to fight any longer.

Friday 2nd

I was around Town with Lieut. Peck of Camp sneed & others from Camp Cumings [*sic*]. Camp sneed is about a mile from Knoxville there is 600 Men not armed all uniformed. Camp Cumings is about 2 Miles from town there is 1200 Men Most of them armed all uniformed I saw 3 trains going to Richmon with 1500 Men.

Saturday 3rd

I went to Camps sneed & Cumings I saw train going to Richmon with 500 Men. Lieut Peck told me that there was 800 men at Cumberland Gap all well armed & had 4–6 pounders & 600 men at Wheelers [*sic*] Gap all well armed

Sunday 4th

I was around Town in the morning. All 11ᵒᶜ I went to the Depot to leave for Cincinnati. During the time I at the Depot, about an hour & a half there was three havey trains went South to Richmon with 3000 Men the 500 Men I saw going to Richmon 3rd Inst were all uniformed & about 400 of them armed

Monday 5th

at Camp Anderson 4 Miles south of Murphyburgh [Murfreesboro] on the Nashville & Chattanooga R.R. there is 3000 Men not armed I arrived at Nashville & put up at the City Hotel to take the 3–30 A.M. train Tuesday. the Clerk told me that Camp Chatham was broke up & that there was 1000 men at Camp Trousdell near the State line.

Tuesday 6th

At 3–30 A.M. I took the train for Louisville. at State line the Engine was off the track was there over an hour. arrived at Louisville about 4–30 P.M between State line & Louisville I saw 3 trains loaded with Pork & Baken [*sic*]. a man in Louisville told me the men that Bought it gave Bonds that they would not ship it to the south. so they shiped [*sic*] it to points near the State line & sold it. it then was shiped south. at about 8^{oc} P.M. I took the train at New albany for Cincinnati.

Wednesday 7th

I arrived at Cincinnati about 6^{oc} A.M. & put up at the Walnut St. House & then went to the office & Reported to Scott.

Tim. Webster

Source: Timothy Webster casebook and field reports, Records of Pinkerton's National Detective Agency, Administrative File, Box 25, Folder 4, Library of Congress.

Appendix IV

Timothy Webster's Reports
from Baltimore, 1861

Thursday 22nd Augt. 1861

About 9ᵒᶜ A.M. I left for Washington City. I arrived & reported to Mr P. at No. 404 E. Street & at about 2–30 P.M. I left for Baltimore again I arrived about 4–30 P.M. & went to the hotel and Earl told me there had been 3 or 4 gentlemen inquiring for me. I Remained around the hotel til 11ᵒᶜ P.M. Drinking & talk with "Sam." Sloan & others. I was laying pipe to get in with "Sam." John Earl told me Jim Gull had left. he got afraid the officers were after him

Friday 23rd

At. 8ᵒᶜ A.M. I went down town on the way I stoped [*sic*] at Merrill's No 239 Baltimore Street I saw Mr Merrill & told him that we thought he ought to let us have the Rifels [*sic*] for something less then [*sic*] 40 Dollars. He said Mr Webster walk in the office I want to talk with you we went in & He said Mr Webster I can not take one cent less then 40 Dollars for if there comes a reaction here I can get 50 Dollars for them with out a word. I asked him if he thought the army (Southern army) would be in Baltimore soon. He said I would not be surprised if they were here in two weeks. I told him we were agoing to clean out Western Virginia before we came to Maryland. He said that is my plan keep a few men around Alexander [*sic*] to keep Lincolns [*sic*] army in a fever & then the main Body of our army cross over above Harpers Ferry & come in to Baltimore then all the arms that I have got would come in play I asked him if many of the citizens of Baltimore were armed. he said I sold a great many Rifels & Guns on the 19th of April & I suppose that we could rase [*sic*] in & right around Baltimore from 6 to 7000 stand of arms. I said & men to use them. he said yes indeed & more men then that. I said well Mr Merrill if we make up our minds to take the Rifels we can get them at a minutes Notice. he said yes. I asked him how many he had. he said about 300 Mr Webster. I said we may want some Bowee [*sic*] Kinfe [*sic*]. He said I have not got many but I can get them by having a few Days Notice. I said very well I will Call again. I then left & went to Allens [*sic*] Eating saloon there I saw Alexander Slayden & others I asked them to take a Drink they did so then Slayden & I went to the Sun office Corner — Slayden said there was from 5 to 6000 stand of arms in Baltimore. he knew that there was 3000 Muskets &

Rifels taken care of the time that old Butler was here & all of our Boys had been geting [sic] Muskets, Rifels & Pistols since were [sic] ever they could Buy them. I said I am D — glad to here [sic] that but what are you agoing to Do for a leader now Kane is locked up. He said oh we have leaders enough there is Col. Shut [Street?] just as good a man as we want & he is ready at any time, & I think he is a Conductor on the Washington Road. about 12ᵒᶜ I went to the Hotel & after Dinner Sloan asked me if I would go to the rases [races] I told him I would I got my horses & we left for the track about 3 Miles East of Town. There we met 10 or 15 we knew we saw the Rases & returned to the Hotel & a party of 8 or 10 Sloan & others Kept me with them. before Sloan & I left for the track He introduced me to D. R. Stiltz, Photography artice [sic] corner Saratoga & Charles Street No 56 North Charles Street. Stiltz said Sloan I am agoing on that trip on Monday. Sloan said you must be very careful or you will get "dated" (spoted [sic]) Stiltz said well how will I work it, Sam. Sloan said I will give you a letter of Introduction to Charles Butler that keeps a China or Crockery store in Washington on Street He is a strong union man & you must talk union like hell Stiltz said I understand that Sam. Sam. then wrote the letter of Introduction & read it to him it read alow [sic] me to introduce to you Mr D. R. Stiltz Mr Stiltz wishes to visit the camps strictly on Business take likeness &c. Sam. said you give him this letter & talk union & he will get you a passport to visit the Camps, then when you come back I will put you strate [sic] on your other track. I then went up strairs [sic] & wrote a Dispatch to Mr Allen to send John Sculey [sic]. I wanted to spot Stiltz to Sculey so he could be piped in Washington. I sent the Dispatch to the office by H.H.L. on the way to the Rase track I asked Sam. if Stiltz was going South after he came back from Washington. He said yes he is going to Washington to get all the points he can then he is going to Manassas & Rickmon [sic]. I said he will have a hard time getting there now. He said as soon as Banks get in camp we will have a Route open some where up by the point of Rocks. He said I run a good many things through by the way of Harpers Ferry before that Route was cut off. When we returned from the track he showed me his waggon in the Millers [sic] Hotel Yard. it is a one horse waggon with a falce [sic] Bottom the whole size of the Bottom of the waggon the space between the two Bottoms is about 2½ or 3 inches. He gave me his likeness taken in company with _____ a *union Man* he is a union man to get points in Baltimore.

Tim. Webster

Source: Timothy Webster casebook and field reports, Records of Pinkerton's National Detective Agency, Administrative File, Box 25, Folder 4, Library of Congress.

Appendix V

Allan Pinkerton's Reports
(from Tim Webster's reports) to
George B. McClellan, 1861–62

Some of the reports (referred to in other reports) no longer exist.

Head Quarters City Guard
Provost Marshals [*sic*] Office
Washington D.C.
November 15th 1861

Major General George B. McClellan
Commanding U.S.A.

General,

I have the honor to report that My Operative (T.W.) the substance of whose report, to me, I have the honor to address to you this day, of his late operations in Virginia, continued his trip through North Hampton and Accomack Counties, on the Eastern shore of Virginia, and the following is the substance of his report of those last mentioned operations, made this day to me, to wit;

That, after landing on the Eastern shore and reaching Eastville as recited more particularly in the latter part of my former report of his operations to you, he procured a conveyance from Tully Wise the Hotel Keeper in Eastville for himself and a Merchant named Price who had come with him from the Western shore and who was going on to Baltimore to buy Goods and that the servant of M^r. Wise drove with them to Drummondtown, Accomack Co. Va.; that there three, principal, roads leading from Eastville in North Hampton County to Drummondtown in Accomack County; that one of those roads in called the "Bayside" road; one is called the "Middle" road; and the other is known as the "Sea Side" road.

That my operative, with Mr Price, took the "Middle" road as it was the one, most travelled, of the three; that he found the distance from Drummondtown to Eastville to be thirty six miles over the road which they travelled; that they arrived at Drummondtown at about four o'Clock in the afternoon of the 12th of November, instant, being Tuesday of the present week; that when about half way between Eastville and Drummondtown they met one Company of Militia coming back from Accomack

153

County to North Hampton County armed with Shot guns and large Bowie Knives the latter being made at Richmond.

That some member of said Company, being known to my operative, were asked by him where they were going; that they replied that the news had come that the Yankees were coming in at Cherrystone Light House and that they had been ordered back to keep them from landing;

That at two different places between Eastville and Drummondtown, there were two insignificant entrenchments being thrown up — one at each place — with ditches 2 to 3 feet deep and four feet wide — across the road — the work being done, as usual, by Negro Slaves; that upon enquiry of the slaves what they were digging them ditches for they replied Oh! Massa digging 'em to bury Yankees in Massa"

That upon arrival at Drummondtown my operative[,] Tully Wise — keeper of the Hotel below — old man Sanders and several others whom he knew; That Tully Wise — a relation of the Governor's of course — said the Yankees were coming down with 5,000 strong, and that the Confederate's [sic] had but 3,000 to meet them with; but that they could lick "10,000 of them";

That on the morning of the 13th Nov.— Wednesday of the present week — Capt. White and other prominent men, at Drummond Town, advised and urged my operative and Mr Merchant Price, to leave their Carpet Sacks at Drummondtown until they returned as the Yankees had a very strong Force across the line and that, seeing them with Carpet Bags, they would be very likely to arrest them; that, to satisfy their friends, they did leave their Carpet Bags and came on without; that Mr Sanders— the Hotel Keeper at Drummondtown — let them have a horse & buggy to go to Balls [sic] farm House opposite Shelltown — telling them to leave the team at Balls [sic] and he (Ball) would send it back; that they would have to go to Oak Hall — Col Smith's Head Quarters— to get a Pass—for Col. S. had issued a proclamation that no one would be allowed to pass across the lines, either way, after the 9th Nov. and, Mr Sanders said, he did not think that Col Smith would let them pass;

That they drove on to the Head Quarters of Col. Smith where they saw Major Cary son-in-law of the M^r. Fisher — Presidential elector, aforesaid, who told them that Col. Smith & Lt. Col Finney had gone out to "reconnoitre"; that my operative told the Major — who was on Col. Smith's staff — that he wanted to pass through the lines; that Dr Thom — with whom my operative was acquainted — stood by and said "Yes, Major, you can give *him* a pass as *time* is of the *utmost importance* to M^r. W— "; that D^r. Thom told us that as all the bridges were burned in Accomack Co. north of there and on the roads leading to Maryland, that they would have to take a by-road which led by a mill at the head of the Creek on which the bridges were before burning; that My Operative saw the Camp of Col. Smith and that not over 900 troops including some companies of militia were in said Camp; that he saw an intelegent [sic] acquantance [sic], formerly from Baltimore, named John Kane who was a private in Col Smith's Regiment who was a fighting man "on his own hook," whom my operative asked where all the "3,000 men," were, that he expected to find there? that Kane replied — calling my operative by name — "there are not over 1500 fighting men in the two Counties— militia and all"; that all these, or nearly all, were in and around the Camp of Col. Smith; that my operative saw one entrenchment being thrown up by some 20 Negro Slaves across the Road between Drummondtown & Oak Hall, like those described henctofore [sic] as having been seen in North-Hampton County;

that when my operative was at Col. Smiths camp, at another time, when on his way to Richmond he saw & heard enough to satisfy himself that there were not over 800 Regular troops in both Counties; and further that my operative is quite sure from his observations that militia included they have not to exceed 2000 fighting men in Accomack and North Hampton Counties; that their arms are Percussion Muskets, Flint Lock Muskets, Shot Guns, Colts [*sic*] Revolvers, old style Cavalry Pistols, Long Richmond Bowie Knives; That my operative heard four brass Cannon and was expecting more over; but that my operative saw none at any time on either trip — that they got their pass, put up up [*sic*] their horse at Ball's who was gone, and arranged with M^r B to have the horse sent back to Sanders; that they went a short distance up the river found a man who with his boat set them across the river, telling them to take to the woods as the Yankees were down about Shelltown; that they followed the Boatman's advice, "took to the woods" and came out at Rohobouth [Rehobeth] Md.; where they procured horse & wagon from Adams, Hotel Keeper, who took them to Princess Anne; that at Princess Anne they heard that the troops of the U.S. were moving from Snow Hill to Accomack County Va; that at Princess Anne they were provided with a team by Mr Wilson whose driver took them to Salisbury Md.

That on the morning of the 14th Thursday of this week 5.30 A.M. they took the train from Salisbury to Wilmington that on the cars they heard the passengers talking about the Federal troops which were moving down to the Eastern shore, some saying there were 3000 some 5000 & some 10,000 troops — that on the road the Merchant, Price, left my operative on the Railroad for Chestertown Kent County Md. which my operative came on to Washington via Baltimore, arriving here as stated in the former part of this report.

All of which is respectfully submitted

Your obedient Servant
E. J. Allen

*   *   *

Head Quarters City Guard
Provost Marshal's Office
Washington D.C.
November 15th 1861

Major General George B. McClellan
Commanding U. S. A.

General.

I have the honor to report that I detailed one of my operatives (T.W.) to leave Baltimore on the 14th of October, last, in company with another of my operatives (W.H.S.) to proceed, via the Eastern Shore of Virginia, until he could find a proper and prudent point for crossing over, into Western Virginia, somewhere in Accomack or North-Hampton Counties and from thence to Gloucester Point — thence across York River to Yorktown — thence to Grove Wharf on James River — thence up James River to Richmond — thence to Manassas Junction — Va. thence to Warrington, the County Seat of Forquir [Fauquier] County Va — thence by way of Turnpike and stone Bridge to Centerville [*sic*] — the Head Quarters of Generals Johnson [*sic*] &

Beauregard — thence, via Richmond and Fredericksburg, to the Head Quarters of Genl. Holmes, at Brook Station on the Richmond, Fredericksburg and Potomac Railroad — thence to retrace his steps, varying as his own judgment and circumstances might require, back to Baltimore and so on to Washington.

That my other operative, already spoken of, (W H S) was to accompany (T.W.) as far down the Eastern Shore, of Virginia, as to the point where the latter should cross over, making his observations in Accomack & North-Hampton Counties and, thence, returning here, to make his report to me — (the substance of which has already been laid before you) — leaving (T.W.) to pursue his operations, in other parts of Virginia, with instructions to make full and thorough investigations into the entire condition of the Rebel Forces; and which, having accomplished, to return here with all reasonable dispatch.

That my said operative (T.W.) returned to these Head Quarters, on last evening, and made his report to me — the substance of which I have the honor to present to you as follows, to wit;

That he parted with my other operative at Eastville, the County seat of North-Hampton County Virginia, on Tuesday October 22nd, and remained at Eastville until Friday the 25th, waiting for "Marshall and his Sloop" to come over — which was detained on account of the brightness of the Moon — Marshall not daring to risk the Federal Gun Boats unless covered by comparative darkness.

That some two or three months ago this man, *Marshall*, had a sloop, of his own, which he used in a daring manner, in running the Federal Blockade; that one day, or night, he was caught, by a calm, near the Western Shore, and his Sloop fell into the hands of the Gun Boats — he himself, very narrowly escaping; that, since that circumstance, Marshall has run a Canoe or "dugout" 31 feet long and 5 ft. 3 inches wide, carrying 3 sails — main, Fore & Jib — from Gloucester Point, York River, to Eastville on the Eastern Shore — carrying the Confederate Mail and passengers, and some goods; that Marshall, being a first rate pilot and very smart man, is frequently employed by the Master's [sic] of Sloops and Schooners, as pilot, with the privilege, to Marshall, of putting his passengers on board such Sloop, or Schooner, as he may engage to pilot across, without charge, to Marshall, for carrying them over; as, also, his mail bag, and his canoe in tow of such sloop or schooner; that Marshall always places a piece of Iron in the Mail bag, before starting, for purpose of sinking it, in case of his being overtaken.

That on Friday evening he (my operative) left Cherry-Stone Light House, in the Canoe of said Marshall with thirteen persons, all told, Eight of whom were from Maryland — most of them from Baltimore and all of which, eight, said they were going to enlist in the Confederate Army and Navy, on their arrival at Richmond, which, he afterwards learned, they did.

That Marshall stood off a short distance from the light house, for some time, before starting across, in order to take observations, and ascertain if the route is clear of Gun boats, and the chances are good for crossing safely.

That Marshall ran due West, about twelve or fourteen miles — the wind blowing a Gale from the East — thence South West by West, about ten or twelve miles, then due west to Gloucester Point — making the whole distance in about three hours and a half — distance, sailing, about thirty miles; that Marshall put my operative on the look out and, when about midway across, he spied a light to which he called Marshall's attention; that Marshall remarked "She is a Gun Boat with a light on her bows; let her come, she cant [*sic*] catch us for, with our present headway, no boat on the river can catch us."

That on landing at Gloucester Point they were hailed by Sentinel, Post No. 1., with the usual "who comes there"; Marshall answered "Marshall, Mail Boat."; The Sentinel, again, "Stand Marshall, give the countersign." Marshall replied "no countersign." The Sentinel, again, "Sergeant of the Guard Post No. 1."

The Sergeant said, to the Sentinel, "who's there"?." the Sentinel, again, "Marshall with mail and passengers."

The Sergeant of the Guard, again, "Sentinel let them pass."; that he went, with the other passengers, to Marshall's shanty built in the encampment, on the Point, to accommodate his passengers.

That on the morning of Saturday, 26th October, he obtained a pass from Col. Crump, for himself and ten others, to go to Richmond; that, before starting, he ascertained that Col Charles A. Crump was commander of the encampment at Gloucester Point Va.; that there are two Regiments of Infantry at that Point; one Regiment in board Shanties, for Winter Quarters, inside the entrenchments; and the other, in canvass tents, about half a mile outside the entrenchments; also two companies of cavalry and one field Battery, of six guns, ranging from six to 12 pounders—four of brass and two of Iron — two, of the brass, 12 pounders— rifled; together with a heavy Earth work, on the beach, with twelve mounted Guns— ranging from 32 to 64 pounders, all Iron, and all, except the one Regiment mentioned, outside, were within the entrenchments.

That these entrenchments comprise an area of about fifteen acres bounded as follows; commencing about one fourth of a mile up the river, from the Battery on the point, aforesaid, and running, somewhat circular in form, till it strikes the York River, again, about a half a mile below the Earth Battery on the Point, aforesaid; that this breastwork is composed of split pine logs set up endways, inside, with an Earth Bank, outside, about twelve feet at the base, the earth being taken from the outside point, thus making a ditch of some five or six feet, at the top, and about as many feet deep; that at about the center of this breastwork, from end to end, there was a sixty four pounder mounted on a high carriage which transverses on a circle, calculated for a sweep of the whole landside of the entrenchments, which is a clear field of about 700 acres, bounded by timber, on the North, and York River on the South.

That, in answer to his inquiry, said Marshall told my Operative that General Magruder had command of that Division — including Gloucester Point, York-Town and all of the Peninsula bounded by James & York Rivers, and extending down to Fortress Monroe; that said Division is composed of 33 Regiments of Infantry and Cavalry.

That about noon, the 26th, Saturday, he crossed York River, to Yorktown, in company with the passengers aforesaid, in a small boat; that the landing, at Yorktown, is in front of a hill which rises, with a slope, some 25 feet, above the beach, on the top of which, in front of the town, is an Earth work mounting six or Eight Guns of 32 to 64 pounders— the sentinel told him "eight" and he saw *six*; that this last named Battery is about three quarters of a mile from the one, on Gloucester point, nearly opposite, but a short distance lower down.

That he learned, there, that General Magruder's Head Quarters were at Yorktown.

That he *then* crossed over the peninsula to Grove wharf, on James River, a distance of about ten miles south of west; That, as no boat would leave there for Richmond until Monday, he took quarters, with the rest of his company, at a farm house near by Grove Wharf.

That on Sunday, the 27th, he, with his company, took a walk, down the River, and fell in with a Lieut. Johnson, formerly of Baltimore and, then, of a Virginia Regiment; that he (my operative) saw, some eight miles down the James River, and about seven miles lower down than where he met the Lieutenant, aforesaid, a point of land which made out into the river, at which point the river is from two to three miles wide, on which point was a battery which, the Lieutenant said, was a very heavy one; and he, also, said that there was another Battery, equally heavy, on the opposite shore, of the river, and directly across, which he, further, said were the best batteries on either York or James River; that he then asked the said Lieutenant how many Regiments Magruder had, under his command, and he replied "Twelve hundred mounted Cavalry and twenty seven Regiments of Infantry["] — armed, for the most part, with Percussion lock muskets— some with Rifles and, very few with flint locks which were used chiefly for Mounting Guard; — with four field batteries— some with four and some with 6 guns, part brass, part Iron — part rifled, part smooth bore; that the Lieutenant further told him that from Yorktown down the Peninsula, toward Fortress Monroe, there were small creeks and inlets running into both the York and James River; that many of the creeks, or inlets, headed near to each other, and ran in opposite directions into the different rivers; that, for nearly fifteen miles, down, from Yorktown, that breastworks were thrown up on the several points of land between the headings, of these various creeks, or inlets, facing towards Fortress Monroe; that on each and every one, of these several breastworks, there were mounted Guns from 18 to 64 pounders; In answer to a question, to the Lieutenant, by my operative, he replied that Magruder's pickets frequently rode out, North, from Gloucester Point, in the direction of the Rappahannock, some 15 miles; but that the region, between Gloucester Point and the Rappahannock, was mostly guarded by the State Militia whose business, for the most part, was to watch the Negroes and see they did not run away.

That the Lieutenant further said, in answer to questions of my operative, that the troops under Magruders command were suffering for nothing, in particular, except Overcoats, which they were expecting soon; that the Lieutenant also further said that some few were wanting shoes, but not many, and that they were expecting some to be distributed, in a few days, which came over from England in the ship Bermuda which ran the Blockade, shortly before, with clothing and munitions of War —for the Confederate Government.

That on Monday morning, the 28th inst. my operative left Grove Wharf, on the regular Steam Packet, for Richmond and, within 30 miles of starting, he saw three heavy earth-works, on the North bank of the River, with heavy Guns mounted; but that he saw no one who could furnish information of the precise number, or weight of metal.

That my operative arrived in Richmond on Monday evening, 28th Oct. and stopped at the Spotswood House.

That on the 29th, Tuesday he was around town making acquaintances, delivering letters, and preparing the way to an interview with the Secretary of War, with the view of getting a pass to go to Manassas and Winchester.

That on the 30th — Wednesday, he was similarly engaged; that on today he was informed by General Jones, Pass adjutant to General Winder, Provost Marshal of Richmond and commander of the Forces at Richmond — that no interview could be had with the Secretary of War except upon business specially connected with the army, as they were daily expecting an attack from the Federal Army of the Potomac, and that the Secretary of War was wholly engaged with officers of the army.

That on the 31st, my operative, having been introduced to William Campbell, a Baltimorean, by means of a letter, from his father, which my operative carried with him to Richmond, took a ride outside of Richmond to visit the Batteries in the vicinity of that City; Mr Campbell was a Contractor, for articles of leather-manufacture, with the Confederate Government, who stands high and was well acquainted with the ordnance Department.

That he found *17 very superior Earth work Batteries around the city*, forming, in connection, nearly a half-circle with either end resting on the James River on its North bank; that the entrenchments all around each of these batteries were from twelve to fourteen feet broad, at the top, and from Eight to ten feet deep; that the outside of the ditches are nearly perpendicular while the inside is on the same slope as the earth work above; that the earth, forming the embankment, is that which was taken from the ditch; and the embankment is about the same size and shape, as the ditch, but rather wider and not so deep.

That these batterries [*sic*] were designed some for *six* Guns and some for *sixteen*; that all these Batteries were nearly completed, and the work upon them was all done by the negro Slaves; that all these Batteries were either mounted, with their full complement, or the guns were being furnished to complete them in the shortest possible time — the caliber varying from 32 to 64 pounders; that the heaviest of these batteries, commanded the turnpikes, and the Railroads leading to Fredericksburg and Manassas; that the ground, around Richmond, is composed of hills and valleys; and the batteries, aforesaid, are on the most elevated and commanding of these hills.

That, after visiting the batteries, my operative went, with Mr Campbell, to the Ordnance Department where the latter introduced the former to several persons who had charge of the ordnance Stores; that among other things seen, by my operative, at said Ordnance Department, were a large lot of Cavalry swords and Enfield Rifles; that upon inquiry, by my operative, he learned of the Col., in charge at said Ordnance Department, that the Bermuda, the English vessel which recently ran the Blockade, had brought, for the Confederate Government, 12,000 Enfield Rifles; a number of Rifled Cannon and a large number of Cavalry Swords; that, upon trial, the rifled Cannon brought from England, aforesaid, were found to be more accurate than any of their brass cannon; that my operative learned that the Confederate Government were making Cannon in Richmond and Memphis; that the same were being rifled and mounted as fast as possible; that on the same evening he went with Mr Campbell aforesaid, to General Jones, of whom, through the agency of Mr Campbell, he & M^r. C. obtained passes to enable them to go to Manassas to visit John Bowen, Express Agent, who was lying sick, of Typhoid Fever, at Manassas, and a gentleman whom he had carried a letter from his father in Baltimore.

That on Friday 7.40 A.M. he & M^r. C. left for Manassas by Railroad; that the train was composed of twelve passenger cars filled with 200 soldiers and citizens, the former of whom had been ordered from Richmond to Manassas and Centerville, they having been on the sick list or on furlough at Richmond; that there were, as he learned, Six Regiments of troops encamped at Richmond under General Winder's command, most of whome [sic] he saw and visited — personally. They appeared to be well provided with uniforms and good overcoats, and were well armed with Rifles and percussion-lock muskets;

These soldiers appeared well pleased with their prospects — sanguine of success — and blamed Genl. Evans for not obeying orders and thus drawing the Federal troops over, at Leesburg, so that General Johnson could have cut them off and taken the whole of them prisoners.

That the people of Richmond seemed well satisfied with Genl. Evan's [sic] course, and regarded it as the best fought and most successful battle since the War commenced.

That my operative arrived at Manassas Junction about 5.00 p.m.; when they found that the Sick Man, Bowen, had been taken down to Richmond — that same day; that Mr Campbell met an acquaintance who told him that if he, and my operative, would go down to Ex. Gov. Smith's camp (he, now, being Col. of a Regiment) they could stay with the Quarter Master who was an acquaintance of Campbells; that they went to Col. Smiths Camp, which was about a mile south of Manassas Junction; that at Manassas Junction and on the way, down to the Camp of Col Smith, My Operative Counted five batteries, of Earth work, mounted with heavy Guns, and nine Regiments of Troops, in Camps — all Infantry.

Arriving at the Camp they were conducted by the Sergeant of the Guard to the tent of Col. Smith's Quarters; that my operative was introduced to Col Smith by M^r. Campbell and the Colonel invited them to take supper with him, which they declined, having taken supper at Manassas.

That Col Smith sent his servant with them to the Quarter Master's quarters, where they spent the night;

That during the evening the Qr. Master, in answer to the question, of my operative, how many such batteries, as those he had passed in coming down from the Junction, the Confederate forces had around that place? answered he did now know how many; but that they had a great many and that they considered *Manassas Junction their strong hold*; that my operative asked the Quarter Master where all their field batteries were; remarking that he had not seen many on his route; that he replied there was none at Manassas, but that they were between Manassas and Centerville — mostly at the latter place.

He asked him how many Regiments there were at Manassas Junction, and he said "10 or 12." "well armed but dam'd [sic] badly off for winter Clothing, but have plenty of ammunition of all kinds."; that they had plenty to eat except Bacon, which they could only serve out twice a week, while they ought to have it, at least, four times; that they had too much fresh meat;

That said Quarter Master said that their was not half the sickness in the army, then, that there was two months previous; that the measles had pretty much disappeared, and what sickness there was, now, was Typhus Fever; that he, further, said that if General Evans had obeyed orders the Confederates would have quartered in Maryland this Winter; that his orders were to "fall back and draw the Yankees in";

that by doing, as ordered, Gen. Johnson would have cut the Right Wing of Gen. McClellan's Army off entirely; that there had been some talk about Court Martialing General Evans; that although he fought well and gained a great victory, still it was nothing when compared with what it would have been if he had obeyed orders; that Genl. Johnson intends to get the Federals to fight, again, on the same ground, if he can, hoping, next time, to be able to accomplish his purpose of drawing them into Manassas where he can bring those batteries to bear upon them.

My Operative further reports that during the night of the 31st, aforesaid, a terrible storm, of rain and wind, came up and blew nearly every tent, in the camp, down; that on the following day there being no comfortable place to stay, and the rain still pouring down, he and Mr Campbell concluded to take the cars and go to Warring-ton — the County Seat of Fauquier County — a distance of about 18 miles South West — and the place where the sick and wounded, from the army about Manassas and elsewhere, are sent to be taken care of; that my operative saw a large number of board Barracks in course of erection, on the west side of the Rail Road, near the Junction, and asked the Quarter Master, what they were intended for and if the troops were going into winter quarter there; that the Qr. Master told him that they had contracted for the putting up of a large number, for the purpose of winter quar-ters, and that they were sending, all over the Country, for Carpenters to come and do the work; He asked the Quarter Master where the 1st Maryland Regiment was, and he replied they were at or near Centerville [*sic*].

That they reached Warrington and put up at the Hotel; that Mr Campbell then introduced my operative to the Mayor of the City — M^r. Bragg; that he saw a large number of soldiers, about town, most of whom appeared to have been sick; that he saw Sergeants come in, from the Regiments, looking after those who were far enough recovered to go on duty again; that the Mayor of the City told him that it would be very difficult to obtain a pass, as he wished, to go to the 1st Maryland Regiment at Centerville, for whose members he had some letters from friends in Batteries; but that he would introduce my operative to the Provost Marshal and see what could be done; that the reason they were so much more stringent, just then, about passes, was because they were anticipating an attack from the Federal Forces and did not wish to grant any persons passes until matters were quiet again.

That on Sunday morning Nov. 3rd. my operative went, after breakfasting with the Mayor, aforesaid, to the office and was, by Mayor Bragg, introduced to the Provost Marshal, who gave him a pass for himself and a M^r. Dempsey — a gentleman who wished, also, to go to Centerville and who was an acquaintance of M^r. Campbell.

That my operative then hired a horse & buggy and, in company with Mr Dempsey, started for Centerville by way of the turnpike on which is situated the Bull's Run Stone Bridge; That they arrived, in Centerville, about 4.00 p.m.; that shortly after crossing the stone bridge aforesaid and about half a mile east of the bridge he came to the first camps which, together with those *further* on, *around, and in Centerville numbered 49 Regiments* of Infantry which he counted, together with 12 Field Bat-teries, Eight of which had Six, and four of which had Eight guns; that the greatest number of these guns was Brass; That he came near to one of these batteries and found that four out of six of the guns were rifled; that he learned, afterwards, that a good many of them were rifled; That he saw some scattering Cavalry but no great number in one body;

That, upon his arrival at Centerville, he was obliged to procure another pass from Provost Marshall [*sic*] Jones before he could get to the 1st Maryland Regiment Col. G. H. Stewart [*sic*]; that he arrived at their camp about Sundown and delivered his letters and received an order from the officer, of the night, to allow a light to be kept up, in one of the tents, *all night*, to enable the men to read their letters and write others to be taken back by my operative, who was to leave the Camp in the Morning; That, during the night, all sorts of conversation was going on; That, among other things, my operative asked the Captain, of one of the companies, where all their cavalary [*sic*] was, about which he had heard so much? That the Captain told him they were Scattered all along the line from Winchester to Genl. Holme's [*sic*] command, at Brook Station; That, upon further enquiry, my operative learned that they had from 10 to 12 Regiments of Cavalry — one of which 1,100 Strong —finely equipped at their own Expense —from Louisiana — had arrived only three days before and were very fine looking indeed; that my operative learned that Forage was scarce and the road being very much cut up, the horses which worked on the wagons, looked badly; that the officers of the Maryland Regiment, aforesaid, were very severe on General Evans for his disobeying orders and, thereby, gaining, though a *glorious*, yet a *very small* advantage *compared* with *what it would have* been if he had obeyed the command of Genl. Johnson.

That this Maryland Regiment was well armed, with percussion lock muskets and Rifles, and they were very well dressed with the exception of some who wanted over- coats.

That my operative further reports that he saw Several of the U.S. Overcoats, which the Soldiers of the Maryland Regiment wore, that they had obtained at the battle of Bulls Run.

That on Monday, Nov 4th, he left the Camp for Centerville, and, as he passed along, he saw *company* and *Regimintal* [*sic*] Drill going on; that their arms all looked well, but their clothing looked bad; that some of them had on *one* colored coat, & some *another* color, with little pretensions to uniform; Some had grey caps; some blue and others slouched hats— all of one Regiment; that the principle clothing was of the Sunfaded Grey —looking as though it had been worn all summer; that each regiment has Sentinels all around their camps to keep the soldiers from passing from one camp to the other without a pass; that on the way to Centerville [*sic*] they passed by the camp of a Mississippi Regiment where Mr. Dempsey —the man who was with my operative —had a friend who was a Lieutenant; that this Lieutenant got into their buggy and rode to Centerville and, while doing so, he pointed out Genl. Beau- regard's Head Quarters, which were in a two story frame farm house painted white. situated near the road leading to Manassas, and about half a mile, nearly west, from Centerville; that he also pointed out the Head Quarter's [*sic*] of Genl. Johnson which were in a large tent, on the East side of the Turnpike, in Centerville.

That my operative saw, while they were driving along near Johnson's tent, four of his aids come out of his Head Quarters, mount their horses and start off, at swift gallop, in the direction of Fairfax Court House; that the Lieut. remarked, "that's the way they have to go when they get Johnson's order's"; that my operative asked the Lieut. if Johnson was the favorite General? He said "no the men think every thing of both, of Beauregard and Johnson; and are willing to follow them any where as they have the utmost confidence in both of them.

My operative further reports that Centerville is situated on an elevated ground gradually sloping to Westward; and the principal encampments are on the western Slope just west of the town; that the ground is, on the whole, sloping to the East, but is somewhat rolling or undulating, while, where the encampments are, the ground is without the undulation; that in going from Fairfax Court House, to Centerville, the main body of the troops could not be seen until a near approach to Centerville; that, in short, Centerville is on a piece of ground higher than its surroundings for a considerable distance from the town; that the whole of Centerville, proper, is made up from about fifteen buildings, all told; that on the wagon road, leading to Manassas, and just outside the buildings in Centerville there are two knolls, of not very considerable size nor elevation, though higher than any other ground in that vicinity, on which they were throwing up small Earth-Works, on which some 15 or 20 men, to each, were at work; that they were not sufficiently advanced for him to judge of their probable design; but, from what was already done, he judged that they were not of, or designed to be, permanent character; that they could not possibly, for want of room for more, have mounted, on them, more than four guns each; that there were no guns there, to be mounted, and that these were the only fortifications which he could see at Centerville; that there were no breast works; for Infantry, nor were there any *certain* indications that they intended to make *that place* their battle field; but that nearly every thing indicated that they designed, if attacked, to fall back on Manassas.

My operative further reports that the same Lieutenant, aforesaid, informed him that, but a few days before, two ladies with, each, a small carpet sack, in her hand, came along, on the Turnpike, from the direction of Washington, and first seen westward, some distance, from Fairfax Court House, who enquired, of their pickets, for the Head Quarters of General Johnson; that these ladies told the pickets that they had passes from the authorities in Washington to cross over and to visit some friends at or near a certain mill, the name of which my operative does not recollect, but situated somewhere within the Federal Lines; that these ladies were passed on by the pickets, to Genl. Johnson's Head Quarters, where, with the General, they remained several hours and that, afterwards, they were passed on to Manassas Junction; that the Lieutenant said the ladies were well dressed; that my operative then drove to the office of Provost Marshal Jones, who gave him a pass to return to Warrington.

That on the following day, Tuesday Nov. 5th, he left Warrington for Richmond in company with M^r. Campbell, aforesaid; that on the way they met an acquaintance of M^r. Campbell — Lieutenant L. H. Routxahn [Routzahn] — who belonged to a Regiment, stationed at Winchester, Va., and, by M^r. Campbell, the Lieutenant was introduced to My Operative; that from the said Lieutenant he learned that, at Winchester, and between Winchester and Martinsburg, there were four Regiments of Infantry and some Militia; that at or near Winchester was one Field Battery of four guns; that at Leesburg there were thirteen Regiments of Infantry, together with two field batteries of six guns each — part brass and part iron; that the Lieutenant told him that he did not know how much cavalry there might be, in the vicinity of Leesburg, for it was so Scattered all along the line to Martinsburg and Winchester, from Leesburg, that he could not tell; that he further told my operative that that Division was under the command of General Evans, and that notwithstanding the concerns of General Johnson, upon General Evans, for his course at Leesburg, yet the whole of the troops, under command of the latter, were well pleased with the plan adopted and its glorious result; that the Lieutenant further stated that it would be very difficult for anyone to go into Maryland, through the lines of General Evans, as he was very cautious about, and to, whom, he issued passes.

That upon arriving in Richmond and stopping at the Spotswood House. over night, he went, on Wednesday Nov. 6th, with Mr. Campbell, to the War Department and called on the Quarter Master General to obtain from him, a list of articles that they were most in need of, which list the Quarter Master General had promised to furnish to my operative a few days before; that the Said Qr. M. Genl., stated that he had not, for want of time, made out such list, and that he did not know of any particular article or articles which did, then, need, *especially*; but they would be very glad to have some "emory cloth" for scouring up their arms &c; that while in said General's office, there came in a Captain of Artillery who had a requisition, which ocupied [*sic*] two pages, and which he handed to the Quarter Master Genl.; that, after looking it over, the General said "Why, Captain, do you want *more guns?*" that the Captain answered "Yes Sir" "I have six guns already — four six pounders and two twelve pound howitzers — and I require two eighteen pounders, beside, as I have 110 men in my company."; that the Quarter Master General replied "I will allow you the two Guns you require, and can only allow you" five hundred rounds to each gun" though your requisition calls for 1000 for each of them, which I will give you an order for and which you can get as you pass through Nashville"; that the Captain said "that may detain me"; that the General said "No, I will telegraph at once";

That my operative shortly afterwards met, on the street, Mr. J. H. Price, a merchant at Warrington, originally from Chester County, Maryland [*sic*], who was on his way to the Pass office of Genl. Jones, aidecamp [aide-de-camp] to Genl. Winder, Provost Marshal, for the purpose of procuring a pass to go to the Maryland line, for the purpose of reaching Baltimore and buying goods to take back to Warrington; that my operative went, with said merchant, to the Pass office and at the same interview, both himself and the merchant procured passes to enable them to pass through General Holme's [*sic*] lines, *with consent of the latter*, to Saint Mary's County Maryland; that on the same day my operative, in company with the said merchant, left Richmond for Fredericksburg, by Railroad, and, reaching there, put up at the Planter's Hotel.

That on Thursday, Nov 7th, my operative was engaged, all day, in calling on sundry persons, in Fredericksburg, and in going thence to Brooks Station the Head Quarters General Holmes about 12 miles North East of Fredericksburg; that, among other persons, he called on Mr. Hazzard chief clerk in the Commissarys Department, at Fredericksburg, to whom he had a letter from his wive's [*sic*] brother — a private in the 1st Maryland Regiment at Centerville.; that his object in calling on Mr. Hazzard was not only to give him the letter, aforesaid, but to obtain all the information possible and, especially, to secure his influence in getting Genl. Holme's consent to pass through his lines, and to aid him in reaching the General, in case he was absent from his Head Quarters, that Mr Hazzard went with him to the Mayor of Fredericksburg to whom the former gave him an introduction; that he showed the Mayor his pass, and told him that his object in going to Maryland was to secure the passage, into Virginia, of certain persons, who wished to come, and whose friends in Virginia wished to have come; as, also, to carry a large number of letters, which he then had, mostly from the 1st Maryland Regiment, and to bring back with him certain kinds of goods which were very much needed by the Confederate Government; that the Mayor thereupon gave him a pass, on the back of his other pass, to Captain Hill, aidecamp to General Holmes, requesting Captain Hill to pass him to General Holmes, wherever he might be; that he then went with Mr. Hazzard to the Quarter Master's Department, where M^r. H. ascertained that Genl. Holmes was at Evansport Va. up the river, from his Head Quarter's, reviewing troops; that he learned from M^r. Hazzard, during the day, that in General Holmes command from the Rappahannock to the Potomac, on the North, and from Chesapeake Bay to the lines of General Beauregard, there were, under the Command of General Holmes, Fourteen Regiments of Infantry, Four Field Batteries and Four very heavy Batteries on the Potomac, known as the Blockading Batteries, at different points along the River, in which Batteries, as he stated, there are from 12 to 15 Very Heavy Guns; that among the said Guns is one which the Confederates call "Long Tom," which was taken at the Battle of Bulls Run; that Mr Hazzard further informed him that he also knew of Batteries on the Rappahannock to guard that River and prevent the passage of Vessels up that stream; but that he did not know where said, last mentioned, Batteries were located, nor what was their capacity; that the lower portion of the peninsula, between the two rivers, aforesaid, was guarded only by Militia, and that the Militia, under General Magruder, reached northward until they were met by those under Command of General Holmes, thus leaving the entire distance, from the mouth of the Potomac to Gloucester Point under guard of Militia alone; that Mr. Hazzard further stated that the troops under General Magruders [*sic*] command were well armed and well supplied with ammunition of all kinds; but that many of the troops were very badly off for Winter clothing; that after requesting my operative to call in the evening and take two letters to his wife's mother, in Baltimore, left, and my operative obtained a team to go to Brook Station, thinking the General might *might* have returned from his review; that he arrived at the Head Quarters of General Holmes about Sundown and learned, immediately, from Captain Hill, to whom he had the letter from the Mayor, aforesaid, that General Holmes was yet absent and might not return for several days; and that, when he did, it was doubtful if the General would give My Operative a pass to cross over into Maryland, through his lines, as Sickles['] Brigade was over, across there, and all along, & he would be almost sure to be taken; that after seeing two Regiments, encamped, close by the General's Head Quarters, he left, on return, that same night, for Fredericksburg; that the roads were very bad very much cut up and the country very Hilly; that he learned of Capt Hill, aforesaid, that the road, from General Holmes['] Head Quarter's, were as bad in every direction.

That on his return he called on M^r. Hazzard, at his house, and they, together, walked up town; that he introduced my operative to Capt. Parker, another aid to General Holmes; that during the evening my operative spoke of the Battle at Leesburg, when he was told by Capt Parker that, not only, General Holmes, but that all the officers, in his Command, censured General Evans for his course at that Battle; stating, further, that a strong flank move ment [*sic*] was to have been made thereby cutting off the Forces, which had crossed over from the Federal side, and, at the same time, General Holmes, with his 12,000 men, were to have crossed over into Maryland.

That Capt Parker there introduced my operative to Surgeon W^m. H. Coffin, of

Genl. Magruder's Staff, who gave him a letter commending him and the Merchant Price, aforesaid, to all persons who might aid them in getting back to Baltimore; that on Friday the 8th Nov. he left Fredericksburg, in the morning, for Richmond, where he obtained a pass to go to Accomack County Va. and so on to Maryland with Genl. Magruder's consent, to be obtained, at Yorktown; that, before leaving Fredericksburg he was told by Capt Parker that they had from 10 to 12 thousand Cavalry along the Potomac from Winchester, on the North, to Brook station, on the South; that my operative asked him if he did not mean that there 10 or 12 Regiments of Cavalry, instead of 10 or 12 thousand, and he replied in the affirmative.

That on the return of my operative to Richmond, as aforesaid, he learned of the arrival of and the triumph of the Fleet at Port Royal, which had depressed the the [sic] people of Richmond, considerably, but they consoled themselves by saying "well they have not got to Charleston yet," "they will have some hard fighting to do before they will get to Charleston."

That on Saturday, the 9th of Nov. my operative reports that he left Richmond for Yorktown & Gloucester Point by way of West Point and York River — to West Point by Rail; that he saw no troops nor Fortifications at West Point except some few — 15 or 20 — who were on the way to Yorktown on Expiring furloughs; that he saw a schooner, then, loaded with Grain, which he was told was brought over by Marshall, together some 15 or 20 passengers, on the night before, from Accomack County, Eastern Virginia, and that Marshall had left West Point, in his Canoe, for Gloucester Point, with the Confederate Mail; that he found that the steamer, from West Point to Gloucester Point, was disabled and he, in company with the Merchant, Price, took passage on a small sloop for, and arrived at Gloucester Point at about sundown and went at once to Marshall's boarding tent, where he learned, from Marshall's brother, that Marshall had gone over, with the mail and two passengers, about an hour and a half before.

That on Sunday morning the 10th November, he went to Col Crump Commanding at Gloucester Point, and showed him the Pass which he was to get sanctioned by General Magruder, and asked Colonel Crump if it was necessary for him to see Gen. M. in order to get his signature to the Pass; that he also showed him the letter, spoken of, from Surgeon Coffin; that, thereupon, Col. Crump told my operative that, as he had seen him before, and that as he had, in addition to the Pass — the letter from Surgeon Coffin, that he need not wait to see Genl. Magruder but that he, himself, would give him a pass and that he could go with M^r. Marshall on his next trip;

That my operative further reports that since he left Gloucester Point, on this same trip, the Confederates had commenced a heavy Earth-Work on an elevation, 50 yards back from the water, and 30 to 35 feet above the water level, and two hundred yards lower down the river, than the first batteries spoken of at Gloucester Point, in another part of this report, with an entrenchment in front — partly finished — 8 to 10 feet wide, at the top, and 5 to 6 feet deep —front perpendicular, and, back, the ordinary slope; that, on this week, there were employed more than 100 Slaves; that he asked Col Clump —for the purpose of drawing out the real object, extent and purpose of this fortification, if that was Infantry Breast Works; that he replied "Oh! No sir it's a *Battery* and we intend to mount six heavy Guns thereon," "four thirty two and two sixty four Pounder's."

That he then returned to Marshalls tent, and that nothing further occurred, during the day, except that he heard considerable complaint among the soldiers about the want of warm clothing and Overcoats.

That on Monday the 11th Nov. about sunrise, Marshall came over with his Canoe bringing, besides the Mail, Mr Fisher — one of the Presidential electors from Eastern Virginia — on his way to Richmond to meet with the Electoral College; that Fisher brought his wife, 2 daughter's and their children, and several slave servants; that Fisher has one farm near Cherrystone Light House, and when Marshall makes it his Head Quarters— on the Eastern shore; that my operative asked Marshall if he was going back that night; that he said "No," he was entirely worn out with running so constantly, night and day, for so long a time; that during the day Marshall left for his family, who are living seven miles north east of Gloucester Point; that, during the day, my operative, while walking around, on the Beach, fell in with one of the Captain's of a sloop which Marshall had piloted across, but shortly before, who told him that he was going back, in the course of two or three nights to carry some Cannon from General Magruder to Col Smith on the Eastern Shore, that about five O'clock, in the evening, Col. Crump sent for him (my operative) to come to his Head Quarters; that, upon going there, Col Crump told him that he had just received a dispatch, from General Magruder, a dispatch for Col Smith, of the Eastern shore, which *must go over that night* and that if they wished (my operative and the Merchant, Price,) they could go over with Marshall, if they would walk to his house — Seven miles distant — which, offer, they very gladly accepted; that they started, with Marshalls brother, who carried the dispatch, for Col Smith, to Marshall; who started with his canoe, and they two, about 11.00 P.M.; that they moved out into the Bay and lay to, until the moon went down, when a heavy North wind commenced to blow, and which raised a very heavy sea; that, notwithstanding, they reached the Eastern Shore, at Mr. Fisher's farm, about 4.30 A.M.; that on arrival Mr Marshall procured a horse from the Overseer, on Fisher's farm, and left for Col Smith's Head Quarter's—*Post Haste*; that at about seven A.M. M^r. James took Mr Price & my operative to the Hotel kept by Tully Wise; that, while at breakfast, the Confederate Post-Master, at that place, came in and asked what the News was in Richmond. that my operative replied "nothing"; that the Post Master further said he had learned, upon good authority, that the "Union Men" of Tennessee had been burning the bridges on the Rail Roads of that state; and the Post Master further said that nearly every man from North Hampton County had gone up to Accomack County to meet the "Yankees," who were coming down, and that a fight was expected, *very shortly*, somewhere near the Maryland line; he (the P.M.) remarking, by the way, that, "in the name of God," he did not see what they were going to do, for they had not enough ammunition to last two days.

In conclusion, of this very lengthy report, General, I beg leave to state that it has been embodied with much haste in order to your speedy possession of its results; and that, consequently it lacks the amount of care, in its execution, except as to facts, figures and circumstances, which might otherwise have been bestowed upon it; that I may also, further, state that the operations and observations, of My Operative, have extended over a month's time and a large extent of Country; and that, from the nature of the case, as, also, from a due regard to his own safety and the success of his mission, he could make no other memorandum than figures; and that, consequently, his report to me, the substance of which is herein embodied, was made up, with that single exception, entirely from memory. I beg leave, further, to State that, on the fourth of October last, I submitted to you a report respecting the amount, kind, condition and number of Enemy's Force; in Virginia, extracts from which I herewith append, and to which I, again, respectfully invite to your attention.

I will, further, respectfully state that in the report of my operative, aforesaid, he states that he observed considerable quantities of Peruvian silver in circulation at Richmond.

And also, further, that my operative reports the following list of prices at Richmond,

> Flour 10 to 12 Dollars per Barrell [*sic*]
> Wheat $2.00 per Bushel
> Oats 75 cents per "
> Corn $1.00   "   "
> Beef — Fresh, at Retail, in market, 8ᶜ to 15ᶜ/lb.
> Bacon Sides 25ᶜ per lb.
> Hams   30   "   "
> Salt Pork none in market
> Salt $15.00 per Sack
> Shoe Thread $4.00 per lb.
> Blk. Lin. Thread $3. "   "   "
> Quinine $4.00 per ounce
> Gents Calf Shoes (Military) $10.00 per pair
> Gents Calf Boots $15.00 to $18.00 per pair
> Blue Soldiers Overcoats $10. to $12. Each
> Decent overcoat $18. to $20.   "
> Hay very Scarce and sold at "all sorts of prices"~
> All of which is respectfully submitted

Your Obedient Servant
E. J. Allen

*   *   *

Head Quarters City Guard
Provost Marshal's Office
Washington Dec 27th 1861

Major General George B. McClellan
Commanding U.S.A.

General,

I have the honor to report that my operative "T.W.," the report of whose operations lately, in Virginia, is already before you, in my report to you of date Dec. 17th inst, being about to start again, to Virginia, called, on Tuesday the 23rd instant, on Captain Wᵐ Winder of 3rd U.S. Artillery, at his residence, or boarding house, on H. st. 296. Washington — kept by Mʳˢ Hutton, to which place he had been fully traced, and with which, has his boarding house, he had been permanently, identified by a most thorough and rigorous "shadowing," with my operatives, from Nov. 30th to the 23rd instant, inclusive:

168

That my operative saw Capt Winder alone, and, after having fully satisfied the Captain of his entire reliability, he then related to him, the account of his interview in Richmond, with Genl. Winder (the Captain's Father), together with his trip to Virginia and connection while there, with Doctor Herndon, substantially as stated to you in my report aforesaid, and which I will briefly recapitulate as follows, to wit;

That my operative had called on General Winder, bearing a letter to the General, from Doctor Herndon, giving my operative a most flattering introduction & making the General to feel that my Operative was a thoroughly reliable man, who had rendered the Doctor great and essential aid in his late escape, as a deserter, from the United States Army, at Washington, and in making his way to Virginia, by way of Leonardtown, Maryland.

That my operative related to Captain Winder substantially, the message of his Father, by my operative, from Richmond, which was about as follows, to wit;

That he learned for the first time, by D^r. Herndon, on his arrival at Richmond, of his son, Capt Wm Winder, having left California for Washington; that he wished my operative to tell his son, on his return from Richmond, that his Father wished him to resign his commission if he *could not find* the *means* of *certain escape* by desertion, and come south;

That his father had much rather he should resign and, if it must be so, lay in jail until the close of the war, or if it should be demanded, that he would rather his son should suffer death of the most ignominious character, than continue to hold his commission and be made to serve the United States in this War against the South.

I have the honor further to report, that Capt Winder received the communication from his father, with great apparent pleasure, telling my operative that all his sympathies were with the South, that his relations and all he held dear, were there, and that, if he had the means, he would go south the very first chance he could get; that his pay, as Captain in the United States Army, was his only means of support for his wife and son.

That the Captain further, told my operative that when he returned to Richmond, he wished him to tell his father, that he might rest assured that he would never fight against the South; that he had met with General McClellan and had told the General, his feelings, and had obtained from him, the offer of returning to duty in California, where he would not be called into action in the present contest; that he would wait the return of my operative from Richmond, and another communication from his father, before determining what course to pursue; that at any rate, his father might depend that *in no possible event* would he *draw his sword against the South*, but that if he could not, on hearing from him again, see his way clear to go South, he would return to California and still retain his place, simply and only, for the purpose of supporting his family; that he had already sent his wife to New Hampshire after their boy — she being formerly, a New Hampshire woman, and that they would all be in Washington on the return of my operative, and that he would be able, by that time, to determine his course.

He further told my operative that he had some land, on the Illinois Central Railroad, which was the only means he possessed, outside of his salary, and that he would try to dispose of it by the time, or before, my operative's return again, from Richmond; that if successful, in the sale of his land, he would be ready to *leave for Virginia, the first chance*, as *all his hopes and wishes and prayers were with the South*.

In Conclusion, General, permit me respectfully, to suggest that I am not sufficiently acquanited [*sic*] with Military rules & law, to know if there be any power which can be exercised in the case of Captain Winder; but that a man who, *for "bread & butter,"* will continue to hold his commission and receive the pay from *the country which has been his benefactor,* while, at *the same time,* he *intends to act* the *traitor's part,* can find *no parallel short of Benedict Arnold,* if indeed, his crime be not yet deeper dyed.

I beg further, respectfully, to suggest that if there be no military rule far-reaching enough to touch his case, that, at least, he be requested to *subscribe* to and *swear allegiance* to *the Country*; not that I have *much confidence* in the *saving power* of *such an Oath,* but for the purpose of testing whether Captain Winder will *add perjury* to the *crime of Treason*

I am, General,

Your obet. Servt.
E. J. Allen

* * *

Head Quarters City Guard
Provost Marshals [*sic*] Office
Washington Jany' 31st 1862

Major General, Geo. B. McClellan
Commanding U.S.A.

General,

I have the honor to report that on yesterday, I submitted to you a brief report of the observations of *my operative "T.W."* during his trip to Virginia & the South, whence he returned on yesterday; and now, beg to submit a more complete and detailed report of the result of his operations during said trip — as indicated in my said report of yesterday.

Said Operative left Washington on December 25th 1861, for Virginia & the South, via Leonardtown Md., reaching which last mentioned place, on Dec. 26th; there he learned that it would be impossible for him to cross the Potomac, because of the extra vigilance on the part of Federal troops stationed in that vicinity.

At Leonardtown, he learned from J.W.J Moore, hotel keeper and strong secessionist, that the only safe chance he (Moore) knew of for crossing the river was near the mouth of Cuckhold Creek from a point called Cob Neck — a point about fourteen miles, airline, from Leonardtown, and about thirty miles by waggon roads.

Cobb Neck — or Cob-Neck is a point extending from the main land some ten miles out, two bays making up from the Potomac into which from the South East runs a creek heading near Allens Fresh, and from the North West, runs another creek called Cuckhold; which two bays, or inlets, make into the Potomac on either side of Cobb Neck point; about one mile from the extreme point of Cob Neck is a small stream called Mill creek, which runs across the Neck from Bay to Bay and is about 100 yards wide & four to five feet water at high tide; on this extreme point is a pine thicket & under brush the land being wet & marshy — not occupied by Federal Pickets nor could be except by boat across Mill Creek.

Maryland Secessionists who are well posted on the points of crossing, consider this, at Cob Neck, the best, now unguarded, on that side of the Potomac; Monroes Creek, on the opposite side, being the only place where persons allowed to pass the rebel lines are permitted to cross the Potomac in the direction of Maryland — excepting at Eastville, or a point on Chesapeake Bay near Eastville, on the Western Shore of Virginia, where the rebels have one only other point of crossing into Maryland, than that mentioned — at Monroes Creek.

The only house on Cob Neck, outside of Mill Creek, is occupied by a Free Negro, farmer, who has a small boat for crossing Mill Creek, and who set my operative across Mill Creek, on his return from Virginia, made, by my operative, to believe he was a Federal Soldier looking to cross over Mill Creek to his camp; Federal Cavalry Pickets being now stationed on Cobb Neck near the main land — scouting out to near Mill Creek.

Friday, 27th, December, *Operative left Leonardtown* and arrived at Cuckhold Creek on the side of Cobb Neck, where he remained making arrangement to cross over, finding no obstacles from Federal guards either in going or coming;

Sunday Night, December 29th, Operative in company with two women & three children was taken across the Potomac in a Canoe and landed four or five miles above the Mouth of Monroes Creek on the Potomac at a place called *Washington's Farm*; the buildings on said farm had all been destroyed by Federal shells from boats passing up & down & by sending men on shore to fire them; reason for destroying Washington's buildings — use made of them to harbor rebels crossing to & from Maryland; no house, now left, within two miles of the Potomac at this point of landing.

Monday 30th December *Operative left Washington's farm* for Richmond; went the first six miles with an Ox Cart; road sandy but bad; remained over night at Arnolds house six miles from Potomac and twenty miles from Hop-yard Wharf on the Rappahannock river — whence by Arnold's team next day, Tuesday 31st December, *to Hop-yard wharf*, aforesaid; thence same night by steamboat Virginia to *Fredericksburg* — the roads from Arnolds to Hop-yard wharf, bad, but being sandy, not as bad as other parts of Virginia.

Wednesday January 1st 1862 Operative was sick, all day, at Fredericksburg; on Thursday January 2nd, *he left Fredericksburg* and arrived in *Richmond* the same day — by railroad.

On the way from Fredericksburg to Richmond, Operative learned from the Captain of a company belonging to a Louisiana Regiment which was stationed at Dumfries, Va, that the Louisiania [*sic*] Regiment, to which said Captain belonged, had been stationed at Dumfries only about six weeks; that during that six weeks, the said Louisiania Regiment had lost 75. men, of whom 28. men had died within four days time; that the cause of so many men dying was "change of climate"

The Captain of said Louisiana Regiment stated further, that the Colonel of said Louisiana regiment, was then in Richmond for the purpose of seeing Jefferson Davis — rebel President — with the view of having said Louisiana Regiment moved to Richmond for Winter Quarters on account of the great mortality attending it while stationed at Dumfries; and the Captain of said Louisiana Regiment stated further that he had learned of arrangements having been made for the removal — that week — of the said Louisiana Regiment from Dumfries to Richmond

The captain of said Louisiana Regt. stated further, that if said Louisiania Regt. was not removed from Dumfries before the 1st of April — one half of said regiment would be in the grave;

The Captain of said Louisiana Regt. also, stated that every one of the regiments on the Potomac, were building winter quarters with logs and mud plaster, moving in to them as soon as finished, while yet green & not dry, thus causing the soldiers to take severe colds and bring upon themselves fearful sickness.

The Captain of said Louisiana Regiment, continuing the conversation with my operative, stated, with apparent earnestness, that he would not remain with his regiment if it was kept at Dumfries, "for" said he, "I would suffer myself to be shot rather than stay there."

The Captain of said Louisiana Regiment stated further that the rebels were abundantly prepared to resist any attack which might be made upon them by the Federal Forces, any where along the line of their Defenses on the lower Potomac, "but" said he, "I am fearful that if no fight is made soon, the Confederate Forces will have to leave the lower Potomac, on account of the dreadful sickness pervading the various camps."

Upon the arrival of my Operative in Richmond, he shortly, made arrangements to obtain passes from the Secretary of War, of the rebel government, to enable him to go to Nashville, Tenn., & to Manassas; before starting for Nashville, *he became sick* and could not leave until *Tuesday January 7th,* when *he started for Nashville,* Tenn, in the Company of William Campbell a Contractor with the rebels [*sic*] Government, for furnishing 5000 Knapsacks, to be made of Canvas & painted black with leather straps; together with belts bayonet Scabbards &c; said Campbell then being on his way west, for the purchase of leather from the *extensive tanneries in Knoxville, Chatanooga* [*sic*] *& Nashville,* to enable him to complete his contract with the rebel government; the manufactory of Campbell is in Richmond and he employs 35 to 40 hands.

Operative found the entire line of railroad, from Richmond through to Bowlingreen [*sic*], in a bad condition, and the average speed of passenger trains, not over ten miles per hour.

Operative arrived at Lynchburg Jany 7th, where were taken into the train going west, bound for Bowlingreen Ky., *six crowded car loads of soldiers,* being a part of Floyd & Wise'[s] command's [*sic*] from Western Virginia which was proceeding under orders to Richmond, but which orders, being countermanded at Lynchburg, these soldiers were ordered to Bowlingreen Ky.

My Operative arrived at Abington, Va. 3.00 P.M. Jany' 8th where, being too sick to go on, he laid over for 24 hours;

During the day — January 8th, *Operative saw a Cavalry regiment,* numbering about 700, including *two pieces — of Artillery—* manned, which had been under *command* of *Floyd* in Western Virginia, or of *Wise,* which, not certainly learned, but were *ordered to Richmond* and the *order* was *countermanded* when they arrived *at Abingdon en-route* for Richmond — ultimate destination not learned; this regiment was *ordered* to *return back to Western Virginia* from Abingdon, Va., it being armed, principally with breech-loading rifles made in Baltimore; each member of said Cavalry having one of Colts Revolvers, Navy Size, and a Sabre; Several of these Cavalry men had large shot guns for buck-shot; *the Artillery attached* to *Said Cavalry was two six pound iron guns—one smoth* [*sic*] *and one rifled.*

Why are you going back to Western Virginia? was asked by my operative, of this Cavalry company; the reply being "we are ordered back to hold the Yankees in check who are coming into Western Virginia and are destroying everything before them."

My operative learned from the soldiers that Forage in Western Virginia was very scarce and that what they had had, before leaving, was necessarily hauled a distance of ten to twelve miles over horrid roads—in fact that the forage was nearly all consumed in regions where the rebel army had been quartered; their horses were in very poor condition, but the men who made up this Cavalry regiment, were looking very hearty, most of them being farmers from the mountain regions

Operative left Abingdon Va. in the morning of Jany.' 9th, *en-route* for Nashville, and *arrived the same evening at Knoxville, Tenn.*, where he was obliged to lay over, for the trains did not run nights owing to the rebels fear of some injury being inflicted by the Union men, of that section between Knoxville and Chatanooga [*sic*].

The bridge at Union Station, which was burned at the time when so many bridges were destroyed sometime ago, and is not yet rebuilt, but about 30 men are at work on the materials for the new bridge; the passengers were obliged to walk about a mile and a half around the railroad crossing, by way of the waggon road bridge, which is lower down the stream than the railroad crossing, and which was sought to be destroyed by Union men.

A company of Infantry is stationed *at Union Station* to guard the material being used for the bridge.

A company of Infantry is stationed at *Jonesboro, Tenn.*, for the purpose of guarding the railroad and of checking any rising up of Union men.

Two companies of Infantry and Two pieces of Light Artillery are stationed at *Greenville* for the purpose of protecting the railroad and for keeping down any rising-up of Union men.

One Company Infantry was stationed at *Russellville, Tenn.*, for the purpose of guarding the railroad and to keep down the up-rising of Union Men.

One Company Infantry was stationed at *Mossy Creek* for the purpose of guarding the railroad and suppressing the Union men.

Guards are stationed at all the railroad *bridges*, small as well large.

One regiment Infantry and Four Pieces Artillery Are stationed at *Knoxville*, men not well armed but well dressed.

My operative learned from a Lieutenant at Knoxville that the belief was, at Knoxville, that if the Soldiers were removed, the Union men would rise again in 24 hours after, and be as "bad as ever"; that the said Lieutenant did not believe there were ten "good southern men" in Knoxville; that said Lieutent [*sic*] would "hang them all" if he had his way, "for," he said, "it cost far more to keep up such a force to guard them, than East Tennessee was worth.

The said Lieutenant was very severe on Parson [William Gannaway] Brownlow, who was lying dangerously ill at home, he having been released from imprisonment on account of his supposed fatal sickness, the Lieutenant remarking that if he had his way he would "hang Old Brownlow that very night."

Provisions at Knoxville—were plenty,

Business at Knoxville—nothing doing excepting in Tanneries

Campbell, the Knapsack contractor who was going west to purchase leather, bought all there was in the tanneries at Knoxville of Harness Leather, and only obtained

Seven hundred dollars worth — the manufactures of leather having sold as fast as they made

Prices of Leather at Knoxville.

> Harness Leather 65¢ per pound
> Bridle Leather   75¢ "   "
> Buff Leather   80¢ "   "

A Tannery at Knoxville Was personally visited by my operative and found to be quite extensive having on hand a considerable quantity of Sole Leather which after only three months in the tan vats, sells at seventy five cents per pound

My *operative left Knoxville, Tenn. Friday Jan'y 10th for Nashville Tenn.*

150 Soldiers were on the same train — en-route *for Bowlingreen* — all Infantry and appeared to be part of the same troops — before spoken of in this report, as being on the way from Western Virginia to Richmond, the order for which, being counter-manded at Lynchburg and the troops being put en-route for Bowlingreen

One Company of Infantry was stationed at *Loudon Tenn.* to *guard* the *railroad* and *keep down Union men.*

One Company of Infantry was stationed at *Mouse Creek*, Tenn., for the sole purpose of *guarding* the *railroad* & *keeping union men in* [illegible] *also one Company at Cleve-land, Tenn.* for the purpose of *guarding* the *railroad* and of *keeping down Union Men.*

My Operative also learned that *west from Chatannooga* [*sic*], Tenn., Union men being fewer, the railroad *bridges only*, and not the railroad, were *guarded.*

My operative arrived at Nashville on January 11th 1862 and found stationed

At Nashville

2 Regiments of Infantry armed with Percussion Muskets
One of these Regiments was encamped *on* the *Fair Ground*
About one mile South East from *Nashville.*
The other of these two Regiments was encamped *across* the *Cumberland River* over *from Nashville* and but a short way from the river

Fortifications about Nashville

My operative learned from the Landlord of the City Hotel — Nashville, Tenn., that about *one mile below* the *City* of *Nashville*, there were being built

Two Earth-work Fortifications one of them on each side of the river, erecting for the purpose of preventing Federal Boats from coming up the Cumberland; slave labor only, being used in the building of said Earth-works

My operative also, *learned at Nashville* that the *railroad* and *suspension bridges* both, were *each guarded* by the soldiers who were stationed at either and on both sides of the Cumberland, being on guard *night and day.*

My operative further, learned that, near to the Depot of the Nashville & Bowlin-green railroad, were *three very large* Ware houses now being used as *hospitals*, all of which were *filled with the sick* — apparently well cared for.

No Leather in Nashville

My Operative learned from Campbell, the Knapsack Contractor aforesaid, that no harness nor bridle leather could be found in Nashville

Percussion Caps

Are being manufactured in Nashville, Tenn, — persons thus employed, 12.

Demoralized Condition of rebel Troops

My operative saw near the R.R. Depot — Nashville 15 to 20 houses of "Ill Fame," where — day & night — in the most public manner and without attempted concealment the business of prostitution, with the soldiers, is carried on to a fearful extent, engendering among the troops the diseases incident to such places. No interference was manifest by civil or military authority, either in relation to houses of Ill Fame or the almost universal drunkenness of the soldiers.

Strictness about passes

At Nashville the very closest scrutiny is exercised in regard to persons wishing to go from Nashville to Bowlingreen. Having the Pass to Nashville of the Secretary of War at Richmond, my operative was enabled, thus, to obtain a pass for Bowlingreen, but for which Pass from Richmond he might not have been able, easily, to pass to Bowlingreen, the Pass from Nashville only permitted my operative to go to the City of Bowlingreen but not to visit the Camps.

Nashville to Bowlingreen

My operative left Nashville for Bowlingreen, on Sunday 12th, January, by railroad which was in bad condition as had been the whole line of railroad from Richmond to Nashville, the trains, on that account, not being run over ten miles an hour

Accident on the Railroad

About Eighteen miles out from Nashville, on the road to Bowlingreen, a switch was displaced, supposed by design, which caused the cars to run off the track, turning completely over and demolishing the Engine and also, one passenger car, but only injuring one man — on the train were *300 Soldiers en-route for Bowlingreen.*

The Conductor of the train told my operative that several other Engines had been thus, of late, destroyed and that at that rate the road would be without Engines

No Bridges guarded between Nashville and Bowlingreen, streams on the route small but much swollen, as had been all rivers & creeks west from Richmond.

Camps around Bowlingreen.

On Monday Jan'y. 13th having obtained a pass from the Provost Marshal of Bowlingreen, my operative went with horse & buggy — finding the roads almost impassable — to visit the *1st Arkansas Regiment*, which was in camp about 3 miles North-West of Bowlingreen — Col Claibourne [*sic*] in Command, with whom, & Major Harris of said Regiment — brother of Gov Harris of Tennessee — my operative had a previous acquaintance.

From Major Harris he learned *Gen. Pillow had resigned* in consequence of a misunderstanding with *Gen Polk and Gov Harris.*

Exaggeration of the number of Troops Stationed at Bowlingreen and under command of Genl Sidney E. Johnson whose Head Quarters are at Bowlingreen, has most undoubtedly been made by Major Harris in his statement of the numbers in and about Bowlingreen — my operative concluding after thorough examination that instead of Eighty, the number under Genl Johnson in the Division of Bowlingreen — all told, would not exceed Sixty Regiments, or about ¾ of the number estimated by Major Harris

My operative learned at the camp in Bowlingreen, that there was *another "1st Arkansas Regiment"* which was stationed at Dumfries in Virginia, this last, regiment being the *"1st Arkansas" proper*; but the one stationed at Bowlingreen, of which Col. Claibourne has command, was the *first regiment raised* in the state of Arkansas, and which without being mustered into the state or Confederate States service, fought "on its own hook" for some three months and then was admitted and mustered into the Confederate service, but not until the "1st Arkansas State Volunteers" had been raised by the state of Arkansas and had been accepted as such, by the rebel Government;

Thus has a struggle of warmth & feeling between these *two claimants to be* the *"1st Arkansas" regiment* been growing up and continued, and the Governor of Arkansas hesitates to decide which shall take precedence as being the "1st Arkansas" regiment fearing thereby he may not please the one decided against.

A case almost entirely analogous to those two mentioned *"1st Arkansas" regiments*, also, exists between *two Tennessee Regiments* each claiming to be the "1st Tennessee" — one being in the Command of Genl Jackson and the other stationed near Manassas.

38 Regiments at and about Bowlingreen were counted by my operative on his trip out to the 1st Arkansas Regiment — Col Claibourne, he having taken a circuitous route for the very purpose of so counting the regiments;

2 Regiments of Cavalry also, were counted by my operative, besides the 38 Regiments, aforesaid, all of which 38, were Infantry.

One of the aforesaid "two Cavalry Regiments" was known as having been of *Ben McCulloughs [sic] Texan Rangers* and when seen at Bowlingreen were armed with large double-barrelled shot guns, for buck-shot, and Colts, Navy size, Revolvers.

These Cavalry Regiments Were stationed, the one about a mile and a half, and the other about two miles and a half from Bowlingreen

7 Field Batteries, near Bowlingreen, Were counted by my operative on his aforesaid, trip from Bowlingreen to visit the "1st Arkansas" Regt. some of these Field Batteries were composed of 4 and some of them, of 6-guns each; the range would average from six to twelve pounders; some of the guns were rifled and some were smooth bore; some of the guns were brass and some were of iron

One, of the Seven Batteries, was entirely Brass and was claimed to be the same as *had by Bragg in the Mexican War*; this Brass Battery is manned and commanded by Arkansas men exclusively.

Forts around Bowlingreen About North West by North from Bowlingreen, and distant — the one about a mile, and the other about a mile and a half from Bowlingreen, were being built, at that time,

Two Earth Works the largest, nearest to and about one mile from Bowlingreen, was to mount 8 heavy guns and the smaller Fort, about one & a half miles from Bowlingreen, was to mount 4 guns; the larger of the two Earth Works, and the one nearest to Bowlingreen, was nearly completed and had two guns mounted.

80 Regiments around Bowlingreen were stated, by *Major Harris of the "1st Arkansas"* regiment, to be the entire force of the rebel army in and about that place, and also, including all the rebel troops between Bowlingreen and Cave City, and at Cave City; which last mentioned, place had recently, been entirely destroyed by the rebel troops, by fire, — every building having been burned down, to prevent their being used by Northern troops;

Col. Hindman, who had lately been commissioned as *a Brigadier General*, was the officer delegated for the destruction of the Railroad Tunnel — north of Cave City, in which service, he was then engaged, having, on his way, reduced Cave City to ashes; said railroad tunnel was on the Nashville & Louisville railroad, North of Cave City.

Major Harris, who is a *brother of the Governor of Tennessee*, further, stated to my operative, that of these 80 Regiments, at and around Bowlingreen, which are meant to include the detachment then away on the mission of destruction to the Tunnel and Cave City, and the entire forces under the command of Genl. Sidney E. Johnson *there were Six or Seven Cavalry regiments.*

The number of Field Batteries was known to Major Harris, but upon talking the matter over between himself and Col. Claibourne they concluded the whole number of guns, in the Field Artillery belonging to these 80 Regiments, at and about Bowlingreen, was between 80 & 90

Speaking of the time of enlistment, Major Harris and others of the 1st Arkansas Regiment, said that they were going home in May "any how," that being the time when their enlistment would expire, "and," they said, "those who have remained at home thus far have got to take our places."

Speaking of Virginia Law, compelling enlistment or of *re-enlistment*, of those who had entered the Army for twelve months, and of her Legislature compelling those, thus enlisted, to serve during the war — *Major Harris and others, of the Said 1st Arkansas Regiment*, said that if said law was enacted by Virginia, the whole force of 12 months volunteers would refuse to re-enlist, as, if such a law was passed by Virginia, most likely the other Southern States would do likewise; that there were *no ten regiments* in the Confederate service which *could prevent the "1st Arkansas Regiment"* from going to their homes at least for sixty days — if after that they should come back.

The general feeling among all the troops seemed to my operative, to be that they would go home at the expiration of their present terms of enlistment, and that not over one half of them would re-enlist unless compelled; that so much is this feeling known to the rebel Government, that they are taking measures to guard against such a contingency by offers of bounty and by anticipation of their terms of enlistment expiring, with furloughs of from thirty to Sixty days, so that the return time of the expiring furlough shall bring the Volunteer back to his Regiment in time to keep the ranks full.

Many are accepting furloughs on these conditions, owing to the long continued bad weather and unpleasant condition of their camps, who would not otherwise — such is their feeling about remaining in the Army.

The clothing of the Troops at and about Bowlingreen, is poor and wearing out; and is composed of all colors & every quality; but where any pretensions are made to uniformity, the prevailing and almost universal color is grey.

The Quarters of the Troops At and around Bowlingreen was mostly in poor canvass tents, which afforded but poor shelter for the comfortless tenants; some few of the regiments were in log shanties.

The Health of the Troops about *Bowlingreen* was better than it was of those Troops at Manassas and Evansport; my operative estimates the relative sickness of Troops about as follows, to wit; —

Bowlingreen & Vicinity	*12* per cent
Manassas & *Centerville* [*sic*]	*15* per cent
Evansport, Dumfries &c	*20* & upwards

The roads around Bowlingreen were almost impassable — so much so that my operative with a strong horse & light buggy, was more than once compelled in returning to Bowlingreen from the surrounding camps, to leave the buggy and lift at the wheels.

Defenses around Bowlingreen

A *very large Fort* is thrown up and *mounted with the heaviest guns* any where in the west, except perhaps at *Columbus*— on the summit of a large hill, the base of which commences close to, and on the east side of Bowlingreen, and is nearly half a mile from base to summit; *this fort commands every approach to the town* by railroad or turnpike.

My operative undertook to ascend the hill and *observe the works*, but was stopt [*sic*] when about half way up, by a guard, and forbid approach to the fort; he was near enough up to the top of the hill to enable him to *see the muzzles of four very large guns.*

Forage at Bowlingreen was scarce, and was brought by waggons a distance of ten to twelve miles

The Head Quarters of Genl. Sidney E. Johnson are at *Bowlingreen* where also, is stationed *Genl. Hardee*— of *"Hardees Tactics."*

My operative left Bowlingreen on Tuesday Jany 14th, first having to obtain a pass *to go to Nashville, en-route for Manassas*, making no stay before reaching Knoxville where only, because the trains run but in the day time, for fear of Union men, he staid [*sic*] over night.

Operative left Knoxville Thursday Jany 16th, *for Lynchburg—en-route for Manassas*; noted nothing new on the way until arriving at *Dublin station*— between Lynchburg & Bristol where, *he saw a small encampment* of *four or five companies of Infantry*, but did not learn why they were stationed there; *he learned before leaving Knoxville* that the day of his arrival there from Bowlingreen, — Jany 15th, the *Drum-Head Court Martial* which had been *sitting in Knoxville* for several weeks, to *try Bridge Burners* and other persons for holding Union Sentiments, had been dissolved for the time being — having already condemned *five* of the reported *bridge burners* who *had* all *been hung*; these bridge burners were farmers who had lived quite a distance up in the mountains and away from the line of the Railroad; the *three* at *Greenville* were *hung on a tree* by the side of the railroad and buried them together by & under the tree — father and son; their friends came afterward and removed the bodies to their previous homes for interment.

My operative arrived at Lynchburg on Friday Jany' 17th, and *left there* the next morning, *for Manassas*, arriving *at Manassas Saturday 18th January.*

Hospitals at Charlottesville, Va., were were [*sic*] built of rough boards one story high, and three of them were each one hundred feet long and thirty feet wide where were received, as also at Warrenton, Gordonsville, Orange Court House and other rail road stations— the sick from the command's [*sic*] of Generals Johnson & Beau-

178

regard; Eight men were seen in charge of an orderly sergeant whom he had been after to Gordonsville, they having overstaid [*sic*] their furloughs, by several days; *$30. reward* was offered *for* the arrest and return of *deserters*.

Roads—Manassas to Centerville were in a very bad condition and my operative, being unable to procure conveyance at Manassas, walked on foot, to Centerville on Sunday Jany' 19th; his object being to see the "1st Maryland" Regt. and make the minutest possible, observations of the rebel troops & defenses.

After reaching *Centerville, my Operative learned* that the "1st Maryland" Regiment had been moved, since his *last visit to Centerville—*about *two months previous—*to a point on the Orange and Alexandria Railroad, about three miles east of Manassas Junction.

Fortifications around Centerville.

The fortifications which were *seen by my Operative*, at and around *Centerville*, were in number, *3*. and described about as follows, to wit; —

There are *two mounds* situated about a quarter of a mile apart and both, in a south east-by south direction from Centerville, — the nearest one being less than 200 yards from the buildings in Centerville, *on Each of which mounds*, are thrown up, *heavy earth-works*, each of which is capable of mounting *four heavy guns*, but having *none yet, mounted—* on January 19th; through there were lying, close by the one, nearest of the two mounds to Centerville, *two 32 pounder guns rifled*; also, there was *one 32 pounder rifled gun* lying close by the Earth-Work on the mound most distant from Centerville.

These two mounds are perhaps, at the extreme, elevated about fifteen feet above the common level of the ground around them — including the artificial Earth-Works in said fifteen feet elevation.

There are between these two Earth-Works and between these two mounds, *two lines of Earth-Work* from seven to eight feet high above the ground surface, and running parallel with each other the whole distance (*about ¼ mile*) from one mound to the other and at sufficient distance from each other, to allow the free working of Field Artillery between said lines of earth-work which *run* parallel to each other *from one of the mounds to the other.*

On the inside of these parallel *lines of Earth-works*, running the whole distance between the two mounds, *are benches of earth-work for riflemen & Infantry*, at sufficient distance from the top of the said parallel lines of earth-work, to answer *as breast works—like* unto *rifle pits.*

These two parallel lines of Earth-work are each pierced with *port holes for Field Artillery* at every *20 to 30 feet, for the quarter mile in length* between the two mounds; each port-hole has a *sliding door* made to work up & down — to be raised by a lever, and falling by its own weight, after the discharge of each gun; each of these *port-hole doors* are made of *heavy pieces of timber* and are covered upon the *outside* with *railroad iron.*

Another Fort, And much larger than either of the two forts, described as being on the top of the mounds aforesaid, *capable of mounting* about *ten heavy guns*, is situated on the North side of the turnpike which runs from Warrenton, via Centerville, to Fairfax Court House, and also, situated a little east of North from Centerville;

No guns are *yet mounted* on this last described fort, but my operative was told at

Centerville by the Soldiers, that the design was to have some 84 pounders mounted upon this largest fort, but that the roads were so very bad that such heavy guns could not be got to Centerville until the railroad was completed from Manassas to Centerville, which would require yet, considerable time.

The Railroad from Manassas to Centerville was nearly all graded — *the work having been performed by slaves*; but having no ties and it being next to impossible to get them until the roads were better, the work upon the railroad from Manassas to Centerville, was not *then*, being completed, as all the teams were required to *haul Forage & provisions* for the army, and could not be diverted from *that object* to the *hauling of ties*.

Other Defenses Were *being built* along the turnpike leading from Centerville to Fairfax Court House, as *heard of*, but *not seen* by my operative.

Other Defenses Still, Were being built along the turnpike in the direction of Bull Run from Centerville, as stated to my operative by, what he deemed, reliable authority; but in consequence of the almost impassable roads, the next to impossible getting of conveyance and the poor health of my operative, at the time, he was deterred from making then, any further examination of the rebel works— north and east of Centerville.

Fortifications around Manassas

On the right hand side of the railroad — going East from Manassas Junction — and from a quarter to half a mile from the Orange & Alexandria railroad, *are two Earth-Works*, one of which, and that, the one farthest from the railroad, being *mounted with four guns—18 to 32 pounders*; the other, and the one nearest to the railroad — about a quarter of a mile distant — being *mounted with three guns—18 to 32 pounders*.

There were two other batteries Situated, the one about ½, and the other about ¾ mile from the Orange & Alexandria railroad on the side of the railroad — in a south easterly direction from the two last above described forts which were located just N. East of Manassas — and too remote from the railroad, to allow my operative to judge of the number and calibre of the guns with which they were mounted.

The largest Fort round about Manassas, was situated just North East of Manassas on both sides of the Orange and Alexandria Railroad — a raised Earth-Work immediately on the railroad *mounting*, on that part lying east and on the right hand side of the railroad, *two guns—32 pounders*— and on the left hand side of the railroad, in both cases coming eastward, *mounting three to four guns*— all but one, *thirty two pounders*— one appearing *larger than 32 pounder*; the wings of this fort, on each side of the said railroad, are made of double rows of hogsheads on top of each other — filled with earth

Troops under Johnson & Beauregard at *Centerville, Manassas &c*

At Centerville,

My operative on 19th January, inst, *counted Ten Regiments*— all *Infantry* no Cavalry seen; these troops are mostly camped in canvas tents but some have log huts and some have board shanty's

Troops at & Around Manassas, Within a radius of 3½ miles— mostly along the line of the Orange & Alexandria railroad — *my operative counted twenty three regi-*

ments; on the road from Centerville [*sic*] to a point 3½ miles east of Manassas, on the Orange & Alexandria railroad, *my operative counted*, in the woods, *three or four regiments of Infantry* and *one regiment of Cavalry*— all either being in or building Winter Quarters.

Other Troops along from Manassas, in the direction of Occoquan, were stationed at different points, as stated to my operative by Col Stewart of the 1st Maryland regiment, but owing the state of the weather, the condition of the roads, and the poor health of my operative, he did not go in person, to visit the troops said to be stationed along in the direction from Manassas to Occoquan, but learned from Col Stewart of the 1st Maryland Regiment, that troops under Genl Johnsons command extended along down from Manassas to near the Potomac, and until met by other, rebel troops under Genl. Holmes.

The entire Force of rebel Army under *Generals Johnson & Beauregard* was stated by *Col Stewart, of the 1st Maryland Regiment*, to be about *seventy two regiments* including what of Cavalry were now acting under command of those generals scattered along from the North line of Genl Holmes['] command, to and beyond Winchester, Va.

The game of "Bluff," Col Stewart stated, had been extensively practiced by the southern men in giving the numbers of the Army, "but," said Col. Stewart, I am, and always was opposed to such a game as that "Bluff"; Col Stewart stated that there had been at *no time, such an array of numbers as had been claimed* in the *Southern Army*

Feeling among the troops.

My operative learned from *personal intercourse* with troops about *Centerville & Manassas*, and from their officers, that owing to the long continued inactivity and want of employment by the by the [*sic*] rebel troops; together with the unsatisfied waiting for the long talked-of and much expected advance by the Federal Army, coupled with the very long continued bad weather — the *rebel troops were completely dispirited at* and *about Centerville*, and those who, on a previous visit of my operative about two months before, were the *bravest* to talk, *were* now *completely changed* and most eager for being released from the rebel Service on some, it mattered to them, little what terms.

The re-enlistment of married men, was considered by my operative, extremely improbable, to any great extent.

Artillery at Centerville was counted by my operative and found to be sixteen guns standing near the main defense, where the port-holes were prepared with doors to cover them.

Artillery at Manassas and vicinity,

My operative counted four field batteries—two with *four*, and *two* with *six guns—* North east of Manassas near the railroad

Health of the rebel Troops.

The first Maryland Regiment is the *most healthy* of any *in* the *rebel service*; its *fall number* as *per roll book* is *707*— rank & file; *this Regiment*, as stated by its *Colonel — Stewart*, was two to one *more healthy than any other* one regiment *in that Command*, the *highest number*, then, *sick* in any *one* of its *companies* or unfit for duty being— *seven*.

"*Very different*," with *other Regiments*, said Col Stewarts, among which is a *fearful* amount of *sickness* and *death*; *caused* as said Col Stewart, *by inactivity* and consequent *demoralization, destroying more*, he firmly believed *than* would be lost in *battle* should they or the Federal Forces advance, and battles ensue; "*such too*," said Col. Stewart, is the *opinion* of *Genl Beauregard* whose *Head Quarters* on the *19th January*, were at or near the *old Battle ground* of *July 21st*, in a *Brick house*.

The Head Quarters of *Genl. Johnson* are at *Centerville*.

Genl. Jackson was at *Romney* when he would go into *Winters Quarters*—as stated by Colonel Stewart.

Tuesday 21st Jany 1862—having spent two days at Centerville & Manassas, *My operative left Manassas* on the railroad train *for Richmond*; arriving *same day* in Richmond, he saw, at the *Petersburg Railroad Depot*, in *Richmond, two very heavy, iron, rifled cannon*, said, there, to be "*84 pounders*" about being loaded onto the cars *to go* around, on account of the burned bridges, by way of Petersburg and Chattanooga, *to Bowlingreen, Kentucky*.

Pass through the Rebel lines.

Wednesday Jany 22nd my operative saw Secretary Benjamin and obtained from him Pass to go through the rebel lines, in the direction of Maryland, only having him to get as he passed, the countersigning of said Pass, by the Generals of Division through which (Divisions) he might have to pass.

Troops at Richmond

Only three regiments are stationed at and about Richmond; one Regiment is on the Fair ground, having Four Pieces Artillery; the other two regiments are lower down than Richmond and about half a mile from James River on the same side with Richmond.

Drunkenness & Desertion

My operative saw in, Richmond, several officers hunting for deserters and men who had overstayed their furloughs; *30 dollars reward* offered *for* the return of *deserters*; Liquors drank freely by soldiers and officers in Richmond

Fortifications around Richmond

There are *seventeen batteries* around *about Richmond* starting above and below the City on James River—quality of earth-works—*the very best.*

Very few guns mounted on *Richmond fortifications.*

Ben. McCullough [sic] in Richmond

My operative was shown Ben. McCullough in Richmond, having on Citizens dress—Jany 23^d 1862

Friday 24th January—operative learned that some *difficulty* had taken place between *Col Jones* of the Passport office, and *Genl Winder*, growing out of, as Col Jones claims, Genl. Winders lack of stringency in regard to recommending persons to have passes, who are of doubtful loyalty in the opinion of Col Jones; *All passes* to go from Richmond to and point *within* the rebel *lines*, are issued by Col Jones for the Secretary of War; and all passes to go *outside* the rebel *lines*, are issued by the *Secretary of War himself* and *great, care, caution* & *stringency* is made use of *in regard to passes*, not only in Richmond but *in all* other *places* where camps are to be visited.

Friday, Jany. 24th my operative left Richmond for the *Maryland line*, via *Fredericksburg*, designing to visit *Brook Station*, the *Head Quarters* of *General Holmes*; Arriving at *Fredericksburg* the same day, *he saw Genl Holmes*, who happened to be *there*, and *who* readily *countersigned the pass*, given to him at Richmond by the Secretary of War *to pass through the rebel lines* in the direction of Maryland; *My operative was kept from* visiting the *Head Quarters of Genl Holmes at Brook Station*, and *also*, the rebel camps at *Evansport* & *Dumfries*, and all their works on *the Lower Potomac*, by his being *out of health*, the *rainy weather*, the *impassable* state of the *roads*, the *impossibility* of *conveyance* being hired at Fredericksburg *and* the fact of *meeting Genl Holmes* at Fredericksburg

Friday Jany 24th. My operative saw Genl. Winder, before leaving *Richmond*, and learned from him that his son *Capt Winder of the U.S.A.* had been sent *back to California*, as he supposed for the purpose of getting him out of the way, as he (*Capt Winder*) was *not* to be *trusted* here in *Washington*, by *Genl McClellan*, on account of his *Southern sentiments*,

Friday Jany 24th at Fredericksburg. My operative saw Dr. Herndon, late deserter from U.S.A.— California Regt. and *now a Medical Director* in the *Division of Genl. Holmes*; Dr Herndon stated that the *sickness* was *fearfully great* in the *Division* of *Genl Holmes*;

Dr Herndon did not know how many *troops* were in *Holme's* [*sic*] *Division* but said that some *stated* the number at *50*, while others said there were *not over 30 Regiments*

Saturday 25th January, my operative left Fredericksburg for Maryland via, *Monroes Creek on the Potomac; he saw on the way* across the country from Hop Yard Landing — Rappahannock River, a *camp* of about *one hundred* rebel *militia* about *five miles East* of *King Georges Court House*; At the last mentioned camp, my operative learned that *six miles North from there*, was *another camp* of *400 Militia* under *Captain Taylor*; and *at Monroes Creek, on* the *Potomac*, he found stationed *30 rebel pickets* in *charge of a Lieutentant*— name not recollected— who *takes up passports* to cross *outside the lines*; no other camps between Monroes creek and *the Hague*, where are stationed under *Major Beale*, about *500 Militia*; *below* the *Hague* and not far above the *mouth* of the *Rappahannock*, is stationed *Capt Forrester* with *one company* of *Artillery* & *four guns*; and *these forces* above stated are *all* the rebel troops which are occupying the *several Counties between* the *Potomac* & *Rappahannock*.

The Lieutent at Monroes Creek stated to my operative that the *rebels* had been obliged to *destroy all the boats* at the Creeks mouths where they had no pickets, to *prevent* the *slaves* from *running away*— relating an instance of late occurrence, where a *dozen slaves* had *drawn* a *boat* for *many miles* by oxen, and were *caught at last* before they had quite reached the Potomac.

Sunday night Jany 26th my *operative* having *arrived* at the *Mouth of Monroe Creek*, was *furnished by* the *Lieutenant* in charge of the Pickets *stationed there two men and a boat* who set him across to *Cob Neck*, landing on the point — *whence* to *Washington* he made his way *avoiding the Union Pickets* and making his way by team or on foot as the case demanded or allowed.

In conclusion I beg respectfully to state that the long distance traveled by my operative by railroad in the south, during his late trip, has enabled him to judge accurately about the condition of their railroads which seemed to him to be gradually but certainly getting into a dilapidated state without corresponding repairs and that not exceeding ten miles an hour is considered safe to run.

I beg also further to report that but for the feeble health of my operative, & the almost impassable roads, & bad weather I should have been able in this report to have given you his observations of the rebel works and camps in the vicinity of the Lower Potomac — Evansport — Dumfries &c —

All of which is respectfully submitted by

Your obedient Servant
E. J. Allen

Source: George Brinton McClellan Papers, 1823–1898, Library of Congress.

Chapter Notes

Introduction

1. George W. Walling, *Recollections of a New York Chief of Police*, 77.

Chapter 1

1. Roland B. Harris, "Sussex, Historic Character Assessment Report: November 2004," 17, http://www.lewes.gov.uk/Files/plan_New haven_EUS_reportpages14to19.pdf; Horsfield, Reverend T. W. Horsfield, *The History and Antiquities of Lewes and its Vicinity*, 336; J.D. Parry, J. D., *Historical and Descriptive Account of the Coast of Sussex*, 189.

2. Timothy Webster Jr.'s year of birth has often been reported as 1821; however, Timothy's sister Esther listed his birth date as March 12, 1822, in a family record book. Where Esther, who wasn't born until 1824, received her information is unknown, but the record of Timothy's baptism on April 7, 1822, at the Church of England church St. Michael seems to confirm her record. Baptisms in the Parish of Newhaven in the County of Sussex in 1822, April 17, Timothy Webster, Parish Records, Newhaven (St. Michael) r1553, East Sussex Record Office; Patricia Goff, *Timothy Webster: The Story of the Civil War Hero and His Family*, 19 and 106–9; Esther Webster Wilgus, *Grandpa and Grandma's Record*.

3. Patricia Goff, *Timothy Webster: The Story of the Civil War Hero and His Family*, 110–12.

4. Ibid., 19 and 112–13; Paul S. Boyer, *The Oxford Companion to United States History*, 87; "Immigration to the United States," eh.net/encyclopedia/article/cohn.immigration.us; 1880 Federal Census for Sacramento, Sacramento County, California: Fannie Frazer and Helen Measure; 1880 Federal Census for New York, New York County, New York: Daniel Webster.

5. Henry W. Farnam and Clive Day (eds.), *Chapters in the History of Social Legislation in the United States to 1860*, 212; Robert Gambee, *Princeton*, 53; Maxine N. Lurie and Marc Mappen (eds.), *Encyclopedia of New Jersey*, 658; "A Brief History of Princeton," http://www.princetonhistory.org/brief_history.cfm.

6. "American Cultural History: 19th Century — : 1820–1829," http://kclibrary.lonestar.edu/19thcentury1820.htm; "American Cultural History: 19th Century — : 1830–1839," http://kclibrary.lonestar.edu/19thcentury1830.htm.

7. Patricia Goff, *Timothy Webster: The Story of the Civil War Hero and His Family*, 13; New Jersey *State Gazette*, October 30, 1841; marriage certificate for Timothy Webster and Charlotte Sprowls, October 23, 1841 (copy), Henry P. H. Bromwell Papers, Illinois History and Lincoln Collection, University of Illinois at Urbana-Champaign, University Library.

8. Patricia Goff, *Timothy Webster: The Story of the Civil War Hero and His Family*, 14; 1850 Federal Census for New York, New York County, New York: Timothy Webster family; 1860 Federal Census for Onarga, Iroquois County, Illinois: Timothy Webster family.

9. Patricia Goff, *Timothy Webster: The Story of the Civil War Hero and His Family*, 12–13.

10. Rodney P. Carlisle and J. Geoffrey Golson (eds.), *Manifest Destiny and the Expansion of America*, 27; Edward Pessen, *Jacksonian America: Society, Personality, and Politics*, 97; William A. Pinkerton and Robert A. Pinkerton, *Timothy Webster: Spy of the Rebellion*, 6.

11. "James K. Polk," www.whitehouse.gov/about/presidents/jamespolk; "The Potato Famine and Irish Immigration to America," www.crf-usa.org/bill-of-rights-in-action/bria-26-2-the-potato-famine-and-irish-immigration-to-america.html; Jerry W. Markham, *A Financial History of the United States*, Vol.

1, 149; William A. Pinkerton and Robert A. Pinkerton, *Timothy Webster: Spy of the Rebellion*, 6.

Chapter 2

1. *Documents of the Board of Councilmen of the City of New York*, Vol. 2, Part 2, Document 45, 12; *New York Times*, December 28, 1855; Robert A. Pinkerton to William A. Pinkerton, May 2, 1907, Records of Pinkerton's National Detective Agency, Timothy Webster's employee record, Administrative file, Box 33, Folder 9, Library of Congress; 1850 Federal Census for New York, New York County, New York: Timothy Webster family.

2. Benson J. Lossing, *History of New York City*, Vol. II, 603 and 605; 1850 Federal Census for New York, New York County, New York.

3. Theodore Ferdinand, introduction for Augustine E. Costello, *Our Police Protectors: A History of the New York Police*, vii; George J. Lankevich, *American Metropolis: A History of New York City*, 84; James F. Richardson, *The New York Police: Colonial Times to 1901*, 49, 64, and 68.

4. Jeffrey A. Kroessler, *New York, Year By Year: A Chronology of the Great Metropolis*, 98; Pryce Lewis and David E. Cronin, "Memoirs of Pryce Lewis as Told to Major David E. Cronin in 1888" (unpublished), 45, Pryce Lewis Collection, Box 5, Folder 2, St. Lawrence University Archives, Owen D. Young Library; William A. Pinkerton and Robert A. Pinkerton, *Timothy Webster: Spy of the Rebellion*, 6.

5. James F. Richardson, *The New York Police: Colonial Times to 1901*, 64.

6. John Hannavy, *Encyclopedia of Nineteenth-century Photography*, Vol. 1, 617.

7. Mark Twain, and Albert Bigelow Paine (ed.), *Mark Twain's Letters*, Vol. 1, 21.

8. William A. Pinkerton and Robert A. Pinkerton, *Timothy Webster: Spy of the Rebellion*, 6.

9. Jeffrey A. Kroessler, *New York, Year By Year: A Chronology of the Great Metropolis*, 92; Stephen E. Maizlish, "The Meaning of Nativism and the Crisis of the Union: The Know-Nothing Movement in the Antebellum North," *Essays on American Politics, 1840–1860*, 166–67; "Know-Nothing Party," http://ohiohistorycentral.org/entry.php?rec=911; "Know-Nothing Party," http://www.britannica.com/EBchecked/topic/320530/Know-Nothing-party.

10. *Documents of the Board of Councilmen of the City of New York*, Vol. 2, Part 2, Document 45, 3 and 6; James F. Richardson, *The New York Police: Colonial Times to 1901*, 70–71; New York *Times*, April 20, 24, and 25, 1855.

11. New York *Times*, April 20, 1855.

12. Ibid., November 27, 1855.

13. New York *Herald*, May 3, 1855. The wording of the testimony differed slightly in the *Times* report but was in substance the same.

14. New York *Times*, May 21, 1855.

15. Ibid., July 2, 1855.

16. *Documents of the Board of Councilmen of the City of New York*, Vol. 2, Part 2, Document 45, 19, 45, 56, 137, and 141.

17. New York *Times*, September 8, 1855.

18. Ibid.

19. New York *Times*, September 8 and 11, 1855; New York *Tribune*, September 14, 1855.

20. New York *Herald*, September 8, 1855; New York *Times*, September 8, 1855. The wording of the testimony varies slightly from paper to paper. In instances where the testimony did not match word for word, the author made a judgment call on which wording to use.

21. New York *Herald*, September 11, 1855; New York *Times*, September 11 and October 26, 1855.

22. James F. Richardson, *The New York Police: Colonial Times to 1901*, 72; New York *Times*, January 21 and March 24, 1856.

23. New York *Times*, December 28, 1855.

Chapter 3

1. James D. Horan, *The Pinkertons: The Detective Dynasty That Made History*, 33; James MacKay, *Allan Pinkerton: The First Private Eye*, 70; Frank Morn, *The Eye That Never Sleeps: A History of the Pinkerton National Detective Agency*, 25; Robert P. Weiss, "Private Detective Agencies and Labour Discipline in the United States, 1855–1946," *The Historical Journal*, 1 March 1986, Vol. 21, 88–89.

2. James D. Horan, *The Pinkertons: The Detective Dynasty That Made History*, 5–6, 10–13, 15–19, 23, 38, and 56; James Mackay, *Allan Pinkerton: The First Private Eye*, 15, 17–18, 28, 48–49, 54, 58–62, 64–65, and 68; Frank Morn, *The Eye That Never Sleeps: A History of the Pinkerton National Detective Agency*, 22–23; "The People's Charter — Representation of the People Act," www.bl.uk/learning/

histcitizen/21cc/utopia/methods1/charter1/
charter.html.

3. http://www.censusrecords.net/cities/
chicago_census.htm.

4. Patricia Goff, *Timothy Webster: The
Story of the Civil War Hero and His Family*, 16;
1860 Federal Census for Onarga, Iroquois
County, Illinois: Timothy Webster family;
1860 Federal Census for Onarga, Iroquois
County, Illinois: Persons who died during the
year ending 1st June, 1860: Timothy Webster,
Sr.

5. John Dowling, *History of Iroquois
County*, 16; www.citytowninfo.com/places/
illinois/onarga.

6. Allan Pinkerton, *Claude Melnotte as a
Detective, and Other Stories*, 235, 246, 247,
255–57, and 260; Sheboygan *Journal*, December 24, 1861.

7. Allan Pinkerton, *Claude Melnotte as a
Detective, and Other Stories*, 254.

8. New York *Times*, September 15, 1883.

9. Alfred Theodore Andreas, *History of
Chicago*, Vol. 1, 534; Allan Pinkerton, *Claude
Melnotte as a Detective, and Other Stories*,
254–55; http://www.agbecker.us/RKSwift.
php.

10. Allan Pinkerton, *Claude Melnotte as a
Detective, and Other Stories*, 255–57.

11. Ibid., 258–59.

12. Ibid., 258–66.

13. Sheboygan *Journal*, December 24, 1861.

14. Henry M. Flint, *The Railroads of the
United States: Their History and Statistics*, 271
and 275; Jennifer Luff, "Surrogate Supervisors:
Railway Spotters and the Origins of Workplace
Surveillance," Duke University Press abstract,
http://labor.dukejournals.org/cgi/content/
abstract/5/1/47; Frank Morn, *The Eye That
Never Sleeps: A History of the Pinkerton
National Detective Agency*, 25; William J. Tenney (ed.), *The Mining Magazine*, Vol. 7, 383.

15. Timothy Webster's casebook, September 11–20, 1857, Timothy Webster casebook
and field reports, Administrative File, Records
of Pinkerton's National Detective Agency, Box
25, Folder 4, Library of Congress.

Chapter 4

1. "An Act for Regulating Schools of
Anatomy, Print, England, 1832," www.
sciencemuseum.org.uk/broughttolife/
objects/display.aspx?id=6870; Brian Bailey,
Burke and Hare: The Year of the Ghouls, 13–

14, 26, and 161; Michael Sappol, *A Traffic of
Dead Bodies*, 2–3.

2. Chicago *Daily Times*, November 8,
1857; Chicago *Tribune*, November 9, 1857.

3. Ibid.

4. Alfred Theodore Andreas, *History of
Chicago*, Vol. 1, 185; Chicago *Tribune*, November 9, 1857; Allan Pinkerton to Russell Green,
December 14, 1857, Chicago City Proceedings
Files, 1833–1871, File 0303A, Illinois Regional
Archives Depository, Ronald Williams Library,
Northwestern University; Ordinance describing city sexton's duties, http://hiddentruths.
northwestern.edu/sexton/sexton_ord.html.

5. Ibid.; Allan Pinkerton, *Criminal Reminiscences and Detective Sketches*, 77 and 79;
Chicago *Daily Times*, November 12, 1857.

6. Allan Pinkerton to Russell Green, December 14, 1857, Chicago City Proceedings
Files, 1833–1871, File 0303A, Illinois Regional
Archives Depository, Ronald Williams Library,
Northwestern University.

7. Allan Pinkerton to Russell Green, December 14, 1857, Chicago City Proceedings
Files, 1833–1871, File 0303A, Illinois Regional
Archives Depository, Ronald Williams Library,
Northwestern University.

8. Allan Pinkerton, *Criminal Reminiscences and Detective Sketches*, 77.

9. Allan Pinkerton to Russell Green, December 14, 1857, Chicago City Proceedings
Files, 1833–1871, File 0303A, Illinois Regional
Archives Depository, Ronald Williams Library,
Northwestern University.

10. Allan Pinkerton, *Criminal Reminiscences and Detective Sketches*, 78.

11. Ibid., 79–80.

12. Ibid., 80–82.

13. Ibid., 82–84.

14. Ibid., 84–85.

15. Ibid., 85–87.

16. Allan Pinkerton to Russell Green, December 14, 1857, Chicago City Proceedings
Files, 1833–1871, File 0303A, Illinois Regional
Archives Depository, Ronald Williams Library,
Northwestern University.

17. Ibid., Chicago *Daily Times*, November
8 and 12, 1857; Chicago *Tribune*, November
9, 1857.

18. Chicago *Daily Times*, November 8,
1857.

19. Ibid., November 8 and 12, 1857; Leslie
B. Arey, *Northwestern University Medical
School, 1859–1959: A Pioneer in Educational
Reform*, 30; Weston A. Goodspeed and Daniel
D. Healy (eds.), *History of Cook County, Illi-*

nois, Vol. 2, 236; Chicago *Tribune*, November 9, 1857; Allan Pinkerton to Russell Green, December 14, 1857, Chicago City Proceedings Files, 1833–1871, File 0303A, Illinois Regional Archives Depository, Ronald Williams Library, Northwestern University.

20. Chicago *Daily Times*, November 22, 1857.

21. James Mackay, *Allan Pinkerton: The First Private Eye*, 70.

22. Chicago *Tribune*, January 12, 1858.

23. John J. Mulheron (ed.), *The Medical Age*, Vol. 2, 39.

Chapter 5

1. 1860 Federal Census for Onarga, Iroquois County, Illinois: Timothy Webster family.

2. Harry E. Downer (ed.), *History of Davenport and Scott County Iowa*, Vol. 1, 339; "James Buchanan," www.whitehouse.gov/about/presidents/jamesbuchanan; Richard M. Ketchum (ed.) and Bruce Catton, *The American Heritage Picture History of the Civil War*, 11; Angus Konstam (ed.), *The American Civil War: A Visual Encyclopedia*, 266.

3. *The Annals of the State Historical Society of Iowa*, 152; Curtis C. Roseman, "History of First Railroad Bridge Across the Mississippi River," http://www.riveraction.org/node/121.

4. Adam Arenson, *The Great Heart of the Republic: St. Louis and the Cultural Civil War*, 3–4; James W. Ely, Jr., "Lincoln and the Rock Island Bridge Case," http://www.indianahistory.org/ihs_press/web_publications/railroad05/Ely1.pdf; David A. Pfeiffer, "Bridging the Mississippi: The Railroad and Steamboats Crash at the Rock Island Bridge," *Prologue*, Summer 2004, Vol. 36, No. 2, http://www.archives.gov/publications/prologue/2004/summer/bridge.html; Benedict K. Zobrist, "Steamboat Men Versus Railroad Men: The First Bridging of the Mississippi River," *Missouri Historical Review*, Vol. 59, No. 2, 161–62 and 166–67.

5. Rock Island *Argus*, April 4, 1860.

6. James W. Ely, Jr., "Lincoln and the Rock Island Bridge Case," http://www.indianahistory.org/ihs_press/web_publications/railroad05/Ely1.pdf; Louis C. Hunter, *Steamboats on the Western Rivers: An Economic and Technological History*, 37; David A. Pfeiffer, "Bridging the Mississippi: The Railroad and Steamboats Crash at the Rock Island Bridge," *Prologu*, Summer 2004, Vol. 36, No. 2, http://www.archives.gov/publications/prologue/2004/summer/bridge.html; James Neal Primm, *Lion of the Valley: St. Louis, Missouri, 1764–1980*, 279; Curtis C. Roseman, "History of First Railroad Bridge Across the Mississippi River," http://www.riveraction.org/node/28; Walter B. Stevens, *St. Louis: The Fourth City, 1764–1911*, Vol. 1, 261; Benedict K. Zobrist, "Steamboat Men Versus Railroad Men: The First Bridging of the Mississippi River," *Missouri Historical Review*, Vol. 59, No. 2, 162.

7. James W. Ely, Jr., "Lincoln and the Rock Island Bridge Case," http://www.indianahistory.org/ihs_press/web_publications/railroad05/Ely1.pdf; Jenry Morsman, "Collision of Interests: The *Effie Afton*, the Rock Island Bridge, and the Making of America," http://www.common-place.org/vol-06/no-04/morsman/; Larry A. Riney, *Hell Gate of the Mississippi: The Effie Afton Trial and Abraham Lincoln's Role in It*, 11; Grant Veeder, "Bridge at Davenport: Abraham Lincoln and the Case of the First Mississippi River Bridge," http://www.iowalincoln200.org/iowa_facts_copy%281%29.htm.

8. Herbert David Donald, *Lincoln*, 157; James W. Ely, Jr., "Lincoln and the Rock Island Bridge Case," http://www.indianahistory.org/ihs_press/web_publications/railroad05/Ely1.pdf; Jenry Morsman, "Collision of Interests: The *Effie Afton*, the Rock Island Bridge, and the Making of America," http://www.common-place.org/vol-06/no-04/morsman/; Stephen B. Oates, *With Malice Toward None: A Life of Abraham Lincoln*, 136; David A. Pfeiffer, "Bridging the Mississippi: The Railroad and Steamboats Crash at the Rock Island Bridge," *Prologue*, Summer 2004, Vol. 36, No. 2, http://www.archives.gov/publications/prologue/2004/summer/bridge.html; Larry A. Riney, *Hell Gate of the Mississippi: The Effie Afton Trial and Abraham Lincoln's Role in It*, 209.

9. Harry E. Downer (ed.), *History of Davenport and Scott County Iowa*, Vol. 1, 340; Benedict K. Zobrist, "Steamboat Men Versus Railroad Men: The First Bridging of the Mississippi River," *Missouri Historical Review*, January 1965, Vol. 59, No. 2, 171; Burlington *Weekly Hawk-Eye*, May 10, 1862; Chicago *Tribune*, December 12, 1860.

10. Harry E. Downer (ed.), *History of Davenport and Scott County Iowa*, Vol. 1, 340; Burlington *Weekly Hawk-Eye*, May 10, 1862;

Chicago *Tribune*, August 9 and December 12, 1860.

11. James D. Horan, *The Pinkertons: The Detective Dynasty That Made History*, 36 and 50.

12. 1860 Federal Census for Davenport, Scott County, Iowa.

13. Burlington *Weekly Hawk-Eye*, May 10, 1862.

14. Patricia Goff, *Timothy Webster: The Story of the Civil War Hero and His Family*, 106; 1860 Federal Census for Onarga, Iroquois County, Illinois: Persons who died during the year ending 1st June, 1860: Timothy Webster, Sr.

15. Harry E. Downer (ed.), *History of Davenport and Scott County Iowa*, Vol. 1, 340.

16. Alfred Theodore Andreas, *History of Chicago*, Vol. 2, 458; Downer, Harry E. Downer (ed.), *History of Davenport and Scott County, Iowa*, Vol. 1, 339; *Daily Democrat and News* (Davenport), December 17, 1860.

17. Chicago *Tribune*, August 9 and December 13, 1860; *Daily Democrat and News* (Davenport), December 17, 1860.

18. Chicago *Tribune*, August 9, 1860; *Daily Democrat and News* (Davenport), December 17, 1860.

19. Partners in Walker, Van Arman, and Dexter were James M. Walker, John Van Arman, and Wirt Dexter. *The American Almanac and Repository of Useful Knowledge for the Year 1859*, 324; Andreas, Alfred Theodore Andreas, *History of Chicago*, Vol. 2, 468; Baldwin, Elmer Baldwin, *History of La Salle County, Illinois*, 245–46; *The Chronicle*, Vol. 21, September 1880–June 1881, 122; Goodspeed, Weston A. Goodspeed (ed.), and Daniel D. Healy (eds.), *History of Cook County, Illinois*, Vol. 2, 207; Wilkie, F. B. Wilkie, *Sketches and Notices of the Chicago Bar; Including the More Prominent Lawyers and Judges of the City and Suburban Towns*, 22; Chicago *Tribune*, December 12, 1860.

20. Chicago *Tribune*, December 12, 1860, and February 11, 1864.

21. Ibid.; *Daily Democrat and News* (Davenport), December 14, 1860.

22. Rowan, Richard Wilmer Rowan, *The Pinkertons: A Detective Dynasty*, 25; Chicago *Tribune*, December 12, 1860.

23. Chicago *Tribune*, December 12, 1860.

24. Ibid.

25. Ibid.

26. Ibid., December 13, 1860.

27. Ibid.; *Daily Democrat and News* (Davenport), December 17, 1860.

28. Chicago *Tribune*, December 13, 1860; *Daily Democrat and News* (Davenport), December 17, 1860.

29. *Daily Democrat and News* (Davenport), December 17, 1860.

30. Ibid.; Andreas, Alfred Theodore Andreas, *History of Chicago*, Vol. 2, 150.

31. *Daily Democrat and News* (Davenport), December 17, 1860.

32. Downer, Harry E. Downer, *History of Davenport and Scott County, Iowa*, Vol. 1, 340; Chicago *Tribune*, December 18, 1860; New York *Times*, December 18, 1860.

33. Chicago *Tribune*, February 11, 1864.

34. Ibid.

Chapter 6

1. Ketchum, Richard M.Richard M. Ketchum (ed.), and Bruce Catton, *The American Heritage Picture History of the Civil War*, 11; Konstam, Angus Konstam (ed.), *The American Civil War: A Visual Encyclopedia*, 266.

2. Ketchum, Richard M.Richard M. Ketchum (ed.), and Bruce Catton, *The American Heritage Picture History of the Civil War*, 12; Mackay, James Mackay, *Allan Pinkerton: The First Private Eye*, 85; Oates, Stephen B. Oates, *To Purge This Land with Blood: A Biography of John Brown*, 212, 265, and 292–93.

3. John Brown Papers, 1842–1910, Chicago Historical Society, Chicago, Illinois.

4. Oates, Stephen B. Oates, *To Purge This Land with Blood: A Biography of John Brown*, 320.

5. Ketchum, Richard M.Richard M. Ketchum (ed.), and Bruce Catton, *The American Heritage Picture History of the Civil War*, 46; Oates, Stephen B. Oates, *To Purge This Land with Blood: A Biography of John Brown*, 310.

6. *The National Cyclopedia of American Biography*, Vol. II, 67; Ketchum, Richard M.Richard M. Ketchum (ed.), and Bruce Catton, *The American Heritage Picture History of the Civil War*, 48; Konstam, Angus Konstam (ed.), *The American Civil War: A Visual Encyclopedia*, 158.

7. Ketchum, Richard M.Richard M. Ketchum (ed.), and Bruce Catton, *The American Heritage Picture History of the Civil War*, 50; Konstam, Angus Konstam (ed.), *The American Civil War: A Visual Encyclopedia*, 136 and 439.

8. Cuthbert, Norma B. Cuthbert (ed.),

Lincoln and the Baltimore Plot, 1861: From Pinkerton Records and Related Papers, 3; Horan, James D. Horan, *The Pinkertons: The Detective Dynasty That Made History*, 52–53; Horan, James D. Horan, and Howard Swiggett, *The Pinkerton Story*, 81; Mackay, James Mackay, *Allan Pinkerton: The First Private Eye*, 97.

9. Cuthbert, Norma B. Norma B. (Cuthbert (ed.), *Lincoln and the Baltimore Plot, 1861: From Pinkerton Records and Related Papers*, 24. The Pinkerton Record book of 1861 was destroyed in the Great Chicago Fire of 1871. However, it was copied in 1866 for William Henry Herndon. Norma Cuthbert published transcriptions of these copies in *Lincoln and the Baltimore Plot*, which is used here in combination with the Herndon-Weik Collection of Lincolniana (with direct quotes coming from Herndon's papers because it is one generation closer to the original reports than Cuthbert's book), from the Huntington Library, San Marino, CA.

10. Cuthbert, Norma B. Norma B. (Cuthbert (ed.), *Lincoln and the Baltimore Plot, 1861: From Pinkerton Records and Related Papers*, 26, 28, 32, 40, 45, and 50; Horan, James D. Horan, and Howard Swiggett, *The Pinkerton Story*, 82; Allan Pinkerton, *History and Evidence of the Passage of Abraham Lincoln from Harrisburg, Pa., to Washington, D.C., on the Twenty-Second and Twenty-Third of February, Eighteen Hundred and Sixty-One*, 9–10. Cuthbert lists the possible operatives who may have been Charles D.C. Williams as Scully, Pryce Lewis, or Samuel Bridgman. Scully, however, would soon be operating in Baltimore using his own name, so it is doubtful he had previously worked in the city under an alias, and Lewis was working on another case in Jackson, Tennessee, at the time, according to: Lewis, Pryce and David E. Cronin in, *Memoirs of Pryce Lewis as Told to Major David E. Cronin in 1888* "Memoirs of Pryce Lewis as Told to Major David E. Cronin in 1888" (unpublished), 2, Pryce Lewis Collection, Box 5, Folder 2; G. H. Bangs to Pryce Lewis, February 18, 1861, Pryce Lewis Collection, Box 2, Folder 1, St. Lawrence University Archives, Owen D. Young Library.

11. Allan Pinkerton to Joseph B. Beale, October 26, 1882, author's collection.

12. Charles W. Mitchell, Charles W., *Maryland Voices of the Civil War*, 483; Allan Pinkerton, to William Herndon, August 5 and 23, 1866, Allan Pinkerton's report, February 15 and 21, 1861, as quoted in Cuthbert, Norma

B. Norma B. (Cuthbert (ed.), *Lincoln and the Baltimore Plot, 1861: From Pinkerton Records and Related Papers*, 2, 5, 32, and 76.

13. Allan Pinkerton, Allan report, February 15, 1861, Herndon-Weik Collection of Lincolniana, LN 2408, Vol. 3, the Huntington Library.

14. Long, Christopher Long, "Knights of the Golden Circle," http://www.tshaonline.org/handbook/online/articles/KK/vbk1.html.

15. Allan Pinkerton, Allan report, February 15, 1861, Herndon-Weik Collection of Lincolniana, LN 2408, Vol. 3, the Huntington Library.

16. 1850 Federal Census for Baltimore, Baltimore County, Maryland: Cipriano Ferrandini; Death Certificate for Cipriano Ferrandini, December 20, 1910, Maryland State Archives, http://www.msa.md.gov/megafile/msa/speccol/sc3500/sc3520/014400/014473/html/14473sources.html.

17. William A. Tidwell, William A., *Come Retribution: The Confederate Secret Service and the Assassination of Lincoln*, 229; U.S. Congress, House of Representatives, *Alleged Hostile Organization Against the Government Within the District of Columbia*, 36th Congress, 2d session, Report 79, 133.

18. Allan Pinkerton, Allan report, February 15, 1861, Herndon-Weik Collection of Lincolniana, LN 2408, Vol. 3, the Huntington Library.

19. William A. Tidwell, William A., *Come Retribution: The Confederate Secret Service and the Assassination of Lincoln*, 229.

20. Allan Pinkerton, Allan report, February 15, 1861, Herndon-Weik Collection of Lincolniana, LN 2408, Vol. 3, the Huntington Library.

21. Allan Pinkerton, Allan report, February 15, 1861, Herndon-Weik Collection of Lincolniana, LN 2408, Vol. 3, the Huntington Library; Tidwell, William A. Tidwell, *Come Retribution: The Confederate Secret Service and the Assassination of Lincoln*, 227.

22. Harry Davies, Harry report, February 12 and 19, Herndon-Weik Collection of Lincolniana, LN 2408, Vol. 3, the Huntington Library.

23. U.S. Congress, House of Representatives, *Alleged Hostile Organization Against the Government Within the District of Columbia*, 36th Congress, 2d session, Report 79, 1 and 144.

24. Harry Davies, Harry report, February 12 and 19, Herndon-Weik Collection of Lin-

colniana, LN 2408, Vol. 3, the Huntington Library.

25. Allan Pinkerton, to William Herndon, August 23, 1866, Herndon-Weik Collection of Lincolniana, LN 2408, Vol. 3, the Huntington Library.

26. Timothy Webster, Timothy report, February 17, Herndon-Weik Collection of Lincolniana, LN 2408, Vol. 3, the Huntington Library.

27. Lamon, Ward H. Lamon, *The Life of Abraham Lincoln: From His Birth to His Inauguration as President*, 505 and 508–10.

28. Mackay, James Mackay, *Allan Pinkerton: The First Private Eye*, 96 and 99–100; Warne, Kate Warne, report, February 19, 1861, as quoted in Cuthbert, Norma B. Norma B. (Cuthbert (ed.), *Lincoln and the Baltimore Plot, 1861: From Pinkerton Records and Related Papers*, 41.

29. Allan Pinkerton, Allan report, February 21, 1861, as quoted in Cuthbert, Norma B. Norma B. (Cuthbert (ed.), *Lincoln and the Baltimore Plot, 1861: From Pinkerton Records and Related Papers*, 52 and 58.

30. Pinkerton, Allan reportAllan Pinkerton, report, February 21, 1861, Herndon-Weik Collection of Lincolniana, LN 2408, Vol. 3, the Huntington Library.

31. Lamon, Ward H. Lamon, *The Life of Abraham Lincoln; : From His Birth to His Inauguration as President*, 520; Pinkerton, Allan reportAllan Pinkerton, report, February 21, 1861, as quoted in Cuthbert, Norma B. Norma B. (Cuthbert (ed.), *Lincoln and the Baltimore Plot, 1861: From Pinkerton Records and Related Papers*, 65–67; S. M. Felton's January 17, 1866, statement, "Lincoln's Secret Journey to Washington in 1861," Abraham Lincoln Presidential Library.

32. Pinkerton, Allan reportAllan Pinkerton, report, February 22, 1861, as quoted in Cuthbert, Norma B. Norma B. (Cuthbert (ed.), *Lincoln and the Baltimore Plot, 1861: From Pinkerton Records and Related Papers*, 69 and 74; Mackay, James Mackay, *Allan Pinkerton: The First Private Eye*, 101; Wilson, William Bender Wilson, *History of the Pennsylvania Railroad Company with Plan of Organization, : Portraits of Officials and Biographical Sketches*, Vol. II, 271.

33. Horan, James D. Horan, and Howard Swiggett, *The Pinkerton Story*, 85–86; Mackay, James Mackay, *Allan Pinkerton: The First Private Eye*, 101; Allan Pinkerton, *History and Evidence of the Passage of Abraham Lincoln from Harrisburg, Pa., to Washington, D.C., on the Twenty-Second and Twenty-Third of February, Eighteen Hundred and Sixty-One*, 20–21.

34. Horan, James D. Horan, and Howard Swiggett, *The Pinkerton Story*, 86; Mackay, James Mackay, *Allan Pinkerton: The First Private Eye*, 74; Pinkerton, Allan reportAllan Pinkerton, report, February 22, 1861, Herndon-Weik Collection of Lincolniana, LN 2408, Vol. 3, the Huntington Library; Rowan, Richard Wilmer Rowan, *The Pinkertons: A Detective Dynasty*, 105.

35. Warne, Kate Warne, report, February 22, 1861, Herndon-Weik Collection of Lincolniana, LN 2408, Vol. 3, the Huntington Library.

36. Mearns, David C. Mearns, *The Lincoln Papers: The Story of the Collection with Selections to July 4, 1861*, 580; Pinkerton, Allan reportAllan Pinkerton, report, February 23, 1861, Herndon-Weik Collection of Lincolniana, LN 2408, Vol. 3, the Huntington Library.

37. Horan, James D. Horan, *The Pinkertons: The Detective Dynasty That Made History*, 54 and 56; Hatch, Frederick Hatch, *Protecting President Lincoln*, 15.

Chapter 7

1. Pinkerton, Allan reportAllan Pinkerton, report, February 23, 1861, Herndon-Weik Collection of Lincolniana, LN 2408, Vol. 3, the Huntington Library.

2. George W. Walling, *Recollections of a New York Chief of Police*, 69; Williams, Charles Williams, report, February 20, 1861, as quoted in Cuthbert, Norma B. Norma B. (Cuthbert (ed.), *Lincoln and the Baltimore Plot, 1861: From Pinkerton Records and Related Papers*, 49.

3. Williams, Charles Williams, report, February 20, 1861, Herndon-Weik Collection of Lincolniana, LN 2408, Vol. 3, the Huntington Library.

4. Pinkerton, Allan reportAllan Pinkerton, report, February 25, 1861, Herndon-Weik Collection of Lincolniana, LN 2408, Vol. 3, the Huntington Library.

5. George W. Walling, *Recollections of a New York Chief of Police*, 69 and 71.

6. Ibid., 71; New York *Times*, April 20, 1901; *The Weekly News-Review*, April 26, 1901.

7. George W. Walling, *Recollections of a New York Chief of Police*, 71–72.

8. Ibid., 72.

9. Ibid., 72–73.

10. Ibid., 73–74.

11. Ibid., 74.

12. Ibid., 74–75.

13. Ibid., 75–77.

14. Pinkerton, Allan reportAllan Pinkerton, report, February 26, 1861, Herndon-Weik Collection of Lincolniana, LN 2408, Vol. 3, the Huntington Library.

15. Webster, Timothy Webster, report, February 26, 1861, Herndon-Weik Collection of Lincolniana, LN 2408, Vol. 3, the Huntington Library.

16. Webster, Timothy Webster, report, February 26, 1861, Herndon-Weik Collection of Lincolniana, LN 2408, Vol. 3, the Huntington Library.

17. Scharf, J. Thomas Scharf, *History of Baltimore City and County from the Earliest Period to the Present Day*, 139.

18. Webster, Timothy Webster, report, February 26, 1861, Herndon-Weik Collection of Lincolniana, LN 2408, Vol. 3, the Huntington Library.

Chapter 8

1. Ketchum, Richard M.Richard M. Ketchum (ed.), and Bruce Catton, *The American Heritage Picture History of the Civil War*, 59–60; Konstam, Angus Konstam (ed.), *The American Civil War: A Visual Encyclopedia*, 108, 151, and 200; Abraham Lincoln's inaugural address, March 4, 1861, www.loc.gov/exhibits/treasures/trt039.html.

2. Allan Pinkerton to Abraham Lincoln, April 21, 1861, Abraham Lincoln Papers, General Correspondence, Library of Congress.

3. Allan Pinkerton, *The Spy of the Rebellion*, 110–12.

4. N. B. Judd to Abraham Lincoln, April 21, 1861, Abraham Lincoln Papers, General Correspondence, Library of Congress.

5. Heidler, David S. Heidler, and Jeanne T. Heidler, *Encyclopedia of the American Civil War: A Political, Social, and Military History*, Vol. 4, 1526; Horan, James D. Horan, *The Pinkertons: The Detective Dynasty That Made History*, 64; Jones, Terry L. Jones, *The A to Z of the Civil War*, Vol. 2, 864; Mackay, James Mackay, *Allan Pinkerton: The First Private Eye*, 108–9; Oates, Stephen B. Oates, *With Malice Toward None: A Life of Abraham Lincoln*, 258.

6. Mackay, James Mackay, *Allan Pinkerton: The First Private Eye*, 110.

7. Allan Pinkerton, *The Spy of the Rebellion*, 143–45.

8. McClellan, George B. McClellan to Winfield Scott, April 23 and 27, 1861, as quoted in Sears, Stephen W. Sears (ed.), *The Civil War Papers of George B. McClellan: Selected Correspondence, 1860–1865*, 7–9 and 12–13; Allan Pinkerton, *The Spy of the Rebellion*, 155; Sears, Stephen W., *George B. McClellan: The Young Napoleon*, 75 and 77.

9. Allan Pinkerton, *The Spy of the Rebellion*, 155.

10. Allan Pinkerton, *The Spy of the Rebellion*, 155; Pinkerton account book, 1861–62, page 70, Records of Pinkerton's National Detective Agency, Box 1, Folder 1, Library of Congress.

11. Allan Pinkerton to Joseph B. Beale, October 26, 1882, author's collection.

12. Pinkerton account book, 1861–62, page 70, Records of Pinkerton's National Detective Agency, Box 1, Folder 1, Library of Congress.

13. Allan Pinkerton, *The Spy of the Rebellion*, 157–59.

14. Ibid., 168.

15. Ibid., 160–66.

16. Ibid., 173–75.

17. Ibid., 160 and 175.

18. Ibid., 176–80.

19. Ibid., 180–81.

20. Timothy Webster's Report, July 23–25, 1861, Timothy Webster casebook and field reports, Records of Pinkerton's National Detective Agency, Administrative File, Box 25, Folder 4, Library of Congress.

21. Angus Konstam, Angus (ed.), *The American Civil War: A Visual Encyclopedia*, 297; "History of Memphis," http://www.memphistn.gov/framework.aspx?page=296; www.census.gov/population/www/documentation/twps0027/tab09.txt.

22. Wright, Marcus J. Wright, *Tennessee in the War, 1861–1865*, 15; Timothy Webster's Report, July 26, 1861, Timothy Webster casebook and field reports, Records of Pinkerton's National Detective Agency, Administrative File, Box 25, Folder 4, Library of Congress.

23. Cutrer, Thomas W. Cutrer, *Ben McCulloch and the Frontier Military Tradition*, 220; Polk, William M., Polk, *Leonidas Polk: Bishop and General*, Vol. 2, 6–7; Timothy Webster's Report, July 27, 1861, Timothy Webster casebook and field reports, Records of Pinkerton's National Detective Agency, Administrative File, Box 25, Folder 4, Library of Congress.

24. Timothy Webster's Report, July 28–29, 1861, Timothy Webster casebook and field reports, Records of Pinkerton's National Detective Agency, Administrative File, Box 25, Folder 4, Library of Congress.

25. Ibid., July 30–31 and August 1, 1861; Stevens, Walter B. Stevens, *Missouri: The Center State, 1821–1915*, Vol. 1, 240.

26. Timothy Webster's Report, August 2–7, 1861, Timothy Webster casebook and field reports, Records of Pinkerton's National Detective Agency, Administrative File, Box 25, Folder 4, Library of Congress.

27. McClellan, George B. McClellan to Mary Ellen McClellan, July 27, 1861, and George B. McClellan to Winfield Scott, August 8, 1861, as quoted in Sears, Stephen W. (ed.), *The Civil War Papers of George B. McClellan: Selected Correspondence, 1860–1865*, 70 and 79–80; Sears, Stephen W., *George B. McClellan: The Young Napoleon*, 98–100 and 102–03.

28. Fishel, Edwin C. Fishel, *The Secret War for the Union: The Untold Story of Military Intelligence in the Civil War*, 89 and 91.

29. Morn, Frank Morn, *The Eye That Never Sleeps: A History of the Pinkerton National Detective Agency*, 45.

30. Fishel, Edwin C. Fishel, "Pinkerton and McClellan: Who Deceived Whom?" *Civil War History*, noNo. 2 (June 1988): 119.

31. Ibid., 117.

Chapter 9

1. Konstam, Angus Konstam (ed.), *The American Civil War: A Visual Encyclopedia*, 31, 78, and 292; McClellan, George B. to Simon Cameron, September 8, 1861, as quoted in Sears, Stephen W. (ed.), *The Civil War Papers of George B. McClellan: Selected Correspondence, 1860–1865*, 95–96; Rowan, Richard Wilmer, *The Pinkertons: A Detective Dynasty*, 136; Sears, Stephen W., *George B. McClellan: The Young Napoleon*, 95–97 and 101.

2. Allan Pinkerton, *The Spy of the Rebellion*, 272.

3. Sears, Stephen W., *George B. McClellan: The Young Napoleon*, 98–99.

4. Pinkerton account book, 1861–62, page 70, Records of Pinkerton's National Detective Agency, Box 1, Folder 1, Library of Congress.

5. Allan Pinkerton, *The Spy of the Rebellion*, 272–73.

6. Timothy Webster's Report, August 22–

23, 1861, Timothy Webster casebook and field reports, Records of Pinkerton's National Detective Agency, Administrative File, Box 25, Folder 4, Library of Congress.

7. Ibid., August 23, 1861.

8. Ibid.

9. Allan Pinkerton, *The Spy of the Rebellion*, 273.

10. Allan Pinkerton, *The Spy of the Rebellion*, 274.

11. Ibid., 277, 279, and 282.

12. Allan Pinkerton, *The Spy of the Rebellion*, 283–85.

13. Ibid., 286–91, 294, and 299–300.

14. Mackay, James Mackay, *Allan Pinkerton: The First Private Eye*, 137–38; Scharf, Colonel J. Thomas Scharf, *The Chronicles of Baltimore; Being a Complete History of "Baltimore Town" and Baltimore City From the Earliest Period to the Present Time*, 617.

Chapter 10

1. E. J. Allen (Allan Pinkerton) to George B. McClellan, November 15, 1861, George Brinton McClellan Papers, 1823–1898, Library of Congress.

2. Ibid.

3. Ibid.; Allan Pinkerton, *The Spy of the Rebellion*, 309–11.

4. Fishel, Edwin C. Fishel, *The Secret War for the Union: The Untold Story of Military Intelligence in the Civil War*, 89; E. J. Allen (Allan Pinkerton) to George B. McClellan, November 15, 1861, George Brinton McClellan Papers, 1823–1898, Library of Congress.

5. E. J. Allen (Allan Pinkerton) to George B. McClellan, November 15, 1861, George Brinton McClellan Papers, 1823–1898, Library of Congress.

6. Richmond *Dispatch*, October 30, 1861.

7. E. J. Allen (Allan Pinkerton) to George B. McClellan, November 15, 1861, George Brinton McClellan Papers, 1823–1898, Library of Congress.

8. *The City Intelligencer; or, Stranger's Guide* (Richmond City Guide, 1862).

9. Dwyer, John L. Dwyer, "Adult Education in Civil War Richmond, January 1861–April 1865," http://scholar.lib.vt.edu/theses/avail able/etd-524414252972830/unrestricted/CSA. PDF, 3 and 22; Konstam, Angus Konstam (ed.), *The American Civil War: A Visual Encyclopedia*, 378; 1860 Federal Census for Richmond, Henrico County, Virginia.

10. E. J. Allen (Allan Pinkerton) to George B. McClellan, November 15, 1861, George Brinton McClellan Papers, 1823–1898, Library of Congress.

11. Ibid.; Allan Pinkerton, *The Spy of the Rebellion*, 315.

12. Fishel, Edwin C. Fishel, *The Secret War for the Union: The Untold Story of Military Intelligence in the Civil War*, 89–90; E. J. Allen (Allan Pinkerton) to George B. McClellan, November 15, 1861, George Brinton McClellan Papers, 1823–1898, Library of Congress.

13. E. J. Allen (Allan Pinkerton) to George B. McClellan, November 15, 1861, George Brinton McClellan Papers, 1823–1898, Library of Congress.

14. Ibid.; "49th Regiment of Virginia Volunteers," http://49thvirginiainfantry.com/49th%20Va%20History.htm.

15. E. J. Allen (Allan Pinkerton) to George B. McClellan, November 15, 1861, George Brinton McClellan Papers, 1823–1898, Library of Congress.

16. Ibid.; Scheel, Eugene Scheel, "The Reconstruction Years: Tales of Leesburg and Warrenton, Virginia," www.loudounhistory.org/history/loudoun-cw-reconstruction-towns.htm.

17. E. J. Allen (Allan Pinkerton) to George B. McClellan, November 15, 1861, George Brinton McClellan Papers, 1823–1898, Library of Congress.

18. Ibid.

19. Ibid.

20. Ibid.

21. Ibid.

22. Ibid.

23. Ibid.; Quinn, S. J. Quinn, *The History of the City of Fredericksburg, Virginia*, 78.

24. E. J. Allen (Allan Pinkerton) to George B. McClellan, November 15, 1861, George Brinton McClellan Papers, 1823–1898, Library of Congress.

25. Ibid.

26. Ibid.

27. Ibid.; Ainsworth, Fred C. and Joseph W. Kirkley, *The War of the Rebellion: A Compilation of the Official Records of the Union and Confederate Armies*, Series IV4, Vol. I, 630.

28. E. J. Allen (Allan Pinkerton) to George B. McClellan, November 15, 1861, George Brinton McClellan Papers, 1823–1898, Library of Congress.

29. Ibid.

30. Ibid.

31. Lewis, Pryce and David E. Cronin, "Memoirs of Pryce Lewis as Told to Major David E. Cronin in 1888" (unpublished), 55, Pryce Lewis Collection, Box 5, Folder 2, St. Lawrence University Archives, Owen D. Young Library.

Chapter 11

1. Ketchum, Richard M.Richard M. Ketchum (ed.), and Bruce Catton, *The American Heritage Picture History of the Civil War*, 114.

2. Sears, Stephen W. Sears (ed.), *The Civil War Papers of George B. McClellan: Selected Correspondence, 1860–1865*, 120; Sears, Stephen W., *George B. McClellan: The Young Napoleon*, 128–30 and 135–38.

3. Allan Pinkerton, *The Spy of the Rebellion*, 326–29, 332–33; New York *Times*, November 21, 1861

4. Ibid.; Scharf, Colonel J. Thomas Scharf, *The Chronicles of Baltimore; Being a Complete History of "Baltimore Town" and Baltimore City from the Earliest Period to the Present Time*, 620; Scharf, J. Thomas Scharf, *History of Baltimore City and County From the Earliest Period to the Present Day*, 139; New York *Times*, November 21, 1861.

5. New York *Times*, November 21, 1861.

6. Allan Pinkerton, *The Spy of the Rebellion*, 337.

7. Allan Pinkerton, *The Spy of the Rebellion*, 337–38.

8. Lanier, Robert S. Lanier (ed.), *The Photographic History of the Civil War In in Ten Vol.s,s.*, Vol. 7, 200; *The War of the Rebellion: A Compilation of the Official Records of the Union and Confederate Armies*, Series 3, Vol. 2, 937.

9. Allan Pinkerton, *The Spy of the Rebellion*, 338.

10. Ibid., 338–39.

11. Ibid., 339–340.

12. Baltimore *American and Commercial Advertiser*, November 22, 1861; That Joseph H. McGee owned Miller's Hotel comes from Scharf, Colonel J. Thomas, *The Chronicles of Baltimore; Being a Complete History of "Baltimore Town" and Baltimore City from the Earliest Period to the Present Time*, 620.

13. Allan Pinkerton, *The Spy of the Rebellion*, 342.

14. Fishel, Edwin C. Fishel, *The Secret War for the Union: The Untold Story of Military In-*

telligence in the Civil War, 97–98; E. J. Allen (Allan Pinkerton) to George B. McClellan, December 27, 1861.

15. Fishel, Edwin C. Fishel, *The Secret War for the Union: The Untold Story of Military Intelligence in the Civil War*, 97 and 336–37; E. J. Allen (Allan Pinkerton) to George B. McClellan, December 27, 1861, George Brinton McClellan Papers, 1823–1898, Library of Congress..

16. E. J. Allen (Allan Pinkerton) to Andrew Porter, December 12, George Brinton McClellan Papers, 1823–1898, Library of Congress.

17. Washington *Star*, December 11, 1862.

18. E. J. Allen (Allan Pinkerton) to George B. McClellan, January 30 and 31, 1862, George Brinton McClellan Papers, 1823–1898, Library of Congress.

19. Ibid., April 20, 1862.

20. Ibid., January 31 and April 20, 1862.

21. Ibid., January 31, 1862, and April 20, 1862.

22. Ibid., January 30 and 31, 1862.

23. Ibid., January 31, 1862.

24. Ibid.

25. Ibid., January 30 and 31, 1862.

26. Ibid., January 30 and 31, 1862.

27. Ibid., January 31, 1862.

28. Ibid.

Chapter 12

1. 1870 Federal Census for Chicago, Cook County, Illinois: John Scully; 1880 Federal Census for Chicago, Cook County, Illinois: John Scully. John Scully, born in Ireland, is listed as a police officer in 1870, a possible profession for a former Pinkerton detective. Further evidence that this is the former detective is the 1880 census information for the same family. In 1880, Scully is listed as a clerk. Testimony in 1876 confirms that John Scully, the former Pinkerton detective, went to work in the City Collector's office and records from that office show that he was a clerk. *Annual Statement of the Finances of the City of Chicago, From April 1, 1875, to December 31, 1875*, 76; *Index to the Miscellaneous Documents of the House of Representatives for the First Session of the Forty-Fourth Congress*, 414; Pryce Lewis confirms that Scully was a father, in Lewis, Pryce and David E. Cronin, "Memoirs of Pryce Lewis as Told to Major David E. Cronin in 1888" (unpublished), 112, Pryce Lewis Collection, Box 5, Folder 2,

St. Lawrence University Archives, Owen D. Young Library.

2. Shoen, Harriet H. Shoen, "Pryce Lewis: Spy for the Union, The True Story of an Ordinary Man Who Had Extraordinary Experiences" (unpublished), 1–2, Pryce Lewis Collection, Box 4, Folder 4, St. Lawrence University Archives, Owen D. Young Library.

3. Allan Pinkerton, *The Spy of the Rebellion*, 492–94.

4. Lewis, Pryce and David E. Cronin, "Memoirs of Pryce Lewis as Told to Major David E. Cronin in 1888" (unpublished), 53–55, Pryce Lewis Collection, Box 5, Folder 2, St. Lawrence University Archives, Owen D. Young Library.

5. Ibid., 56–57.

6. Ibid., 58; Allan Pinkerton, *The Spy of the Rebellion*, 495.

7. Lewis, Pryce and David E. Cronin, "Memoirs of Pryce Lewis as Told to Major David E. Cronin in 1888" (unpublished), 67, Pryce Lewis Collection, Box 5, Folder 2, St. Lawrence University Archives, Owen D. Young Library; Allan Pinkerton, *The Spy of the Rebellion*, 501; Rowan, Richard Wilmer Rowan, *The Pinkertons: A Detective Dynasty*, 168.

8. Lewis, Pryce and David E. Cronin, "Memoirs of Pryce Lewis as Told to Major David E. Cronin in 1888" (unpublished), 67, Pryce Lewis Collection, Box 5, Folder 2, St. Lawrence University Archives, Owen D. Young Library; Allan Pinkerton, *The Spy of the Rebellion*, 502.

9. Lewis, Pryce and David E. Cronin, "Memoirs of Pryce Lewis as Told to Major David E. Cronin in 1888" (unpublished), 67–68, Pryce Lewis Collection, Box 5, Folder 2, St. Lawrence University Archives, Owen D. Young Library.

10. Fishel, Edwin C. Fishel, *The Secret War for the Union: The Untold Story of Military Intelligence in the Civil War*, 149; Lewis, Pryce, and David E. Cronin, *Memoirs of Pryce Lewis as Told to Major David E. Cronin in 1888* "Memoirs of Pryce Lewis as Told to Major David E. Cronin in 1888" (unpublished), 69, Pryce Lewis Collection, Box 5, Folder 2, St. Lawrence University Archives, Owen D. Young Library; Allan Pinkerton, *The Spy of the Rebellion*, 503.

11. Lewis, Pryce, and David E. Cronin, *Memoirs of Pryce Lewis as Told to Major David E. Cronin in 1888* "Memoirs of Pryce Lewis as Told to Major David E. Cronin in 1888" (un-

published), 69–70, Pryce Lewis Collection, Box 5, Folder 2, St. Lawrence University Archives, Owen D. Young Library.

12. Ibid., 70–71.

13. Ibid., 71.

14. Ibid., 71–72.

15. Allan Pinkerton, *The Spy of the Rebellion*, 505–506.

16. Lewis, Pryce, and David E. Cronin, *Memoirs of Pryce Lewis as Told to Major David E. Cronin in 1888* "Memoirs of Pryce Lewis as Told to Major David E. Cronin in 1888" (unpublished), 72–73, Pryce Lewis Collection, Box 5, Folder 2, St. Lawrence University Archives, Owen D. Young Library.

17. Ibid., 73; Allan Pinkerton, *The Spy of the Rebellion*, 506; Rowan, Richard Wilmer Rowan, *The Pinkertons: A Detective Dynasty*, 172.

18. Allan Pinkerton, *The Spy of the Rebellion*, 301 and 306–307; Tyler, Lyon G. Tyler, *William and Mary College Quarterly Historical Magazine*, Vol. XIII13, 275; *Biographical Directory of the United States Congress:*, "Morton, Jackson, (1794–1874)," http://bioguide.congress.gov/scripts/biodisplay.pl?index=M001015.

19. Lewis, Pryce, and David E. Cronin, *Memoirs of Pryce Lewis as Told to Major David E. Cronin in 1888* "Memoirs of Pryce Lewis as Told to Major David E. Cronin in 1888" (unpublished), 73–74, Pryce Lewis Collection, Box 5, Folder 2, St. Lawrence University Archives, Owen D. Young Library; Allan Pinkerton, *The Spy of the Rebellion*, 506.

20. Lewis, Pryce, and David E. Cronin, *Memoirs of Pryce Lewis as Told to Major David E. Cronin in 1888* "Memoirs of Pryce Lewis as Told to Major David E. Cronin in 1888" (unpublished), 74–75, Pryce Lewis Collection, Box 5, Folder 2, St. Lawrence University Archives, Owen D. Young Library.

21. Ibid., 75.

22. Ibid., 75–76.

23. Ibid., 76–77.

24. Richmond *Dispatch*, March 3, 1861.

25. Lewis, Pryce, and David E. Cronin, *Memoirs of Pryce Lewis as Told to Major David E. Cronin in 1888* "Memoirs of Pryce Lewis as Told to Major David E. Cronin in 1888" (unpublished), 77–78, Pryce Lewis Collection, Box 5, Folder 2, St. Lawrence University Archives, Owen D. Young Library.

26. Ibid., 78.

27. Ibid., 79; E. J. Allen (Allan Pinkerton) to George B. McClellan, April 20, 1862,

George Brinton McClellan Papers, 1823–1898, Library of Congress.

28. Lewis, Pryce, and David E. Cronin, *Memoirs of Pryce Lewis as Told to Major David E. Cronin in 1888* "Memoirs of Pryce Lewis as Told to Major David E. Cronin in 1888" (unpublished), 79, Pryce Lewis Collection, Box 5, Folder 2, St. Lawrence University Archives, Owen D. Young Library.

29. Allan Pinkerton, *The Spy of the Rebellion*, 532–33.

30. Ibid., 510–11; Lewis, Pryce, and David E. Cronin, *Memoirs of Pryce Lewis as Told to Major David E. Cronin in 1888* "Memoirs of Pryce Lewis as Told to Major David E. Cronin in 1888" (unpublished), 80–81, Pryce Lewis Collection, Box 5, Folder 2, St. Lawrence University Archives, Owen D. Young Library.

31. Lewis, Pryce, and David E. Cronin, *Memoirs of Pryce Lewis as Told to Major David E. Cronin in 1888* "Memoirs of Pryce Lewis as Told to Major David E. Cronin in 1888" (unpublished), 84–85, Pryce Lewis Collection, Box 5, Folder 2, St. Lawrence University Archives, Owen D. Young Library.

32. Ibid., 84–87 and 89–90.

33. Ibid., 90–93; Richmond *Dispatch*, March 20, 1862.

34. Lewis, Pryce, and David E. Cronin, *Memoirs of Pryce Lewis as Told to Major David E. Cronin in 1888* "Memoirs of Pryce Lewis as Told to Major David E. Cronin in 1888" (unpublished), 93–96, 100 and 102–103, Pryce Lewis Collection, Box 5, Folder 2, St. Lawrence University Archives, Owen D. Young Library; Richmond *Dispatch*, March 21 and 24, 1862.

35. Lewis, Pryce, and David E. Cronin, *Memoirs of Pryce Lewis as Told to Major David E. Cronin in 1888* "Memoirs of Pryce Lewis as Told to Major David E. Cronin in 1888" (unpublished), 106, Pryce Lewis Collection, Box 5, Folder 2, St. Lawrence University Archives, Owen D. Young Library; Allan Pinkerton, *The Spy of the Rebellion*, 523 and 535.

36. Lewis, Pryce, and David E. Cronin, *Memoirs of Pryce Lewis as Told to Major David E. Cronin in 1888* "Memoirs of Pryce Lewis as Told to Major David E. Cronin in 1888" (unpublished), 106–107, Pryce Lewis Collection, Box 5, Folder 2, St. Lawrence University Archives, Owen D. Young Library.

37. Wagner, Margaret E. Wagner, Gary W. Gallagher, and Paul Finkelman, *The Library of Congress Civil War Desk Reference*, 594;

"Castle Godwin," http://www.mdgorman. com/prisons/castle_godwin.htm.

38. Lewis, Pryce, and David E. Cronin, *Memoirs of Pryce Lewis as Told to Major David E. Cronin in 1888* "Memoirs of Pryce Lewis as Told to Major David E. Cronin in 1888" (unpublished), 108, Pryce Lewis Collection, Box 5, Folder 2, St. Lawrence University Archives, Owen D. Young Library.

39. Ibid., 108–109.

40. Ibid., 109–111.

41. Ibid., 111.

42. Ibid., 112–15; Fogarty, Gerald P. Fogarty, *Commonwealth Catholicism: A History of the Catholic Church in Virginia*, 199.

43. Lewis, Pryce, and David E. Cronin, *Memoirs of Pryce Lewis as Told to Major David E. Cronin in 1888* "Memoirs of Pryce Lewis as Told to Major David E. Cronin in 1888" (unpublished), 115, Pryce Lewis Collection, Box 5, Folder 2, St. Lawrence University Archives, Owen D. Young Library; *Sadlier's Catholic Almanac and Ordo for the Year of Our Lord 1865*, 83.

44. Lewis, Pryce, and David E. Cronin, *Memoirs of Pryce Lewis as Told to Major David E. Cronin in 1888* "Memoirs of Pryce Lewis as Told to Major David E. Cronin in 1888" (unpublished), 115–17, Pryce Lewis Collection, Box 5, Folder 2, St. Lawrence University Archives, Owen D. Young Library.

45. Ibid., 117–18.

46. Ibid., 118–22; Horan, James D. Horan, *The Pinkertons: The Detective Dynasty That Made History*, 107.

47. Lewis, Pryce, and David E. Cronin, *Memoirs of Pryce Lewis as Told to Major David E. Cronin in 1888* "Memoirs of Pryce Lewis as Told to Major David E. Cronin in 1888" (unpublished), 121–22, Pryce Lewis Collection, Box 5, Folder 2, St. Lawrence University Archives, Owen D. Young Library.

48. E. J. Allen (Allan Pinkerton) to George B. McClellan, April 20, 1862, George Brinton McClellan Papers, 1823–1898, Library of Congress.

49. Lewis, Pryce, and David E. Cronin, *Memoirs of Pryce Lewis as Told to Major David E. Cronin in 1888* "Memoirs of Pryce Lewis as Told to Major David E. Cronin in 1888" (unpublished), 122, Pryce Lewis Collection, Box 5, Folder 2, St. Lawrence University Archives, Owen D. Young Library.

50. Allan Pinkerton, *The Spy of the Rebellion*, 533–34.

51. Ibid., 538, and 539–540; Alan Axelrod,

Alan, *The War Between the Spies: A History of Espionage During the American Civil War*, 143.

52. Richmond *Dispatch*, April 4 and 10, 1862.

Chapter 13

1. Lewis, Pryce, and David E. Cronin, *Memoirs of Pryce Lewis as Told to Major David E. Cronin in 1888* "Memoirs of Pryce Lewis as Told to Major David E. Cronin in 1888" (unpublished), 124–26, Pryce Lewis Collection, Box 5, Folder 2, St. Lawrence University Archives, Owen D. Young Library.

2. Ibid., 129–131.

3. Allan Pinkerton, *The Spy of the Rebellion*, 529.

4. Richmond *Dispatch*, April 5, 1862.

5. Lewis, Pryce, and David E. Cronin, *Memoirs of Pryce Lewis as Told to Major David E. Cronin in 1888* "Memoirs of Pryce Lewis as Told to Major David E. Cronin in 1888" (unpublished), 134, Pryce Lewis Collection, Box 5, Folder 2, St. Lawrence University Archives, Owen D. Young Library.

6. Richmond *Dispatch*, April 10, 22, 28, and 30, 1862.

7. Lewis, Pryce, and David E. Cronin, *Memoirs of Pryce Lewis as Told to Major David E. Cronin in 1888* "Memoirs of Pryce Lewis as Told to Major David E. Cronin in 1888" (unpublished), 131–32, Pryce Lewis Collection, Box 5, Folder 2, St. Lawrence University Archives, Owen D. Young Library.

8. Ibid., 134.

9. Ibid., 135.

10. Richmond *Dispatch*, April 30, 1862; Proceedings of Court Martial in the Case of Timothy Webster, Spy, Papers of and Relating to Military and Civilian Personnel, compiled 1874–1899, documenting the period 1861–1865, Record Group 109, Unfiled Papers and Slips Belonging in Confederate Compiled Service Records, M347, National Archives and Records Administration.

11. Allan Pinkerton, *The Spy of the Rebellion*, 544.

12. E. J. Allen (Allan Pinkerton) to George B. McClellan, April 20, 1862, George Brinton McClellan Papers, 1823–1898, Library of Congress.

13. Allan Pinkerton, *The Spy of the Rebellion*, 542 and 546–47. Pinkerton's reports to McClellan confirm that he left the camp at

Yorktown after receiving the news of Webster's arrest.

14. Ibid., 547.

15. Ibid., 547 and 549–550.

16. Ibid., 551.

17. Frosst, George Washington Frosst, "A South Berwick Yankee Behind Confederate Lines," Part 1, Old Berwick Historical Society, http://www.obhs.net/index.php?option=com_content&view=article&id=256&Itemid=266.

18. Fisher, George D. Fisher, *History and Reminiscences of the Monumental Church, Richmond, VA.*, 256; Hanna, J. Marshall Hanna, "Castle Thunder in Bellum Days," *Southern Opinion*, November 3, 1867, 1; "A Memorial. Moses Drury Hoge, D. D., LL. D.," www.mdgorman.com/Written_Accounts/Periodicals/a_memorial_moes_drury_hoge_d_d.htm.

Allan Pinkerton, *The Spy of the Rebellion*, 552–58; Richmond *Dispatch*, April 30, 1862; Richmond *Examiner*, April 30 and May 6, 1862.

Chapter 14

1. Richmond *Examiner*, April 30, 1862.

2. Allan Pinkerton, *The Spy of the Rebellion*, 558–59.

3. Richmond *Examiner*, April 30, 1862.

4. Richmond *Dispatch*, April 30, 1862; Richmond *Enquirer*, May 6, 1862.

5. Richmond *Dispatch*, December 11, 1862.

6. Ibid.

7. Markle, Donald E. Markle, *Spies and Spymasters of the Civil War*, 91–93.

8. Allan Pinkerton to Abraham Lincoln, June 5, 1863, Abraham Lincoln Papers, Library of Congress.

9. Abraham Lincoln Papers at the Library of Congress website, http://cweb2.loc.gov/cgi-bin/query/r?ammem/mal:@field(DOCID+@lit(d2389000)).

10. *Annual Statement of the Finances of the City of Chicago, From April 1, 1875, to December 31, 1875*, 76; *Index to the Miscellaneous Documents of the House of Representatives for the First Session of the Forty-Fourth Congress*, 414; Lewis, Pryce, and David E. Cronin, *Memoirs of Pryce Lewis as Told to Major David E. Cronin in 1888* "Memoirs of Pryce Lewis as Told to Major David E. Cronin in 1888" (unpublished), 112,

Pryce Lewis Collection, Box 5, Folder 2, St. Lawrence University Archives, Owen D. Young Library; Chicago *Tribune*, December 15, 1902; Allan Pinkerton to Abraham Lincoln, June 5, 1863, Abraham Lincoln Papers, Library of Congress; Cook County Coroner's Inquest Records for John Scully, December 15, 1902, Illinois Regional Archives Depository, Ronald Williams Library, Northwestern University; 1870 Federal Census for Chicago, Cook County, Illinois: John Scully; 1880 Federal Census for Chicago, Cook County, Illinois: John Scully; 1910 Federal Census for Chicago, Cook County, Illinois: Julia Scully.

11. Inglis, William Inglis, "A Republic's Gratitude: What Pryce Lewis Did for the United States Government, and How the United States Government Rewarded Him," *Harper's Weekly*, December 30, 1911; New York *Times*, December 10, 1911; 1870 Federal Census for Chicago, Cook County, Illinois: Pryce Lewis; 1900 Federal Census for Jersey City, Hudson County, New Jersey: Pryce Lewis.

12. Jones, Terry L. Jones, *The A to Z of the Civil War*, Vol. 2, 865–66; Konstam, Angus Konstam (ed.), *The American Civil War: A Visual Encyclopedia*, 292, 347, and 443; Oates, Stephen B. Oates, *With Malice Toward None: A Life of Abraham Lincoln*, 304; Rowan, Richard Wilmer Rowan, *The Pinkertons: A Detective Dynasty*, 182–85; Sandburg, Carl Sandburg, and Edward C. Goodman, *Abraham Lincoln, The Illustrated Edition: The Prairie Years and the War Years*, 210; Sears, Stephen W. (ed.), *The Civil War Papers of George B. McClellan: Selected Correspondence, 1860–1865*, 204; Sears, Stephen W., *George B. McClellan: The Young Napoleon*, 206.

13. MacKay, James MacKay, *Allan Pinkerton: The First Private Eye*, 167; Rowan, Richard Wilmer Rowan, *The Pinkertons: A Detective Dynasty*, 185–86.

14. Horan, James D. Horan, *The Pinkertons: The Detective Dynasty That Made History*, 50; MacKay, James MacKay, *Allan Pinkerton: The First Private Eye*, 209–10, 214–22, and 236–37; "Pinkerton National Detective Agency," encyclopedia.chicagohistory.org/pages/2813.html.

15. Patricia Goff, *Timothy Webster: The Story of the Civil War Hero and His Family*, 76 and 109–110.

16. Horan, James D. Horan, *The Pinkertons: The Detective Dynasty That Made History*, 92–93.

Sources

Books

Ainsworth, Fred C., and Joseph W. Kirkley. *The War of the Rebellion: A Compilation of the Official Records of the Union and Confederate Armies*, Series IV, Vol. I. Washington, D.C.: Government Printing Office, 1900.

The American Almanac Repository of Useful Knowledge for the Year 1859. Boston: Crosby, Nichols, 1859.

Andreas, Alfred Theodore. *History of Chicago*. Chicago: A. T. Andreas, 1884.

Annals of the State Historical Society of Iowa. Iowa City: Jerome B. Duncan, 1863.

Annual Statement of the Finances of the City of Chicago, From April 1, 1875, to December 31, 1875. Chicago: Geo. J. Titus' (Inter Ocean) Book and Job Print, 1876.

Arenson, Adam. *The Great Heart of the Republic: St. Louis and the Cultural Civil War*. Cambridge: Harvard University Press, 2011.

Arey, Leslie B. *Northwestern University Medical School, 1859–1959: A Pioneer in Educational Reform*. Evanston: Northwestern University, 1959.

Axelrod, Alan. *The War Between the Spies: A History of Espionage During the American Civil War*. New York: Atlantic Monthly Press, 1992.

Bailey, Brian. *Burke and Hare: The Year of the Ghouls*. Edinburgh: Mainstream, 2002.

Baldwin, Elmer. *History of La Salle County, Illinois*. Chicago: Rand McNally, 1877.

Boyer, Paul S. *The Oxford Companion to United States History*. New York: Oxford University Press, 2001.

Bryan, George S. *The Spy in America*. Philadelphia: J.B. Lippincott, 1943.

Carlisle, Rodney P., and J. Geoffrey Golson (eds.). *Manifest Destiny and the Expansion of America*. Santa Barbara: ABC-CLIO, 2007.

The Chronicle. Vol. 21, September 1880–June 1881. Ann Arbor, MI: Chronicle Association, 1881.

The City Intelligencer; or, Stranger's Guide. Richmond: MacFarlane and Fergusson, 1862.

Costello, Augustine E. *Our Police Protectors: A History of the New York Police*. Montclair, NJ: Patterson Smith, 1972.

Cuthbert, Norma B. (ed.). *Lincoln and the Baltimore Plot, 1861: From Pinkerton Records and Related Papers*. San Marino, CA: Huntington Library, 1949.

Cutrer, Thomas W. *Ben McCulloch and the Frontier Military Tradition*. Chapel Hill: University of North Carolina Press, 1993.

Davis, James D. *History of Memphis: The History of the City of Memphis*. Memphis: Hite, Crumpton and Kelly, 1873.

Documents of the Board of Councilmen of the City of New York. Vol. 2, Part 2. New York: McSpedon and Baker, Printers to the Common Council, 1855.

Donald, Herbert David. *Lincoln*. New York: Simon and Schuster, 1995.

Dowling, John. *History of Iroquois County*. Watseka, IL: Iroquois County Board of Supervisors, 1968.

Downer, Harry E. (ed.). *History of Davenport and Scott County, Iowa*, Vol. 1. Chicago: S. J. Clarke, 1910.

Farnam, Henry W., and Clive Day (ed.). *Chapters in the History of Social Legislation in the United States to 1860*. Union, New Jersey: Lawbook Exchange, 2000.

Fishel, Edwin C. *The Secret War for the Union: The Untold Story of Military Intelligence in the Civil War*. Boston: Houghton Mifflin, 1996.

Fisher, George B. *History and Reminiscences of the Monumental Church, Richmond, VA., from 1814 to 1878*. Richmond: Whittet and Shepperson, 1880.

Flint, Henry M. *The Railroads of the United States: Their History and Statistics*. Philadelphia: John E. Potter, 1868.

Fogarty, Gerald P. *Commonwealth Catholicism: A History of the Catholic Church in Virginia*. Notre Dame: University of Notre Dame Press, 2001.

Freeman, Douglas S. *Lee's Lieutenants: A Study in Command*. New York: Simon and Schuster, 1998.

Gambee, Robert. *Princeton*. New York: W. W. Norton, 1987.

Goff, Patricia. *Timothy Webster: The Story of the Civil War Hero and His Family*. Elgin, IL: Goff, 2000.

Goodspeed, Weston A., and Daniel D. Healy (eds.). *History of Cook County, Illinois*, Vol. 2. Chicago: Goodspeed Historical Association, 1909.

Hannavy, John. *Encyclopedia of Nineteenth-century Photography*. New York: Taylor and Francis, 2008.

Hatch, Frederick. *Protecting President Lincoln*. Jefferson, NC: McFarland, 2011.

Heidler, David S., and Jeanne T. Heidler. *Encyclopedia of the American Civil War: A Political, Social, and Military History*. Santa Barbara: ABC-CLIO, 2000.

Horan, James D. *The Pinkertons: The Detective Dynasty That Made History*. New York: Crown, 1967.

_____, and Howard Swiggett. *The Pinkerton Story*. New York: Van Rees Press, 1951.

Horsfield, T. W. *The History and Antiquities of Lewes and Its Vicinity*. Lewes: J. Baxter, 1824.

Hunter, Louis C. *Steamboats on the Western Rivers: An Economic and Technological History*. Cambridge: Harvard University Press, 1949.

Index to the Miscellaneous Documents of the House of Representatives for the First Session of the Forty-Fourth Congress. Washington: Government Printing Office, 1876.

Johnson, Robert Underwood, and Clarence Clough Buel. *Battles and Leaders of the Civil War*, Vol. III. New York: Century, 1888.

Jones, Terry L. *The A to Z of the Civil War*. Lanham, Maryland: Scarecrow Press, 2006.

Ketchum, Richard M. (ed.), and Bruce Catton. *The American Heritage Picture History of the Civil War*. New York: American Heritage, 1960.

Konstam, Angus (ed.). *The American Civil War: A Visual Encyclopedia*. London: PRC Publishing, 2001.

Kroessler, Jeffrey A. *New York, Year By Year: A Chronology of the Great Metropolis*. New York: New York University Press, 2002.

Lamon, Ward H. *The Life of Abraham Lincoln; From His Birth to His Inauguration as President*. Lincoln: University of Nebraska Press, reprint of 1872 edition, 1999.

Lanier, Robert S., and Francis Trevelyan Miller (eds.). *The Photographic History of the Civil War in Ten Volumes*, Vol. Seven. New York: Review of Reviews Co., 1912.

Lankevich, George J. *American Metropolis: A History of New York City*. New York: New York University Press, 1998.

Lossing, Benson J. *History of New York City*, Vol. II. New York: Perine Engraving and Publishing, 1884.

Lurie, Maxine N., and Marc Mappen (eds.). *Encyclopedia of New Jersey*. New Brunswick: Rutgers University Press, 2004.

MacKay, James. *Allan Pinkerton: The First Private Eye*. Edison, NJ: Castle Books, 2007.

Maizlish, Stephen, and John J. Kushma (eds.). *Essays on American Antebellum Politics, 1840–1860*. College Station: Texas A&M University Press, 1982.

Manarin, Louis H. *Richmond on the James*. Charleston: Arcadia, 2001.

Markham, Jerry W. *A Financial History of the United States*, Vol. 1. Armonk, NY: M. E. Sharpe, 2002.

Markle, Donald E. *Spies and Spymasters of the Civil War*. New York: Hippocrene Books, 1994.

Mearns, David C. *The Lincoln Papers: The Story of the Collection with Selections to July 4, 1861*. New York: Doubleday, 1948.

Mitchell, Charles W. *Maryland Voices of the Civil War*. Baltimore: Johns Hopkins University Press, 2007.

Morn, Frank. *The Eye That Never Sleeps: A History of the Pinkerton National Detective Agency*. Bloomington: Indiana University Press, 1982.

Mortimer, Gavin. *Double Death: The True Story of Pryce Lewis, The Civil War's Most Daring Spy*. New York: Walker and Company, 2010.

Mulheron, John J. (ed.). *The Medical Age*, Vol. 2. Detroit: George S. Davis, 1884.

National Cyclopedia of American Biography, Vol. II. New York: James T. White, 1895.

Oates, Stephen B. *To Purge This Land with Blood: A Biography of John Brown*. Amherst: University of Massachusetts Press, Second Edition, 1984.

_____. *With Malice Toward None: A Life of Abraham Lincoln*. New York: Harper and Row, 1977.

Official Records of the Union and Confederate Navies in the War of the Rebellion, Series 1, Vol. 5. Washington: Government Printing Office, 1897.

Parry, J. D. *Historical and Descriptive Account of the Coast of Sussex*. Brighton: Wright and Son, 1833.

Pessen, Edward. *Jacksonian America: Society, Personality, and Politics* (Revised Edition). Urbana: University of Illinois Press, 1985.

Photographic History of the Civil War in Ten Volumes, Vol. 7. New York: Review of Reviews, 1912.

Pinkerton, Allan. *Claude Melnotte as a Detective, and Other Stories*. New York: Dillingham Co., 1875.

_____. *Criminal Reminiscences and Detective Sketches*. New York, G. W. Dillingham Co., 1878.

_____. *History and Evidence of the Passage of Abraham Lincoln from Harrisburg, Pa., to Washington, D.C., on the Twenty-Second and Twenty-Third of February, Eighteen Hundred and Sixty-One*. New York: Rode and Brand, 1907.

_____. *The Spy of the Rebellion*. New York: G. W. Carleton, 1883.

Pinkerton, William A., and Robert A. Pinkerton. *Timothy Webster: Spy of the Rebellion*. Chicago: Pinkerton's National Detective Agency, 1906.

Polk, William M. *Leonidas Polk: Bishop and General*. London: Longmans, Green, 1893.

Primm, James Neal. *Lion of the Valley: St. Louis, Missouri, 1764–1980*. St. Louis: Missouri Historical Society Press, 1998.

Quinn, S. J. *The History of the City of Fredericksburg, Virginia*. Richmond: Hermitage Press, 1908.

Richardson, James F. *The New York Police: Colonial Times to 1901*. New York: Oxford University Press, 1970.

Riney, Larry A. *Hell Gate of the Mississippi: The Effie Afton Trial and Abraham Lincoln's Role in It*. Geneseo, IL: Talisman Press, 2006.

Rowan, Richard Wilmer. *The Pinkertons: A Detective Dynasty*. Boston: Little, Brown, 1931.

Sadlier's Catholic Almanac and Ordo for the Year of Our Lord 1865. New York: D. & J. Sadlier, 1865.

Sandburg, Carl, and Edward C. Goodman. *Abraham Lincoln, The Illustrated Edition: The Prairie Years and the War Years*. New York: Sterling, 2007.

Sappol, Michael. *A Traffic of Dead Bodies*. Princeton, NJ: Princeton University Press, 2002.

Scharf, Colonel J. Thomas. *The Chronicles of Baltimore; Being a Complete History of "Baltimore Town" and Baltimore City from the Earliest Period to the Present Time*. Baltimore: Turnbull Brothers, 1874.

_____. *History of Baltimore City and County from the Earliest Period to the Present Day*. Philadelphia: Louis H. Everts, 1881.

Sears, Stephen W. (ed.). *The Civil War Papers of George B. McClellan: Selected Correspondence, 1860–1865*. New York: Ticknor and Fields, 1989.

_____. *George B. McClellan: The Young Napoleon*. New York: Da Capo Press, 1999.

Stevens, Walter B., *Missouri: The Center State, 1821–1915*. St. Louis: S. J. Clarke, 1915.

_____. *St. Louis: The Fourth City, 1764–1911*, Vol. 1. St. Louis: S. J. Clarke, 1911.

Tenney, William J. (ed.). *The Mining Magazine*, Vol. VII. New York: John F. Trow, 1856.

Tidwell, William A. *Come Retribution: The Confederate Secret Service and the Assassination of Lincoln*. Jackson: University Press of Mississippi, 2001 edition.

Tillinghast, B. F. *Rock Island Arsenal: In Peace and in War*. Chicago: Henry O. Shepard, 1898.

Twain, Mark, and Albert Bigelow Paine (ed.). *Mark Twain's Letters*, Vol. 1. New York: Harper and Brothers, 1917.

Tyler, Lyon G. *William and Mary College Quarterly Historical Magazine*, Vol. 13. Richmond: Whittet and Shepperson, 1905.

U.S. Congress, House of Representatives. *Alleged Hostile Organization Against the Government Within the District of Columbia*, 36th Congress, 2d Session, Report 79.

Wagner, Margaret E., Gary W. Gallagher, and Paul Finkelman. *The Library of Congress Civil War Desk Reference*. New York: Simon and Schuster, 2002.

Walling, George W. *Recollections of a New York Chief of Police*. New York: Caxton Book Concern, 1887.

The War of the Rebellion: A Compilation of the Official Records of the Union and Confederate Armies. Washington: Government Printing Office, 1899.

Wilkie, F. B. *Sketches and Notices of the*

Chicago Bar; Including the More Prominent Lawyers and Judges of the City and Suburban Towns. Chicago: Western News, 1872.

Wilson, William Bender. *History of the Pennsylvania Railroad Company with Plan of Organization, Portraits of Officials and Biographical Sketches*, Vol. II. Philadelphia: Henry T. Coates, 1895.

Wood's Baltimore City Directory. Baltimore: John W. Woods, 1860.

Wright, Marcus J. *Tennessee in the War, 1861–1865.* New York: Ambrose Lee, 1908.

Articles

"A Brief History of Princeton." http://www.princetonhistory.org/brief_history.cfm.

"The Crystal Palace Police." *Gleason's Pictorial Drawing Room Companion.*

Ely, James W., Jr. "Lincoln and the Rock Island Bridge Case," http://www.indianahistory.org/ihs_press/web_publications/railroad05/Ely1.pdf.

Fishel, Edwin C. "Pinkerton and McClellan: Who Deceived Whom?" *Civil War History*, No. 2 (June 1988).

Frosst, George Washington. "A South Berwick Yankee Behind Confederate Lines," Part 1, Old Berwick Historical Society, http://www.obhs.net/index.php?option=com_content&view=article&id=256&Itemid=266.

Hanna, J. Marshall. "Castle Thunder in Bellum Days," *Southern Opinion*, November 3, 1867.

Harris, Roland B. "Sussex, Historic Character Assessment Report: November 2004." East Sussex County Council, West Sussex County Council, and Brighton and Hove City Council, 2004, http://www.lewes.gov.uk/Files/plan_Newhaven_EUS_report pages14to19.pdf.

"Immigration to the United States." eh.net/encyclopedia/article/cohn.immigration.us.

Inglis, William. "A Republic's Gratitude: What Pryce Lewis Did for the United States Government, and How the United States Government Rewarded Him," *Harper's Weekly*, December 30, 1911.

"Know-Nothing Party." *Encyclopedia Britannica*, http://www.britannica.com/EBchecked/topic/320530/Know-Nothing-party.

"Know-Nothing Party." Ohio History Central, http://www.ohiohistorycentral.org/entry.php?rec=911.

Long, Christopher. "Knights of the Golden Circle," *Handbook of Texas Online*, http://www.tshaonline.org/handbook/online/articles/KK/vbk1.html.

Luff, Jennifer. "Surrogate Supervisors: Railway Spotters and the Origins of Workplace Surveillance," Duke University Press abstract, http://labor.dukejournals.org/cgi/content/abstract/5/1/47.

"Memorial. Moses Drury Hoge, D.D., LL.D., A." www.mdgorman.com/Written_Accounts/Periodicals/a_memorial_moes_drury_hoge_d_d.htm.

Morsman, Jenry. "The *Effie Afton*, the Rock Island Bridge, and the Making of America," http://www.common-place.org/vol-06/no-04/morsman/.

Pfeiffer, David A. "Bridging the Mississippi: The Railroads and Steamboats Clash at the Rock Island Bridge," Summer 2004, Vol. 36, No. 2, http://www.archives.gov/publications/prologue/2004/summer/bridge.html.

"Pinkerton National Detective Agency." encyclopedia.chicagohistory.org/pages/2813.html.

"The Potato Famine and Irish Immigration to America," www.crf-usa.org/bill-of-rights-in-action/bria-26-2-the-potato-famine-and-irish-immigration-to-america.html.

Roseman, Curtis C. "History of First Railroad Bridge Across the Mississippi River," http://www.riveraction.org/node/28.

Scheel, Eugene. "The Reconstruction Years: Tales of Leesburg and Warrenton, Virginia," www.loudounhistory.org/history/loudoun-cw-reconstruction-towns.htm.

Veeder, Grant. "Bridge at Davenport: Abraham Lincoln and the Case of the First Mississippi River Bridge," http://www.iowalincoln200.org/iowa_facts_copy%281%29.htm.

Weiss, Robert P. "Private Detective Agencies and Labour Discipline in the United States, 1855–1946," *The Historical Journal*, 1 March 1986, Vol. 21, Cambridge University Press.

Zobrist, Benedict K. "Steamboat Men Versus Railroad Men: The First Bridging of the Mississippi River," *Missouri Historical Review*, January 1965, Vol. 59, No. 2.

Unpublished Documents

Abraham Lincoln Papers, Manuscript Division, Library of Congress.

Allan Pinkerton Letters to Joseph Beale, 1882–83, Author's Collection.

Allan Pinkerton Papers, Chicago Historical Society, Chicago, Illinois.

Baptisms in the Parish of Newhaven in the County of Sussex in 1822: April 17, Timothy Webster, Parish Records, Newhaven: (St. Michael) r1553, East Sussex Record Office.

Chicago City Proceedings Files, 1833–1871, File 0303A, Illinois Regional Archives Depository, Ronald Williams Library, Northwestern University.

Cook County Coroner's Inquest Records for John Scully, December 15, 1902, Illinois Regional Archives Depository, Ronald Williams Library, Northwestern University.

Death Certificate for Cipriano Ferrandini, December 20, 1910, Maryland State Archives.

Dwyer, John L. "Adult Education in Civil War Richmond, January 1861–April 1865 (dissertation), http://scholar.lib.vt.edu/theses/available/etd-524414252972830/unrestricted/CSA.PDF.

Felton, Samuel M., January 17, 1866, statement, "Lincoln's Secret Journey to Washington in 1861," Abraham Lincoln Presidential Library, Springfield, Illinois.

George Brinton McClellan Papers, 1823–1898. Manuscript Division, Library of Congress.

Henry P. H. Bromwell Papers, Illinois History and Lincoln Collections, University of Illinois at Urbana–Champaign, University Library.

Herndon-Weik Collection of Lincolniana, The Huntington Library, San Marino, California.

John Brown Papers, 1842–1910, Chicago Historical Society, Chicago, Illinois.

Lewis, Pryce, and David E. Cronin. "Memoirs of Pryce Lewis as Told to Major David E. Cronin in 1888." Pryce Lewis Collection, St. Lawrence University Archives, Owen D. Young Library.

Proceedings of Court-Martial in the Case of Timothy Webster, Spy, Papers of and Relating to Military and Civilian Personnel, compiled 1874–1899, documenting the period 1861–1865, Record Group 109, Unfiled Papers and Slips Belonging in Confederate Compiled Service Records, M347, National Archives and Records Administration.

Pryce Lewis Collection, St. Lawrence University Archives, Owen D. Young Library.

Records of Pinkerton's National Detective Agency, Manuscript Division, Library of Congress.

U.S. Census

1850 Federal Census for Baltimore, Baltimore County, Maryland: Cipriano Ferrandini.

1850 Federal Census for New York, New York County, New York.

1850 Federal Census for New York, New York County, New York: Timothy Webster family.

1860 Federal Census for Davenport, Scott County, Iowa.

1860 Federal Census for Onarga, Iroquois County, Illinois: Timothy Webster family.

1860 Federal Census for Onarga, Iroquois County, Illinois: Persons who died during the year ending 1st June, 1860: Timothy Webster, Sr.

1860 Federal Census for Richmond, Henrico County, Virginia.

1870 Federal Census for Chicago, Cook County, Illinois: John Scully.

1870 Federal Census for Chicago, Cook County, Illinois: Pryce Lewis.

1880 Federal Census for Chicago, Cook County, Illinois: John Scully.

1880 Federal Census for Sacramento, Sacramento County, California: Fannie Frazer and Helen Measure.

1880 Federal Census for New York, New York County, New York: Daniel Webster.

1900 Federal Census for Jersey City, Hudson County, New Jersey: Pryce Lewis.

1910 Federal Census for Chicago, Cook County, Illinois: Julia Scully.

Wilgus, Esther Webster. *Grandpa and Grandma's Record*, courtesy of Lucille Campbell, Elk Grove, California.

Newspapers

Baltimore *American and Commercial Advertiser*

Baltimore *Sun*

Burlington *Weekly Hawk-eye*

Chicago *Daily Times*

Chicago *Tribune*

Daily Democrat and News (Davenport, Iowa)

New Jersey *State Gazette*

New York *Herald*

New York *Times*

New York *Tribune*

Richmond *Dispatch*

Richmond *Enquirer*

Richmond *Examiner*

Rock Island *Argus*
Sheboygan (Wisconsin) *Journal*
Washington *Star*

Websites

Abraham Lincoln Papers at the Library of Congress website, lcweb2.loc.gov/ammem/alhtml/malhome.html.
Abraham Lincoln's inaugural address, March 4, 1861, www.loc.gov/exhibits/treasures/trt039.html.
"A. G. Becker & Co., Incorporated," http://www.agbecker.us/RKSwift.php.
American Cultural History, Kingwood College, "American Cultural History, 19th Century: 1820–1829," http://kclibrary.lonestar.edu/19thcentury1820.htm.
"American Cultural History, 19th Century: 1830–1839," http://kclibrary.lonestar.edu/19thcentury1830.htm
ancestry.com
Biographical Directory of the United States Congress, "Morton, Jackson (1794–1874)," http://bioguide.congress.gov/scripts/biodisplay.pl?index=M001015.
British Library: "The People's Charter: Representation of the People Act," www.bl.uk/learning/histcitizen/21cc/utopia/methods1/charter1/charter.html.
census.gov
censusrecords.net
citytowninfo.com/places/illinois/onarga
Civil War Richmond: mdgorman.com, http://www.mdgorman.com/Prisons/castle_godwin.htm.
Eastville, Virginia, www.easternshoretowns.com/eastvill/eastvill.shtml.
"49th Regiment of Virginia Volunteers," http://49thvirginiainfantry.com/49th%20Va%20History.htm.
hiddentruths.northwestern.edu
loc.gov/exhibits/treasures/trt039.html, Abraham Lincoln's Inaugural Address, March 4, 1861.
memphishistory.org
memphistn.gov
newspaperarchive.com
Whitehouse.gov: "James Buchanan," www.whitehouse.gov/about/presidents/jamesbuchanan; James K. Polk, www.whitehouse.gov/about/presidents/jamespolk.

Libraries and Archives

Abraham Lincoln Presidential Library, Springfield, Illinois.
Alderman Library, University of Virginia, Charlottesville, Virginia.
Allen County Public Library Genealogy Center, Fort Wayne, Indiana.
Charles E. Young Library, University of California in Los Angeles, Westwood, California.
Chicago Historical Society, Chicago, Illinois.
Chicago Public Library, Chicago, Illinois.
Cincinnati Museum Center, Cincinnati, Ohio.
Cleveland Health Sciences Library, Case Western Reserve University, Cleveland, Ohio.
Cleveland Heights: University Heights Public Library, Cleveland Heights, Ohio.
Cleveland Public Library, Cleveland, Ohio.
David Rumsey Map Collection, www.davidrumsey.com.
Don L. Love Memorial Library, University of Nebraska–Lincoln, Lincoln, Nebraska.
East Sussex Record Office, Lewes, East Sussex, UK.
Frances Howard Goldwyn Public Library, Hollywood, California.
Grasselli Library and Breen Learning Center, John Carroll University, University Heights, Ohio.
Harvard Libraries, Cambridge, Massachusetts.
Historical Society of Princeton, Princeton, New Jersey.
Historical Society of Washington, D.C.
Hugh M. Morris Library, University of Delaware, Newark, Delaware.
Huntington Library, San Marino, California.
Joseph Regenstein Library, University of Chicago, Chicago, Illinois.
Kelvin Smith Library, Case Western Reserve University, Cleveland, Ohio.
Kent State Main Library, Kent, Ohio.
Lakewood Public Library, Lakewood, Ohio.
Library of Congress, Washington, D.C.
Los Angeles Public Library, Los Angeles, California.
Maryland State Archives, Annapolis, Maryland.
Memorial Library, University of Wisconsin–Madison, Madison, Wisconsin.
Memphis Public Library, Memphis, Tennessee.
Museum of the Confederacy, Richmond, Virginia.

National Archives and Records Administration, College Park, Maryland.

New York Public Library, New York, New York.

Northern Regional Library Facility, University of California, Richmond, California.

Putnam Museum, Davenport, Iowa.

Robert Crown Law Library, Stanford Law School, Stanford, California.

Ronald Williams Library, Northwestern University, Chicago, Illinois.

Roscoe L. West Library, College of New Jersey, Ewing, New Jersey.

St. Lawrence University Archives, Owen D. Young Library, Canton, New York.

Seymour Library, Knox College, Galesburg, Illinois.

University Libraries, University of Arkansas, Fayetteville, Arkansas.

University Library, University of Illinois at Urbana–Champaign, Urbana, Illinois.

University of Georgia Libraries, Main Library, Athens, Georgia.

Virginia Historical Society, Richmond, Virginia.

Webster Groves Public Library, Webster Groves, Missouri.

William T. Young Library, University of Kentucky, Lexington, Kentucky.

Zach S. Henderson Library, Statesboro, Georgia.

Index

Numbers in *bold italics* indicate pages with photographs.

Aberdeen, Md. 144
Abingdon, Va. 106, 172–73
Accomack County, Va. 92, 99, 153–56, 166, 167
Adams,_____ 155
Alabama 50, 60
Albany, N.Y. 55
Alexander, Captain_____ 104
Alexandria, Va. 86, 151
Allen's Eating Saloon 88, 151
Allen's Fresh, Md. 90, 170
American Civil War 6, 68, 135
American Party 16
American Telegraph Company 57
Anatomy Act of 1832 29
Annette Travis's brothel 53
Antietam *134*
Arkansas 50
Army of the Potomac 80, 101, 133–34, 159
Astor Place Riot 16

Bagby, George 148
Ball (of Ball's Farm)_____ 154–55
Baltimore, Md. 25, 51, 52, 53, 54, 55–56, 57, 59, 60, 62, 63, 64–66, 68, 76, 85, 86–88, *87*, 90, 92, 98, 100, 101, 103–4, 144–45, 149, 151, 153, 155, 156, 164, 165, 166, 172
Baltimore *American and Commercial Advertiser* 103
Baltimore Street, Baltimore, Md. 65, 86, *87*, 145, 151
Bangs, George H. *25*, 25–27, 30, 34, 137
Barr's Saloon 52
Baugh, Richard D. 79, 148, 149
Bayside Road, Accomack County, Va. 153
Beale, Joseph B. 75
Beals, Major_____ 117
Beauregard, Pierre G.T. 155–56, 162, 165, 178–79, 181, 182
Benedict, Md. 90
Benjamin, Judah P. 6, 94, 106, 107, 159, 172, 175, 182–83

Bissell, Josiah W. 43–48
Blake, Thomas 9
Booth, John Wilkes 58
Bowen, John 95–96, 159–60
Bowling Green, Ky. 75, 106–7, 172, 174, 175–78, 182
Bradley, Cyprus P. 43–44, 45–47, 48
Bradley, William H. 47
Brady Street, Davenport, Iowa *43*
Bragg, Braxton 176
Bragg, Charles 97, 161
Brainard, Daniel 34
Breckinridge, John C. 50
Bridgman, Samuel 190n10
Briggs, John H. 16–21, 139–43
Bristol, Va. 178
Brook Station, Va. 97, 98, 156, 162, 164, 165, 166, 183
Brown, George William 90
Brown, John 23, 49–50
Brownlow, Jim 149
Brownlow, William Gannaway 149, 173
Brownlow's Knoxville *Whig* 149
Buffalo, N.Y. 55
Bull Run, First Battle of 85, 162, 165
Bull Run, Va. 79, 97, 148, 161, 180
Burke, William 29
Burton, Dr._____ 77
Butler, Charles 88

Cabbagetown, N.J. 9
California 104, 108, 169, 183
Calvert, John S. 148
Camden and Amboy Railroad 8
Cameron, Simon 85
Camp Anderson 149
Camp Boone 147
Camp Chatham 149
Camp Cummings 149
Camp Lee, Richmond, Va. 130
Camp Rector 77
Camp Sneed 149

Camp Trousdell 149
Campbell, William 94–97, 98, 106, 126, 159–61, 163–64, 172, 173, 174
Caphart, John 130
Capitol Building, Washington, D.C. **66**
Capitol Square, Richmond, Va. 94, **115**
Carter, Artemus 29
Cary, Major_____ 154
Cashmeyer, Philip 126
Castle Godwin 125, 126
Cave City, Ky. 177
Central America 52
Centreville, Va. 97–98, 101, 107, 155, 160, 161–63, 164, 178, 179–81, 182
Chadwick, Walter E. 43–45, 46–47, 48
Chapin, John P. 47
Charles Street, Baltimore, Md. 88, 152
Charleston, S.C. 25, 65, 68, 145, 166
Charlotte Hall, Md. 90
Charlottesville, Va. 178
Chartism 22
Chattanooga, Tenn. 77, 79, 106, 113, 116, 149, 172, 173, 174, 182
Cherrystone Lighthouse 92, 154, 156, 167
Chesapeake Bay 89, 92, 99, 165, 171
Chestertown, Md. 100, 155
Chicago, Ill. 5, 23, 25, 26, 29, **35**, 38, 40, 41, 44, 47, 48, 72, 133, 134; Great Chicago Fire 25
Chicago and Rock Island Railroad 40, 44
Chicago Avenue, Chicago, Ill. 33
Chicago Cemetery 29–31, 33; map **36**
Chicago Courthouse and City Hall **37**
Chicago *Daily Times* 34
Chicago River 33
Cincinnati, Ohio 54, 72, 73, **74**, 75, 78, 80, 147, 149, 150
City Hotel, Nashville, Tenn. 149, 174
Clackner, George 119–20, 122
Clark Street, Chicago, Ill. 33
Clarksville, Tenn. 75, 76, 147
Claude Melnotte as a Detective, and Other Stories 25
Cleburne, Patrick R. 175–76, 177
Cleveland, Ohio 54
Cleveland, Tenn. 106, 174
Cobb Neck, Md. 105, 110, 170–71, 183
Coffin, William H. 99, 165–66
Columbus, Ohio 54
Columbus, Tenn. 178
Confederate States of America 50, 68, 73, 94, 125, 129; map **83**
Connor, Lieutenant_____ 79, 148
Constitutional Guards 52
Cook, Burton C. 44

Cook County 23, 44
Cooper, James 94
Cooper, William 94
Corinth, Miss. 149
Corsica 52
Cridland, John Frederick 126
Crump, Charles A. 92–93, 99, 102, 157, 166, 167
Crystal Palace Exhibition 5, 13–14
Crystal Palace, New York, N.Y. 5, 13, **14**, **15**, 26
Cuckold Creek, Md. 105, 170
Cumberland Gap, Tenn. 149
Cumberland River 147, 174
Curtin, Andrew G. 57

Daly, Charles P. 19
Dart, John? 47
Davenport, Iowa 39–40, 41, 42, **43**
Davies, Harry W. 51, 53–54, 136
Davis, Jefferson 40, 68, 127, **129**, 131, 171
Davis, Varina 129
Dearborn, Luther 23
Delaware and Raritan Canal 8
Democratic Party 10, 50
Dempsey,_____ 97–98, 161, 162
Dennis, Paul H. 44, 47
Department of Ohio 72
Detroit, Mich. 26
De Voe, Ely 59–61, 62–64
Dexter, Wirt 189n19
District of Columbia 104–5; map **93**
Dix, Dorothea 57
Douglas, Stephen A. 43, 50
Douglass, Frederick 23
Dred Scott decision 39
Drummondtown, Va. 100, 153–54
Dublin, Va. 178
Dumfries, Va. 106, 171–72, 176, 178, 183, 184
Dundee, Ill. 23

E Street, Washington, D.C. 86, 151
Earl, John 86, 101–2, 151
Eastville, Va. 92, 99–100, 153–54, 156, 171
Effie Afton 41
Ellis,_____ 66–67, 145–46
Equitable Life Assurance Society 133
Evans, General_____ 160–61, 162, 163–64, 165
Evansport, Va. 165, 178, 183
Evergreen, Calif. 136
E.W. Clark & Bro. 26
Exchange Hotel 114

Fairhaven, Md. 89
Fauquier County, Va. 97, 155, 161
FBI Criminal Identification Bureau 134–35
Felton, Samuel 50–51, 55
Ferrandini, Cipriano 52–53, 55, 58, 59
Finncan, James 30, 33–34
Finney, Colonel_____ 154
First Arkansas Regiment 107, 175, 176–77
First Maryland Regiment 97, 107, 161, 162, 164–65, 179, 181–82
First Tennessee Regiment 176
Fishel, Edwin C. 80–1
Fisher,_____ 154, 167
Fletcher, S. D. 94
Flint, J. C. 45
Florida 50
Floyd, John B. 172
Ford, James 94
Forrester, Captain_____ 183
Fort Claiborne 148
Fort Dover 147
Fort Henry 147
Fort McHenry 103
Fort Monroe 133, 157, 158
Fort Sumter 68
Forward,_____ 65, 145
Fox River 23
Franciscus, George C. 57
Frank, Whitney 45, 46
Fredericksburg, Va. 98, 105–6, 108, 111, 156, 159, 164, 165–66, 171, 183
Friendship, Md. 89
Front Street, Memphis, Tenn. *79*

Gage, George W. 47
Garland, Samuel 149
Gay, Alexander *see* Imbert, Jules
Georgia 50
Glasgow, Scotland 22
Gloucester Point, Va. 92–93, 99, 155, 156–58, 165, 166–67
Gorbals, Glasgow, Scotland 22
Gordonsville, Va. 178, 179
Grand Junction, Tenn. 77, 79, 149
Grave robbing, 5, 29, 38
Great Britain 125
Great Miami River 73
Green, Russell 29, 33
Greenville, Tenn. 173
Grove Wharf, Va. 94, 155, 158
Gull, Jim 151

H Street, Washington, D.C. 168
Hague, Va. 183
Hamilton, Mich. 26

Hardee, William J. 79, 148, 178
Hare, William 29
Harpers Ferry, Va. 49–50, 86, 89, 151, 152
Harris, Isham G. 175, 177
Harris, James 175–77
Harrisburg, Pa. 55, 56
Haskill, Colonel_____ 65, 144
Haven, Carlos 44
Havre-de-Grace, Md. 67, 146
Hays, Captain_____ 60
Hazzard,_____ 98–99, 164–65
Henrico County Jail 122, 123–24, *124*
Herndon, Dr._____ 104, 108–9, 169, 183
Hicks, Thomas H. 54
Hill,_____ 78, 148
Hill, Captain_____ 165
Hillard, Otis K. 53–54, 55
Hindman, Thomas C. 177
Hoge, Moses D. 130, 132
Holmes, Theophilus H. 97, 98–99, 108–9, 156, 162, 164–65, 181, 183
Hop-Yard Landing, Va. 183
Hop-Yard Wharf, Va. 105, 171
Howard, James R. 30
Howard House 65, 145
Humboldt, Tenn. 77–78, 147
Hunt, James C. 148
Hurd, Jacob 41

I Street, Washington, D.C. 85
Illinois 5, 6, 22, 72, 137
Illinois Central Railroad 24, 28, 72, 169
Imbert, Jules 5, 25–27
Indiana 22, 72
Indianapolis, Ind. 54
Iowa 42, 45
Ireland 10, 111, 125

Jackson, Andrew 7, 10
Jackson, Claiborne F. 79, 149
Jackson, Thomas J. 176, 182
Jackson, Tenn. 77, 190*n*10
James,_____ 167
James River 94, 155, 158, 159
January, Derrick A. 47
Johnson, Lieutenant_____ 158
Johnson, Sidney E. 175–76, 177, 178
Johnston, Joseph E. 155–56, 160, 161, 162, 163, 178, 181, 182
Jones, John B. 95, 98, 159, 161, 162, 163, 164, 182
Jonesboro, Tenn. 173
Judd, Norman B. 41, 55–57, *56*, 64, 72
Juka Camp 149

Kane, George P. 88, 152
Kane, John 100, 154
Kane County, Ill. 23
Kansas 39
Kansas-Nebraska Act 39, 49
Keen, Captain_____ 66–67, 144, 145–46
Kentucky 73, 74, 80, 147; map *109*
Key West, Fla. 25
Knights of Liberty 90
Knights of the Golden Circle 52, 90
Knox, Joseph 41, 44
Knoxville, Tenn. 79–80, 106, 107, 147, 149,
    172, 173–74, 178

Lake Michigan 31, 46
Lake Street, Chicago, Ill. *35*
Lamon, Ward 57
Lee, Robert E. 49
Leesburg, Va. 98, 160, 163, 165
Leonard, James 14
Leonardtown, Md. 90, 105, 169, 170–71
Lewis, Hattie 51, 65–66, 75, 86, 88, 102,
    111, 114, 115–16, 122, 126, 127, 128, 129–
    30, 131, 132–33, 136, 145, 152
Lewis, James T. 148
Lewis, Pryce 13, 75, 100, 111–26, **114**, 127–
    28, 132, 133, 136, 137, 190*n*10; map *124*
Lincoln, Abraham 5, 41, 50, 52, 53, 54–58,
    55, 59, 60, 65, **66**, 67, 68, 72, 83–84, 101,
    118, 129, *134*, 136, 144, 145; letter to *70*, *71*
Loudon, Tenn. 174
Loudon Railroad Bridge 149
Louisiana 50
Louisville, Ky. 75, 78, 80, 147, 149–50
Louisville and Nashville Railroad 177
Lowenbach, Joseph 94
Lowenbach, Lewis 94
Luckett, James H. 51–52, 59
Lynchburg, Va. 106, 107, 172, 174, 178

Maddox, Joseph H. 104
Magruder, John B. 93–94, 99, 157, 158,
    165–66, 167
Main Street, Memphis, Tenn. 78
Main Street, Richmond, Va. 117, 120, 122,
    148
Manassas, Va. 79, 88, 95–96, 101, 107, 148,
    152, 154, 155, 159–61, 162, 163, 172, 176,
    178, 179, 180–81, 182
Marshall,_____ 92, 99, 156–57, 166–67
Martinsburg, Va. 98, 163
Mary Washington 89
Maryland 50, 51, 53, 54, 59, 67, 85, 86, 94,
    98–99, 105, 107, 146, 151, 154, 160, 164,
    165, 166, 167, 171, 183; map *93*, *108*

Matsell, George W. 15, 16–17, 18–19, 21
McAllister, William 44, 47
McCann, Michael 18, 19, 21
McClellan, George B. 6, 72, *73*, 80, 83–84,
    85, 91, 97, 101, 104, 108, 110, 112, 113, 114,
    116, 128, 133–34, 153, 169, 183
McClellan, Mary Ellen 84
McClernand, John A. *134*
McCubbin, Samuel 116–18, 120, 121–22
McCulloch, Benjamin 79, 148, 176, 182
McDowell, Irvin 85
McGee, Joseph H. 103
McKellar, William 17, 18, 19, 21, 139, 140,
    143
McMullen, Augustine L. 125–26, 127
McPhail, James L. 103
Melodeon Concert Hall 60
Memphis, Tenn. 74–75, 76, 77–78, *79*, 80,
    128, 147–48, 159
Mercer County, N.J. 8
Merrill,_____ 86–88, 151
Mexican-American War 10, 176
Mexico 52
Micheal, James 67, 145–46
Michigan 22
Michigan Street, Chicago, Ill. 34
Mill Creek, Md. 170–71
Miller's Hotel 86, 88, 89, 102, 103, 152
Milliken, Isaac L. 34
Mississippi 50
Mississippi and Missouri Railroad 40
Mississippi River 39, 40, *42*
Missouri 79, 148–49
Monmouth County, N.J. 9
Monroe Creek 105, 109, 171, 183
Montreal, Canada 23, 26–27
Monumental Hotel *115*, 117
Morris, J. W. J. 105, 170
Morton, Elizabeth 113, 119
Morton, Jackson 113, 119
Morton, William Chase 119–21
Morton family (of Jackson and Elizabeth)
    113, 122, 124, 125
Mossy Creek, Tenn. 173
Mound City, Tenn. 77, 78, 148
Mouse Creek, Tenn. 174
Municipal Police Act 12
Murfreesboro, Tenn. 149
Myers,_____ 147

Nashville, Tenn. 73–74, 80, 106–7, 149,
    164, 172, 173, 174–75, 178
Nashville and Chattanooga Railroad 149
Nassau Street, Princeton, N.J. *11*
National Hotel 78, 147

National Volunteers 53, 59–61, 63
New Albany, Indiana 80, 150
New Hampshire 169
New Jersey 6
New Madrid, Mo. 149
New York, N.Y. 9, 12–14, 16, 25, 50, 55, 133
New York City Hall *18*
New York *Herald* 17
New York Police Department 5, 12–13, *13*,
   14–15, 16–17, 21
New York *Times* 17, 18, 19, 102
Newhaven, England 7
North Avenue, Chicago, Ill. 33
North Carolina 50
North Hampton County, Va. 92, 153–56
North Western Police Agency *see* Pinker-
   ton's National Detective Agency

Oak Hall, Va. 154
Occoquan, Va. 181
Offutt, John F. C. 94
O'Grady,_____ 30, 31–33
Ohio 72, 73
Ohio and Mississippi Railroad 78, 147
Ohio River 73, 147
Old Capitol Prison 133
Onarga, Ill. 23–24, 42, *136*, 137
Orange and Alexandria Railroad 179, 180–
   81
Orange Courthouse 178
Oregon 10

Parker, Captain_____ 99, 165–66
Peck, Lieutenant_____ 149
Peninsula Bank of Detroit 26
Peninsula Campaign 6, 84, 133
Pennsylvania Railroad 57
Perry Street, Davenport, Iowa *43*
Perrymansville, Md. 51, 54, 64, 65, 66–67,
   144, 145
Petersburg, Va. 148, 182
Petersburg Railroad Depot, Richmond, Va.
   182
Philadelphia, Pa. 51, 55, 72
Philadelphia, Wilmington and Baltimore
   Railroad 50, 144
Pillow, Gideon 73, 78, 79, 147–48, 149, 175
Pinkerton, Allan 10, *24*, 45, 49, 60, 63–64,
   75, *84*, 127, 131, *134*; as author 25, 30, 75,
   119; Civil War service 6, 68–74, 78, 80,
   84, 85, 86, 88, 89, 90–91, 97, 100, 101,
   103, 104–5, 110, 111–14, 116, 117, 122, 126,
   128–29, 133–34, 151, 152; *Claude Melnotte as a Detective, and Other Stories* 25;
   *Criminal Reminiscences and Detective

Sketches 30; death 135; early years 22–23;
   guilt over Webster's death 137; head of
   Pinkerton's National Detective Agency
   22, 23, 25–26, 29, 30–33, 45, 47, 134–35;
   investigating plot to assassinate Abraham Lincoln 5–6, 50–53, 54–57, 59, 64–
   65, 136, 144–45; letters from *70, 71*;
   meeting Webster 5, 14; reports to Gen-
   eral McClellan 153–84; *The Spy of the
   Rebellion* 51, 69–71, 72, 74–76, 77, 86,
   88–91, 101–3, 111–12, 119, 122, 124–25,
   126
Pinkerton, Joan (Carfrae) 22–23, *24*
Pinkerton, William 23
Pinkerton & Co. *see* Pinkerton's National
   Detective Agency
Pinkerton's National Detective Agency 5,
   21, 22, 23, 24–25, 26, 27–28, 29, 30, 38,
   41–42, 44, 68–69, 75, 133, 134–35
Pittsburgh, Pa. 54, 72
Planter's Hotel 164
Polk, Leonidas E. 78, 147–48, 175
Port Royal Sound, South Carolina 166
Potomac River 104, 105, 110, 116, 117, 165,
   166, 170–71, 172, 181, 183
Price, J. H. 98, 99–100, 115–16, 119, 153,
   154, 155, 164, 166, 167
Prince Frederick, Md. 90
Princess Anne, Md. 100, 155
Princeton, N.J. 8–9, *11*
Pryer, Roger A. 148

Quinlan, Martin 29–30, 33–34, 38

Rambaut,_____ 148
Randolph, Tenn. 148
Rappahannock River 105, 165, 171, 183
Rector, Henry M. 176
Rehobeth, Md. 100, 155
Republican Party 50
Resurrectionists 29, 38
Richmond, Va. 6, 80, 84, 85, 88, 91, 92,
   94–95, *96*, 98, 99, 101, 102, 104, 105–6,
   107, 111, 112–15, 117, 119, 122, 124, 128, 131,
   133, *135*, 137, 149, 152, 155–57, 158–60,
   163–64, 166, 167, 168, 169, 171, 172, 174,
   175, 182, 183
Richmond *Dispatch* 94, 115, 116, 122, 127,
   128, 131, 132
Richmond *Examiner* 131–32
Richmond, Fredericksburg and Potomac
   Railroad 156
Richmond House, Chicago, Ill. 44, 45, 47
Ritchie, William 148
R.K. Swift, Brothers & Johnson 25–26

Rock Island, Illinois 39–40, 44, 46, 47
Rock Island *Argus* 39–40
Rock Island Bridge 5, 39–41, *42*, 43, 44, 46, 47–48
Rock Island Bridge Company 41, 46
Romney, Va. 182
Ross, Anthony P. 94
Routzahn, L. H. 163
Rowley, Bob 78, 147, 148
Rucker, Edward A. 35–38
Rush Medical College 34
Russellville, Tenn. 173

St. Louis, Mo. 25, 26, 27, 40, 48, 78, 148
St. Louis Chamber of Commerce 43, 44, 45, 47
St. Mary's County, Md. 164
St. Michael (church) *8, 9*
Salisbury, Md. 100, 155
Sampson, Tom 6, 59–64, *63*
Sanders,_____ 154, 155
Sanford, Henry 57
Saratoga Street, Baltimore, Md. 88, 152
Scobell, John 75
Scotland 22, 29
Scott, Joseph 94
Scott, Roger B. 79, 148
Scott, William H. 90, 92, 114, 119, 133, 136, 150, 156
Scott, Winfield 57, 72, 73, 80, 101
Scully, John 88–90, 111–12, 113–23, 124–26, 127–28, 132, 133, 136, 137, 152, 195n1
Scully, Julia 111, 133
Second Street, Davenport, Iowa *43*
The Secret War for the Union: The Untold Story of Military Intelligence in the Civil War 80–81
Seely, Colonel_____ 78–79, 147–48
Seward, William 118
Shelltown, Md. 100, 154, 155
Sherrington,_____ 60, 64–65, 144–45
Sherwood Hotel 64, 65, 145
Sickles, Daniel 165
Slaughter, Montgomery 98, 164–65
Slayden, Alexander 88, 151–52
Sloan, Sam 86, 88–89, 90, 101, 103, 151, 152
Sly,_____ 149
Smith, Charles 99, 100
Smith, Lewis 94
Smith, William 96, 154–55, 160, 167
Snow Hill, Va. 155
South Carolina 50
South Street, Baltimore, Md. 52
Spotswood Hotel 94, *95*, 98, 114, 158, 164
Springer,_____ 54, 65–66, 144, 145

Springfield, Ill. 54
The Spy of the Rebellion 51, 72, 75
Stanton, Edwin 129
Stanton, O. C. 123–24
State Street, Chicago, Ill. *35*, 46
Stebbins, Charles 148
Stein, E. H. 105, 122, 128
Steuart, George H. 162, 181–82
Stiltz, Daniel R. 88–89, 152
Street, Colonel_____ 152
Swift, Richard K. 26

Taylor,_____ 54, 144
Taylor, Captain_____ 183
Taylor's Saloon 67, 146
Tennessee 50, 73, 74, 80, 101, 147, 173; map *109*
Tennessee River 147
Texas 50
Thom, Dr. _____ 154
Tillman, Colonel_____ 147
Toledo, Ohio 54
Tracy, John F. 44, 45, 47
Trenton, N.J. 55
Tucker, William 19–20, 141–43
Turner, William H. H. 52–53
Twain, Mark 14

Union *see* United States
Union City, Tenn. 78, 147, 148
Union Station, Tenn. 173
United Kingdom 29
United States 6, 7, 10, 16, 29, 39, 48, 49–50, 51, 52, 67, 68, 101, 129, 133, 137, 146; map *83*
United States House of Representatives 41, 53
United States Supreme Court 39, 48

Van Arman, John 189n19
Virginia 50, 80, 86, 89, 90, 92, 101, 104, 105, 133, 151, 153, 155, 156, 164, 166, 168, 169, 170, 171, 172, 173, 174, 177; map *83*, *93*, *108*, *109*
Virginia (steamboat) 171

Wabash Avenue, Chicago, Ill. 46
Wales 111, 125
Walker, James 189n19
Walker, Van Arman, and Dexter 44, 189n19
Walling, George Washington 60, 61–62
Walnut Street House 150
Warne, Kate 51, 55, 57, 136
Warrenton, Va. 97, 98, 155, 161, 163, 178, 179

Warsaw, Ill. 23

Washington, D.C. 50, 52, 53, 54, 56, 57, 60, 61, 63, 65, *67*, 72, 80, 85, 86, 88, 89, 90, 100, 101, 104–5, 110, 111, 113, 114, 116, 119, 120–21, 122, 128–29, 133, 144, 145, 148, 151, 152, 155, 156, 163, 168, 169, 170, 183

Washington *Star* 104–5

Washington Street, Chicago, Ill. 46

Washington's Farm, Va. 105, 171

Webster, Charlotte (Sprowls) 9, 10, 12, 39, 135–36, *135*

Webster, Daniel 8, 12

Webster, Eleanor 12

Webster, Elizabeth 8

Webster, Esther 7–8

Webster, Eva Lewes 39, 135–36

Webster, Fanny 8

Webster, Frances 7–8, 9

Webster, Godfrey 7

Webster, Helen 8, 23–24

Webster, James 7, 12

Webster, Jonathan 7–8

Webster, Maria 7–8

Webster, Mary 7–8

Webster, Samuel 7–8

Webster, Sarah 9

Webster, Timothy (II) *51*; arrest and confinement 126, 128–30, 133; body 131, 137; confined to bed in Richmond 115–17, 118, 119–20, 122, 133; court martial 127–28; description 51, 69–70; early life 6, 7–11, 185*n*2; execution 130, 136–37; family life 6, 12, 23–24, 39, 42, 135–36; grave *137*; investigating grave robberies 5, 30–31, 33–34; investigating plot to assassinate Abraham Lincoln 5–6, 51, 54, 64–67, 136, 144–46; investigating plot to destroy Rock Island Bridge 5, 39, 41–44, 47; letter delivered to Abraham Lincoln *70*, *71*; marriage 6; meets Allan Pinkerton 5; missing 111, 112, 114–15; as New York City police officer 5, 12–21; as private detective 5, 23, 24–28; as railroad detective 5, 27–28; reaction to execution of 131–32; reports *27*, *81*, *82*, 85, 144–52; saving Tom Sampson and Ely De Voe 61–64; testimony in front of New York City Board of Alderman 17–21, 139–43; tracking Jules Imbert 25–26; as Union spy 6, 69–83, 85–104, 105–11, 122, 136, 147–84; witness in Scully's defense 124–25

Webster, Timothy, Sr. 7–8, *10*, 23–24, 42

Webster, Timothy (III) 9, 136, 137; grave *137*

West Indies 25, 52

West Point, Va. 99, 166

West Virginia 50; map *83*, *109*

Wheeler Gap, Tenn. 149

Wheeling, Va. 73

White, Captain_____ 154

White Beer Brewery 64–65, 144–45

Wight, J. Pierson 94

Willard's Hotel 61, 63, *64*

Williams, Charles D. C. 51, 59–60, 64–65, 136, 144, 145, 190*n*10

Wilmington, N.C. 25, 155

Wilson,_____ 155

Wilson, Henry 104

Winchester, Va. 97, 98, 159, 162, 163, 166, 181

Winder, John H. 95, 104, 108, 116, 117–18, *118*, 120–22, 126, 131, 159, 160, 164, 169, 182–83

Winder, William 104, 108, 168–70, 183

Wisconsin 22

Wise, Henry A. 172

Wise, Tully 100, 153, 154, 167

Woodbridge, George 129, 130

Woodruff, Lewis B. 21

World Building, New York, N.Y. 133

Worsham House 77, 78, 148

Wright and Currier's livery stable 34

York, Eli 34–38

York River 93, 99, 155, 156, 157, 158, 166

Yorktown, Va. 93–94, 128, 133, 155, 157, 158, 166

5/24